# Reminiscences of

# Rear Admiral Donald J. MacDonald

# U.S. Navy (Retired)

U.S. Naval Institute

Annapolis, Maryland

1986

## PREFACE

In the oral memoir that follows, Admiral Donald J. MacDonald, USN(Ret.) recounts his varied career that included ship command during one of the most intense naval campaigns of World War II and command of the presidential yacht during a bygone era when President Truman could come aboard often for lunch and all-night poker games.

Admiral MacDonald was an eyewitness to many historic events. As a special naval observer attached to the U.S. Embassy in London from 1940 to 1942, he watched the Battle of Britain from the roof of his hotel. Later, from his perspective as executive officer and commanding officer of the destroyer _O'Bannon_ (DD-450), he offers an excellent account of the fierce naval battle at Guadalcanal in November 1942. Remaining in the Guadalcanal area after that action, _O'Bannon_ became part of Cactus Striking Force that attempted to intercept the Tokyo Express.

When MacDonald entered Germany shortly after that country's surrender, he was appalled by the corruption he saw as Americans snapped up German stocks and art treasures for personal gain. He was also unhappy with American policies that denigrated Germany as an unworthy opponent.

Command of Truman's presidential yacht, _Williamsburg_, after the war was more enjoyable duty. The President took full advantage of this vessel, often inviting skipper MacDonald to join him for lunch and using him as a sounding board, one example being right before his decision to fire General MacArthur. Collateral duty included being in charge of Shangri-La, the presidential retreat in the Maryland mountains and the Little White House in Key West, Florida.

Also in this volume are thorough discussions of his duty as a White House aide during FDR's administration, battleship duty in *California* (BB-44) in the mid-1930s, and later tours as a department head at the Naval Academy and in the Office of the Chief of Naval Operations prior to his retirement in 1959.

These interviews were conducted by Dr. John T. Mason, Jr., former director of the Naval Institute's oral history department. The smooth typing was done by Mrs. Deborah Reid.

Susan B. Sweeney
Oral History Department
U.S. Naval Institute
December 1986

Rear Admiral Donald John MacDonald
United States Navy (Retired)

Donald John MacDonald was born in DuBois, Pennsylvania, on July 25, 1908, and was graduated from the DuBois High School as an honor student in 1926. He attended Werntz Preparatory School, Annapolis, Maryland, before his appointment to the Naval Academy from the 23rd District of Pennsylvania in 1927. While on the Naval Academy varsity soccer team, he won class numerals in that sport and in tennis, baseball, and basketball. Graduated and commissioned ensign on June 4, 1931, he subsequently attained the rank of captain to date from July 1, 1950. On October 1, 1959, he was transferred to the retired list and was advanced to the rank of rear admiral on the basis of combat awards.

After graduation in 1931, he served consecutively in the destroyers Hulbert (DD-342) and Truxtun (DD-229) until June 1933, when he was transferred to the USS California (BB-44). He received two letters of commendation for service in that battleship. Detached in the fall of 1937, he served in the USS Salinas (AO-19) until April 1938. He reported in May to the Office of the Chief of Naval Operations, Navy Department, Washington, D.C., and during that tour of duty had additional duty as a White House aide until August 1940. He then served for 18 months as special naval observer, American Embassy, London, England, with additional duty as aide to Vice Admiral Robert Lee Ghormley, USN, then special naval observer in London. He was in London during the Battle of Britain and the bombing of London.

Returning to the United States in February 1942, he reported in March to the plant of the Bath Iron Works Corporation, Bath, Maine, where the USS O'Bannon (DD-450) was being fitted out. He served as her executive officer from commissioning, June 26, 1942, until January 1943, when he assumed command. The O'Bannon, during his service, participated in the capture and defense of Guadalcanal, August 10, 1942 to February 8, 1943; Guadalcanal Third Savo, November 12 to 15, 1942; and the Rennel Island Operation, January 29-30, 1943; the consolidation of the Solomons February 8 to June 20, 1943; New Georgia-Rendova Occupation, March 25, 1943; Kula Gulf action, May and June 1943; Kolombangara action, July 12-13, 1943; Vella LaVella occupation, August 15 to October 16, 1943; and action off Vella LaVella, October 6-7, 1943.

For heroism and distinguished service as executive officer and later commanding officer of the O'Bannon, he was awarded the Navy Cross and gold star in lieu of a second Navy Cross; the Legion of Merit and a gold star in lieu of a second Legion of Merit; the Silver Star Medal and two gold stars in lieu of the second and third Silver Star Medal; and the Bronze Star Medal and a gold star in lieu of the Second Bronze Star Medal. The citations which follow show, in chronological order, the actions for which the awards were made:

Silver Star Medal: "For conspicuous gallantry and intrepidity as executive officer of the USS O'BANNON during action against enemy Japanese naval forces in the Guadalcanal-Tulagi Area on November 12-13, 1942. Although his ship was under tremendous aerial bombardment and engaged at close quarters with an outnumbering force of Japanese warships, [he] successfully maintained position in the battle line, and ... continued to lead our column into the face of superior enemy fire power at extremely close range. By maneuvering his ship with fearless skill, he directed the fire of her guns and torpedoes into a Japanese battleship and inflicted considerable damage on that enemy vessel . . ."

Gold Star in lieu of second Bronze Star Medal: "For heroic service as Commanding Officer of the USS O'BANNON in action against enemy Japanese forces in the Solomon Islands Area during January and February 1943 . . . operating in support of our assault troops on Guadalcanal Island, [he] expertly directed the bombardment from his vessel, thereby contributing materially to the destruction or evacuation of all Japanese forces on the island . . ."

Legion of Merit: "For exceptionally meritorious conduct . . . as Commanding Officer of the USS O'BANNON in action against enemy Japanese forces in the Solomon Islands from January 19 to March 6, 1943. In this period of intense activity, [he] skillfully directed the operation of his ship in continuous anti-submarine patrols and bombardments of enemy shore positions . . . the O'BANNON was of invaluable service to the task force in helping disrupt numerous enemy air attacks, and participated in one daylight and three night bombardments against Guadalcanal, New Georgia and Kolombangara Islands, performing her varied and difficult tasks with outstanding merit."

Gold star in lieu of second Legion of Merit: "For exceptionally meritorious conduct in . . . action against enemy Japanese forces in the Solomon Islands in April 1943. During extremely hazardous night operations in enemy waters, [he] maneuvered his vessel into an advantageous striking position and, with excellent judgment and splendid leadership launched a determined attack upon a hostile submarine, probably sinking it by well-coordinated depth charges and gunfire. His expert seamanship and fine tactical skill enabled the O'BANNON to come through the engagement unscathed and without injury to personnel."

Bronze Star Medal: "For distinguishing himself . . . as Commanding Officer of a destroyer operating as a unit of a task force during combined minelaying expeditions and bombardments of Japanese shore installations in the Kolombangara and New Georgia areas, British Solomon Islands, on the nights of May 7 and 13, 1943, operating under cover of darkness in poorly charted waters, [he] skillfully executed his assigned maneuvers and brought his ship through without damage. By his cool courage and able seamanship, he contributed materially to the successful mining of waters used extensively by the Japanese surface forces and to the destruction of enemy shore installations . . ."

Navy Cross: "For extraordinary heroism as commanding officer of the USS O'BANNON in action against enemy Japanese forces in the Solomon Islands, July 4, 5, and 6, 1943. When a cruiser of his task force was torpedoed during an effective bombardment of enemy positions off Kula Gulf, [he] skillfully maneuvered the O'BANNON close to the sinking vessel in order to screen another destroyer assisting in the hazardous rescue operations . . . enabled this destroyer to carry out her mission undamaged, although his own ship was being subjected to intense fire from enemy coastal batteries and the entire rescue detachment bombed by hostile aircraft. Twenty-four hours later, the same task group participated in a fierce engagement with a numerically superior Japanese naval force, and succeeded in sinking or severely damaging all of the hostile vessels . . . [He] contributed in large measure to the success of our forces in these vital campaign . . ."

Gold star in lieu of a second Silver Star Medal: "For conspicuous gallantry and intrepidity in action as commanding officer of the USS O'BANNON in the van of a small Task Force during an engagement with enemy Japanese surface vessels off Kolombangara Island, Solomon Islands on the night of July 12-13, 1943. When his ship encountered a covering force of Japanese cruisers and destroyers [he] . . . launched an aggressive and determined torpedo and gunfire attack in coordination with other destroyers in the task force. While at least four hostile ships were destroyed and two damaged and forced to retire as a result of this action, he and his gallant command brought the O'BANNON through the engagement unscathed. . ."

Gold star in lieu of second Navy Cross: "For extraordinary heroism and distinguished service . . . during the engagement with Japanese naval forces north of Vella Gulf, British Solomon Islands, on the night of August 17-18, 1943. His ship was a unit of a task group which participated in the interception and routing of an enemy force . . . which was endeavoring to reinforce the enemy garrisons in the Vella LaVella-Kolombangara area. [His] ship attacked the Japanese force in the face of continuous gun and torpedo fire . . . [and] he materially contributed to the destruction of two destroyers, four large barges and a number of smaller ones, and damage to a third destroyer without damage to his ship . . ."

Gold star in lieu of a third Silver Star Medal: ". . . during the night engagement with Japanese naval forces in the Solomon Islands area on October 6-7, 1943 . . . His skillful attack with torpedoes and gunfire materially contributed to the sinking of one or more enemy vessels and the damaging of three additional ships. As a result of the determined attacks, the enemy's mission was frustrated, his force greatly damaged and compelled to retire . . ."

He is also entitled to the ribbon for, and a facsimile of, the Presidential Unit Citation to the USS O'Bannon, for "outstanding performance in combat against enemy Japanese forces in the South Pacific from October 7, 1942, to October 7, 1943 . . ."

In April 1944 he reported for duty on the staff of Commander in Chief, United States Fleet, at Headquarters, Navy Department, Washington, D.C. From August 1944 to June 1945, he had duty as operations and plans officer on the staff of Commander U.S. Naval Forces, France, and was attached to the staff of the Supreme Commander, Allied Expeditionary Force (General of the Army Dwight D. Eisenhower), from June until November of that year. For seven months thereafter, he served as deputy chief of staff to Commander Naval Forces, Germany.

Returning to the United States in June 1946, he was in charge of organizing the Support Section, Operational Intelligence Branch, Office of the Chief of Naval Operations, Navy Department, and served as chief of that section until June 1948. He next commanded the presidential yacht USS Williamsburg (AGC-369) and received a special letter of commendation from President Harry S Truman. In September 1951 he was transferred to command of the USS Marquette (AKA-95).

Between November 1952 and August 1955, he was head of the Department of Foreign Languages at the Naval Academy, after which he served as Commander Destroyer Squadron 34. In October 1956 he was assigned to the Office of the Chief of Naval Operations, Navy Department, where he served as assistant director of the Undersea Warfare Division and later as assistant director of the General Planning Group, until his retirement on October 1, 1959.

In addition to the Navy Cross with gold star, the Silver Star Medal with two gold stars, the Legion of Merit with gold star, the Bronze Star Medal with gold star, and the Presidential Unit

Citation Ribbon, Admiral MacDonald has the American Defense Service Medal, Base Clasp; the Asiatic-Pacific Campaign Medal with silver star (five operations); the American Campaign Medal; the European-African-Middle Eastern Campaign Medal; the World War II Victory Medal and the National Defense Service Medal. He has also been awarded the Order of the Crown (rank of Officer) and the Croix de Guerre with Palm from the Government of Belgium; and the Croix de Guerre with Star from the French Government for his part in the liberation of France and Belgium, the Rhine River crossing and the elimination of the German pockets in France and the Channel Islands. For his part in representing the Navy at the wedding of Grace Kelly and the Prince of Monaco, he was presented with a special medal commemorating the event.

Authorization

The U.S. Naval Institute is hereby authorized to make available to libraries and other repositories of its choosing the transcripts of seven oral history interviews concerning the life and career of the undersigned. The seven interviews were recorded on 22 May 1974, 23 July 1974, 5 August 1974, 10 September 1974, 5 December 1974, 30 January 1975 and 27 December 1979 in collaboration with Dr. John T. Mason, Jr. of the U.S. Naval Institute.

The undersigned does hereby release and assign to the U.S. Naval Institute all right, title, restrictions, and interest in these seven interviews. The copyright in both the oral and transcribed versions shall be the sole property of the U.S. Naval Institute. The tape recordings of the interviews are and will remain the property of the U.S. Naval Institute.

Signed and sealed this 19th day of November, 1984

Donald J. MacDonald

Donald J. MacDonald
Rear Admiral, U.S. Navy (Retired)

Interview Number 1 with Rear Admiral Donald J. MacDonald, U.S. Navy (Retired)

Place: Admiral MacDonald's residence in Washington, D.C.

Date: Wednesday morning, 22 May 1974

Subject: Biography

Interviewer: John T. Mason, Jr.

Q: Admiral, I've been looking forward to this series with you for quite some time, ever since Ed Hooper told me about you, so I wonder if you'd begin in the proper way with a biography by giving me the date and place of your birth and then a thumbnail sketch of your early life, your early education, something about your family background, perhaps?*

Admiral MacDonald: Thank you, Doctor. I was born in Du Bois, Pennsylvania, on 25 July 1908. I was graduated from Du Bois High School as an honor student, valedictorian of the class, also president of the class.

Q: Tell me something about your family background, about your father. What was his business?

Admiral MacDonald: My father was a graduate of the Colorado

---

*Vice Admiral Edwin B. Hooper, USN (Ret.), who was Director of Naval History at the time of the interview. Hooper and MacDonald were classmates in the Naval Academy's class of 1931.

School of Mines, and his business turned out to be handling his deceased father's property. Instead of remaining in the West, where he had been spending some time as a civil engineer building railroads, he came back to handle his mother's property.

Q: You say your father had been in the mining business in the Far West?

Admiral MacDonald: Well, he was a graduate of the Colorado School of Mines, as I mentioned before, but also, I might point out, he was captain of the football and baseball teams, because this has a bearing on why I went to the Naval Academy.

My grandfather, Donald John MacDonald, was a Canadian who came into this country lumbering. He unfortunately died at a rather young age but was lumbering in the northwest part of Pennsylvania and had also acquired properties in Wisconsin, lumber properties, and contemplated moving out in that direction, but he died. My father had to then handle the situation, and he sold all of that except he went into the mining business in northwest Pennsylvania. We lived in Du Bois in what you might call a very nice environment and also a family that didn't need anything.

Q: This was anthracite mining?

Admiral MacDonald: No, soft-coal mining. We also owned a lot of property which he had to handle, including a hotel and a few other things.

In my last year at Du Bois High School, my father being fairly well known politically and so forth, found out that the congressman from the 23rd district had an appointment, so he gave it to me. I hastily took the exams and didn't pass English in my original exam.

Q: Had you been thinking about the Naval Academy up to then?

Admiral MacDonald: No, I hadn't, really.

Q: It was simply an opportunity to get an appointment to a service academy?

Admiral MacDonald: That's right. So, when the congressman heard that I had failed the first year he said, "Well, I'll give Donald the principal appointment for next year," in which case I had to make up my mind to go to the Naval Academy and study, and my mind was sort of influenced by the fact that the director of athletics at the Naval Academy at that time, 1926 or 1927, was my father's roommate at the Colorado School of Mines, Commodore

McCandless.* Of course, my father being an athlete, thought that maybe my going to the Naval Academy under his old friend and pal would be helpful.

Needless to say, I was too small really to be much of an athlete, although I did work at it.

Q: Did you have brothers?

Admiral MacDonald: Yes, I had two brothers. One, later, was in the class of 1933 at the Naval Academy.** He sort of had my father's athletic ability and also brain. The younger brother tried to get into the Naval Academy and had the appointment, but, finally, due to the fact that the congressman felt that my father hadn't donated enough money or something, took the appointment away from him.*** So he went into the Air Force, the Army Air Corps.

Q: Well, sir, you got the principal appointment, and then you had to bone up for the examination.

---

*Commodore Byron McCandless, USN. As a commander, McCandless was Director of Athletics at the Naval Academy from 1923 to 1925.

**Midshipman Harold Alexander MacDonald, USN.

***This brother was Charles H. MacDonald.

Admiral MacDonald: I then went to prep school for one year.

Q: Where did you go?

Admiral MacDonald: To a Naval Academy preparatory school, which was run by Bobby Werntz.*

Q: Bobby Werntz's factory, wasn't it?

Admiral MacDonald: That's right, it was a real factory, and I passed without difficulty the next year. I entered the Naval Academy and was graduated from there in 1931.

Q: How did you like the life of discipline at the Academy?

Admiral MacDonald: I wasn't too enthusiastic about it at all! I think some of the people took an interest in making it hard for me.

Q: You mean hazing or something?

---

*Robert L. Werntz. Werntz graduated from the Naval Academy in 1884, resigned his commission in 1890, and later established the Werntz Preparatory School on Maryland Avenue in Annapolis. After his death in 1931, the school continued until a fire in 1937 destroyed the building.

Admiral MacDonald: In terms of hazing, yes. It was a new life for me, there's no doubt about it. However, academically I made out fairly well. It wasn't difficult, nor was the discipline too hard.

Q: Did you enjoy the summer cruises?

Admiral MacDonald: Yes, I really did enjoy the summer cruises. I think it's a great thing for the midshipmen to get away and travel around a bit.

Q: What did they entail? Where did you go?

Admiral MacDonald: Our freshman cruise was just up and down the East Coast, up to Newport, Maine, New York, and Guantanamo. As a matter of fact, that cruise was not too good.

Q: Rather disappointing, wasn't it?

Admiral MacDonald: Very disappointing, but the next cruise went to Europe, and that was a very satisfactory arrangement, because I was able to claim relatives and so forth in different places, and they would allow me to take more time off than they would allow most other people. We traveled all around Europe. That was very good.

Q: Did the summer cruises help solidify your desire to stay in the service, a naval career?

Admiral MacDonald: Now that you bring up that thought, even though I went to the Naval Academy and did go out for football and other sports, it was quite evident that I wasn't going to be a great football player. I never really seriously thought of staying in the Navy at that time. My father being an engineer and also having his own construction company, it more or less looked like I would come out after the Naval Academy and go into engineering. I even had the possibility of a job at that time with some friends of his in New York, Stone and Webster. It wasn't until we were virtually graduated and the conditions of the economy of the country were such . . .

Q: You graduated in the midst of the Depression.

Admiral MacDonald: Yes, in the middle of the Depression more or less, and I definitely decided to stay in, although I still thought that, maybe, after a while, when conditions improved, I might leave the service.

Q: During Academy days, you weren't attracted, then, towards aviation or anything specific in the naval service?

Admiral MacDonald: Not particularly. There was a lot of aviation. I enjoyed flying, but at the time I was somewhat nearsighted and would not have been able to qualify physically for the eye examination that was required at that time. The condition of my eyes has never gotten very bad and actually has improved as time went on. I didn't have to wear glasses except occasionally for reading. But that just eliminated the thought of going into aviation at the time, so I never thought of that.

Q: Did you concentrate on engineering while you were at the Academy?

Admiral MacDonald: Well, engineering, of course, was at that time one of the majors, you might call them. It wasn't too difficult for me at the time. One thing that seemed to be more difficult for me was English. Why, I don't know, but it was.

Q: Probably some lack of preparation in high school?

Admiral MacDonald: Possibly so. I found out later, after being at the Naval Academy, that this is not an unusual thing. The professors of English more or less indicated that the best way of learning English is to learn a foreign language. Then you really know how to put a sentence together.

Q: Well, that's perfectly right. When you learn a foreign language, you learn grammar and structure, and unfortunately we don't do so much of that when we learn English.

Admiral MacDonald: We did at the time. I guess I never spent enough time reading books and so forth. I was always sort of out playing golf, tennis, and anything else. That probably was part of it.

Q: Did McCandless more or less look after your athletic interests while you were there?

Admiral MacDonald: I used to go out and see him. I went out for the usual teams--football, baseball, basketball--and so forth, which were the majors at the time, but I realized after the first year that physically I was not large enough to get in there and compete with those boys. So I went out for other sports like soccer, and I got a letter there. And I played tennis, baseball, basketball, got numerals there.

Q: Did you play lacrosse?

Admiral MacDonald: No, but lacrosse was one sport where everyone had an equal chance usually, going there, except the boys from Baltimore who were quite able. They'd been playing this for a long time, they knew all about it, they moved right in. So when my brother moved into the Naval Academy, I told him that lacrosse was a sport, and he immediately made the varsity. He went out for lacrosse and passed up football. He went out for soccer.

It was a nice period there, and socially it was a lot of fun. We were tied down; we didn't have the freedom then that they have today, but I think the people there were well-motivated. I think we graduated a class of about 340-some, and my standing was in the upper quarter, I guess 50.*

It's a funny thing, I used to be in some sections with Admiral Rivero.** He stood at the top of the class, and one of the prominent ones in my class was Jack McCain, who was Commander in Chief Pacific recently.*** Jack McCain stood way down at the bottom, so you can see class standing in a way doesn't dictate where you're going to end up.

Q: No. It's a fair yardstick, but some men are late bloomers, so to speak.

Admiral MacDonald: Yes. Jack, of course, was a fine officer and

---

*MacDonald stood number 85 in a graduating class of 441.

**Midshipman Horacio Rivero, Jr., USN, graduated number three. Rivero was Vice Chief of Naval Operations from 1964 to 1968. Admiral Rivero's oral history is in the Naval Institute collection.

***Midshipman John S. McCain, Jr., USN, stood number 424. He served as Commander in Chief Pacific from 1968 to 1972.

well-motivated; he's always been well-motivated. I think the fact that his family background was all Navy helped a great deal.

From there I was in the group that was ordered to destroyers from the Naval Academy.

Q: There was no question of commissions for your class, was there?

Admiral MacDonald: No, that came along later, in 1933, when only half the class was commissioned.* My brother was way up at the top; he didn't have to worry about that. All of our people who wanted commissions were able to get them. However, some of the people did leave the Navy at that time, some of our prominent classmates, because jobs offered them on the outside were quite attractive then. People used to come down there from various corporations and interview midshipmen, and they convinced quite a few of them to leave.

Q: The graduates weren't obligated to spend . . .

---

*As an austerity measure necessitated by the Depression, it was decided in the fall of 1932 that only the top half of the Naval Academy's class of 1933, and subsequent classes, would be commissioned. This policy was to remain in effect until the number of line officers, at that time approximately 5,700, was reduced to the authorized level of 5,449. With the advent of the Roosevelt Administration, the new President was eventually able to commission the entire class of 1934 and to offer commissions to those discharged in 1933.

Admiral MacDonald: We weren't obligated at that time to spend any time in the service. We could get out if we wanted to, and a goodly number did leave the service then.

Q: But at that point you weren't tempted?

Admiral MacDonald: No, no, oh no, not at that time. Conditions didn't look good to me at all on the outside.

I was ordered to a destroyer based in San Diego. After a month's leave or something, I very vividly can remember arriving on board on a Saturday morning, the day I was supposed to report, and there was only one officer on the ship at the time. She was tied up to a mooring buoy in San Diego Harbor, and that officer, who was the executive officer, turned to me and said, "You have the weekend duty," and off he went. He informed me that there were books that I could read to see what had to be done, but I would have the weekend duty for that ship. Well, I hastily started to read up on what I was supposed to do, being an ensign on board . . .

Q: And just a fresh one, too!

Admiral MacDonald: . . . and it seemed like that Monday the whole division was supposed to go out for different drills and maneuvers. I got through everything all right and was prepared to do what the book said. When all the officers started pouring back on Monday morning, we had to have the ship ready to get under way. The captain cleared us from the buoy. I always thought that someone was going to relieve me. I didn't feel that this responsibility was going to hang on indefinitely, but it seems that the person who has the weekend duty has the first watch. So, off to sea we went, and, after the captain turned the ship over to me, I turned around and started looking for someone to bail me out! No one did, and the captain finally came over to me and said, "You know, I don't want anyone on this ship who doesn't carry his own weight, so you're going to start standing watches right away."

The next thing I knew, we'd cleared the buoy off Point Loma, and someone started shouting "Man overboard." From that moment on, it was hectic. After the man-overboard drill, the comment was that I'd either run over the man or we lost him or something. Then the fire drill and so forth. Then everyone went down below, except myself.

After it quieted down, I felt great.

Q: You had survived!

Admiral MacDonald: Survived, but this put me in good step, because my classmates who went to the other ships in the division weren't allowed to take the watch. A lot of them weren't even watchstanders for a year.

Q: Still, it was pretty rough at first?

Admiral MacDonald: Oh, it was terrible.

Q: Who was the skipper who had this policy?

Admiral MacDonald: Pinky Powers, Lieutenant Commander Pinky Powers, and he had funny ideas, a pretty tough hombre.* I think he retired as a lieutenant commander at that time and later had cancer or something and died.

This did really help me and gave me a great boost in connection with confidence. Later, I was assigned as assistant gunnery officer, communications officer, and so forth.

Q: How many officers were on board the destroyer?

Admiral MacDonald: The captain, the executive officer, who was Geiselman, the gunnery officer, engineer--we had seven or eight.**

Q: This was the _Hulbert_, was it?

---

*Lieutenant Commander Frederick D. Powers, USN.
**Lieutenant Ellis H. Geiselman, USN.

Admiral MacDonald: Yes, the *Hulbert*. Seven or eight officers and most of them were married. There was only one bachelor, and his name was Midtlyng.* He was the engineer officer.

We operated for a year, and they then put in a program of rotating ships in reserve. The *Hulbert* was then put into reserve in a year, about 1933, I guess. We were then shifted over to a ship called the *Truxtun*. Geiselman, who was the executive officer, took over another ship, and there was another captain, who had never served in destroyers and took over, I guess it was, the *Truxtun*. All the rest of the officers in the *Hulbert* shifted over under him, and the old gunnery officer became the exec.

One interesting thing here was when we shifted over, we were up in the Navy Yard, Mare Island, and the captain who was taking over the command asked our skipper, Powers, who he thought was the best watchstander or deck officer for him, because he wanted him to take over from the beginning and take the ship out of Mare Island. And he did say that I, he felt, was the most qualified to do it, in which case, when we finally put to sea--when we were ready and put to sea--he asked me to take the deck and take the ship out for him. All these things certainly helped a lot in building up confidence.

*Lieutenant (junior grade) Carl R. Midtlyng, USN.

Q: Well, that shows the wisdom of the skipper, doesn't it? I mean putting you through the . . .

Admiral MacDonald: It did and it also--a lot of these people like several lieutenants who felt a little disturbed that some sort of ensign should usurp their sort of prerogative of seniority in watchstanding and so forth. I don't think there was any real bad feeling about it, but I think they had hurt feelings.

We did an awful lot of maneuvering in fog, because every summer we used to go up to Port Angeles, in the state of Washington, and we had to do an awful lot of maneuvering in fog.

Q: That was the purpose of it?

Admiral MacDonald: No, weather conditions were more favorable in the summer up there and it's pretty quiet. It also is a sort of liberty recreation area, where they could do other things, and the fact that you could get out and there was plenty of room where you could do a lot of training in a few minutes or something.

Q: Did you go up to Alaska at all?

Admiral MacDonald: No, I never went up there on a destroyer.

Q: So it was a real learning period?

Admiral MacDonald: It was, and I suppose the fact of being bachelors you have to take the duty of a lot of the married men an awful lot, who couldn't see their families too much and always wanted to get home when they could. It was a fine experience.

Q: It was a motivation for finding a wife, wasn't it?

Admiral MacDonald: Well, I'd decided a long time before that I wouldn't marry in the Navy. You could have too good a time being an independent officer. Marriage didn't appeal to me at the time, although I certainly spent a lot of time dashing around to parties, dancing, and all that sort of thing. Life was very pleasant then for a naval officer. You were accepted wherever you went, not exactly always respected, but at least accepted. Naval officers were almost looked upon as catches for the daughters, because we had a little bit of stability and also independence.

Q: And there was a certain amount of glamour attached to the career?

Admiral MacDonald: Oh, yes, and the traveling around was interesting. But it's a hard working arrangement, you know, 24 hours a day, seven days a week most of the time.

I think the indoctrination in any of the military services is a wonderful start for any young boy, wonderful.

Q: It helps him to organize his life, doesn't it?

Admiral MacDonald: It helps him to organize his life. He receives a discipline that is very helpful later on in life, and he sort of understands such things as loyalty, obedience, trustworthiness, and a few things like that.

Then, after destroyer duty, I was sent to . . .

Q: And that was when? Two years?

Admiral MacDonald: Yes. I guess it was there because I went to California.

Q: In June of 1933.

Admiral MacDonald: In June of '33 I went to the California; that's right. I ended up being the senior classmate who was attached to the USS California, so my chores immediately became president of the JO mess, and my assignment at that time was ship's secretary to Captain Wilson Brown.

I want to point out this thing, president of the JO mess.

They had the regular officers' mess and then all officers who had less than three years, because there are so many officers on a battleship, had their own JO mess, junior officers' mess, and the senior one is always president. All young officers do mess in that mess.

Q: Did you have the responsibility for the type of food?

Admiral MacDonald: Yes. The executive officer held you responsible for the whole junior officers' quarters and everything, and when we had an inspection and there was something wrong, the president was always the one to get the blame and have to do something about it.

Q: This was in the chain of command.

Admiral MacDonald: That's right, and the sort of interesting point here was we had the staff of Commander U.S. Battle Force on board the California.

Q: Was that Wilson Brown?

Admiral MacDonald: No, no, Wilson Brown was the commanding officer at the time.

Q: He was the captain?

Admiral MacDonald: Yes. Joseph Mason Reeves was commander of the Battle Force, and he flew his flag in the USS California.* Now, his staff, the communicators, had about four of my classmates on board, three of them . . .

Q: And they joined the JO mess?

Admiral MacDonald: Yes, they all were in the JO mess, and three of them stood higher than I did in the class, but, being attached to the staff, they were not responsible for anything in the ship. Rivero was one, Allan Reed, and J.B. Colwell, who all stood higher in my class than I did.** Then, being president of the mess, I had to boss them around!

Wilson Brown at that time had Parkinson's Disease. He couldn't write his name, and I was the only one who could carry his correspondence to his cabin to be signed as ship's secretary and watch him as he tried to make a "WB."

Q: How did he manage to stay in the service?

---

*Admiral Joseph M. Reeves, USN, Commander Battle Force from 1933 to 1934.

**Ensign Allan L. Reed, USN, stood number five in the class of 1931. Ensign John B. Colwell, USN, whose oral history is also in the Naval Institute collection, stood number six.

Admiral MacDonald: Well, this is rather interesting. I guess he fought it until he completed that job. He later became a rear admiral, and he also later became an aide to President Roosevelt, a naval aide to President Roosevelt, but I understand that by that time this thing had cleared up.* Whether this was a temporary thing, I don't know, but he would not allow anyone in the cabin when he would sign the papers except me.

Q: That was a part of your duty as ship's secretary, was it?

Admiral MacDonald: Yes, for one year. The following year I moved up into the wardroom and I became fourth division officer. I had the number four turret and also became catapult officer. Of course, any time you're a turret officer, you're one of the senior watch officers on the bridge, so I never stood a JO watch on a battleship. I moved right into the top standing of watches.

Q: Again, traced back to the skipper of the <u>Hulbert</u>.

Admiral MacDonald: Yes. We had a series of captains and I moved along. After Wilson Brown there was Blackburn and Stephen Rowan.** I was there for about four years, and I continued to be

---

*As a captain, Wilson Brown was naval aide to the President from 1934 to 1936; as a vice admiral he held the post from 1943 to 1945.

**Captain Paul P. Blackburn, USN; Captain Stephen C. Rowan, USN.

the fourth division officer. We had wonderful success in a lot of ways, firing the catapults, guns, and so forth.

Q: The California was considered the . . .

Admiral MacDonald: We were right up there in competition for the top all the time.

It was very nice duty; I enjoyed it very much.

Q: Did she operate always in the Pacific?

Admiral MacDonald: No, we came around to the East Coast on one cruise in 1934, as I recall. We cruised up and down the East Coast, went through maneuvers, and then out to Hawaii on another cruise. They always had one annual cruise set up to different places, the Panama Canal, Hawaii, or down in the Caribbean.

Q: This was the locale for war games, too?

Admiral MacDonald: War games, yes, that is what I mean. Other than that, you did a lot of training on your own, firing your own practices, which are all required practices, and, of course, we did sort of have a routine arrangement. If we were on the West Coast, we'd go up to the Bremerton area, the Puget Sound area during part of the summer and drift down, ending up in San

Francisco usually around Labor Day, then back to San Pedro. We were anchored in the San Pedro area all the time.

Q: Were battleships required to participate in certain civilian celebrations along the coast?

Admiral MacDonald: Yes, they usually did. One thing about being on one of the senior flags, we usually had priority in moorings, priority in tying up at a dock, or anything like that, which was always a big help. But you had a lot of difficulty in connection with this thing of flagships, of always having officers calling, and honors were very important. Particularly having a quarterdeck division, you were constantly making sure it was very clean and everything.

There's one thing I do remember now about Reeves. He lived on board ship. He was a very wonderful officer, there's no doubt about it. He never seemed to be disturbed about anything. But later Admiral Leahy came on, and he used to arrive very early in the morning and it was always a very confusing arrangement.* Just about when you were getting ready for colors, here was the admiral arriving at the ship.

---

*Admiral William D. Leahy, USN, Commander Battle Force from March 1936 until December of that same year, when he was relieved in order to become Chief of Naval Operations. He officially took office as CNO on 2 January 1937.

Q: From his quarters on shore?

Admiral MacDonald: That's right, his flag barge coming out, and it was always a little hectic, which one was going to arrive first, whether you'd have to sound colors or you were going to have to greet the admiral.

Anyway, Leahy had a wonderful habit--he arrived early, he would then have lunch and take a nap, get up at 3:00 o'clock, and every day he'd leave the ship at 3:00 o'clock. It was a very interesting thing, but during that period the quarterdeck division could not do any heavy work while he was resting. That was my point, really. Between certain hours, we couldn't do any work overhead.

Q: Couldn't disturb the admiral! That was a fairly peaceful existence he had, didn't he, fairly easy?

Admiral MacDonald: Yes, and he had some good skippers. They were all excellent skippers. Stephen Rowan stood way up at the top of his class.* I remember I used to play golf with him a lot, and he was on the golf course the day he got the word that he had not been selected. He just stopped our golf that day when he got the word and requested permission to go to Washington and

*Captain Rowan graduated number five in the class of 1903.

find out why. When he got to Washington, he found out that maybe his executive officer had created such an impression of the ship that people weren't too happy with it, particularly some of the staff officers there. He didn't know this and, of course, he didn't take it very easily because he never did realize that maybe some of the people were very unhappy in his ship. This was quite a blow to him and he was an outstanding officer. He was never selected.

Q: Tell me something about Admiral Reeves.

Admiral MacDonald: You know, he was a quiet, unassuming man but very brilliant and, as far as aviation was concerned, he was way ahead of everyone else. He was the one who started night operations from carriers. Everyone else would have given it up, because they thought it was too daring and too dangerous. But he insisted on it in some of the war games and so forth, and sooner or later it became the thing. He was farsighted in a lot of ways like that, and very cool, calm, and collected. I never saw him frustrated. Many times when I had the watch he'd be just walking up and down. He very seldom ever left the ship. He was a wonderful naval officer in that nothing seemed to disturb him. I used to walk with him, back and forth on his walks, parading the quarterdeck. He never disturbed anyone that I know of. He may have caused a little trouble via his chief of staff, who was

Adolphus Andrews.* Adolphus did cause the exec difficulty about certain things.

Reeves worked out this carrier airplane business in the Navy, where I would imagine that you could almost say he was the one who really put aviation on the upstream.

Q: And yet he was not a pilot himself, was he?

Admiral MacDonald: No, he was not a pilot himself. At least, I don't think he was a pilot at any time, but he certainly saw the advantage of enhancing the air side of the Navy at the time.** Really, we only had two carriers then that were anything, the Lexington and the Saratoga.

Q: So, his support at that crucial moment was important for naval aviation?

Admiral MacDonald: Very important, by his making them fly missions and perform tasks that they hadn't done before. It advanced a lot of techniques and made aviation a more powerful weapon.

---

*Captain Adolphus Andrews, USN.

**Although never a pilot, in 1925 at age 53, Reeves qualified as a naval aviation observer.

Q: This was demonstrated in part, was it not, in exercises surrounding the defense of the canal?

Admiral MacDonald: Oh, yes, definitely. All the war exercises that I recall--well, basically, at that time, the sort of strategy was battle-line strategy, and all the war games were set up for it. Two opposing battle lines would come in, try to maneuver for the best position, and everything . . .

Q: Then slug it out?

Admiral MacDonald: Then slug it out. The ships at that time all carried scouting planes. We carried four scouting planes, and we'd launch them at different hours to try to get advance information on the opposing force. That necessitated the development of a technique which also came along very well of picking these craft up after you had launched them. Launching became easy, but trying to get them back on board safely on the battleships and cruisers became a problem. Doing all these maneuvers and everything, techniques of turns, trying to calm down the sea so they could land and pick up rapidly with cranes--we used to try all kinds of things, booms extended, coming up in cargo nets, and then hooking on, then all of a sudden coming right up astern. We developed these techniques during that period.

Q: The plane required new techniques?

Admiral MacDonald: That's right. It required new techniques altogether, particularly in the launching. We'd have to launch before we shot. Before you opened up your gunfire, you'd have to have all your planes in the air; otherwise, the pressure when you fired would blow the planes. So they'd have to be launched. It required a great deal of training to cut down on the time required to do all of this and, of course, this was part of the competitive things that we did all the time.

Q: What about your contingent of aviators on board ship? Were they integrated into the--did they stand watch?

Admiral MacDonald: They were supposed to, but they fought against it all the time because they never really got too well qualified for standing. They did stand a few watches, as I remember, on board when we were cruising normally, but they were opposed to it from the point of view that their main job was flying those airplanes and so forth. They did stand watches in port; there's no doubt about that. But at sea this was one of the problems. They would go up there, and some of them had to stand--even though they were lieutenants and so forth, they had to stand JO watches on the bridge until they qualified to stand a deck watch under way. Of course, after a certain period of indoctrination they were able to do it, but they fought it.

Q: They didn't learn that in Pensacola?

Admiral MacDonald: No. You had your regular watch officers. In our case it was the four turret officers who were the regular watch officers. We had some wonderful aviators on board, including at one time John Crommelin, who has caused the Navy so much trouble.* He was one of our senior aviators, but at that time he was no difficulty at all.

Q: Were there any exercises that involved the Hawaiian Islands?

Admiral MacDonald: Yes. I don't recall too well our cruise around the Hawaiian Islands in the California, because it always comes back to cruising around in the destroyer, but we did have one cruise out there. We anchored in Lahaina Roads for a while and also tied up, I guess, in Pearl Harbor at one time. That was in the California, but, for some reason or other, outside of some of the social life, I don't recall too much in the way of . . .

---

*Lieutenant John G. Crommelin, Jr., USN. In the late 1940s, Crommelin was an outspoken critic of the Green Bowlers, a secret society formed at the Naval Academy which chose a select few from each class and supposedly helped one another throughout their careers. Crommelin used the media to expose the members and charged that favoritism was shown among society members in promotions.

Q: Well, this was early in the decade of the Thirties and I suppose the . . .

Admiral MacDonald: Oh, Honolulu was a great place at that time. I mean, there were only about three hotels along Waikiki Beach, the Royal Hawaiian, the Halekulani, and one other. The beach was great, and the people invited the Navy to some rather nice parties. It was just a small place at the time. I do recall very vividly coming to the conclusion that I'd never want to really live in Honolulu or on the island of Oahu because it's too constricting. You can travel from one end to the other in half a day.

Q: It's 2,000 miles from anywhere, isn't it?

Admiral MacDonald: That's right. At that time they weren't flying out there. The only way you could go out was on a ship, and it seemed like it was very isolated and very restricted, so I enjoyed going there for a short period of time, but I never thought it would be a place I'd want to live.

After the <u>California</u> duty . . .

Q: That contributed a lot to your education as a naval officer, didn't it?

Admiral MacDonald: Oh, yes. I will say that there was one period in the _California_ when I was ship's secretary and had to prepare the ship's papers all the time, a daily paper and all schedules, business. The executive, Howard Lammers, was really a stickler for everything, even a comma omitted.* He'd call me up, and we might have to reprint all the finished schedules. If you ever made a mistake, he was just a terrible guy, and this was one of the things that Stephen Rowan didn't know. Well, at one time I did seriously think of resigning under him.

Q: The pressure was too much?

Admiral MacDonald: It was pretty great. I'd have to stay aboard every night to make sure this paper was perfect, and off he would go.

Q: How was the news gathered for the paper?

Admiral MacDonald: We printed a daily routine every day of what would take place the next day.

Q: Oh, I see, a kind of log.

---

*Commander Howard M. Lammers, USN.

Admiral MacDonald: According to what divisions did this and what hour you did that and what drills had to take place. This thing didn't really come down ready to go until everyone else was about ready to leave, and if there was ever any mistake in it--that was only part of the thing. The other thing was the preparation of all their letters, all the correspondence for the ship.

Q: You had to write the letters?

Admiral MacDonald: Sort of initially draft them.

Q: Sounds like a full-time job.

Admiral MacDonald: Oh, it was, and including all the confidential publications. I was responsible for all of that.

Q: On board ship they can't very well get away, can they?

Admiral MacDonald: Yes, but they do. The person I relieved in the job had lost a publication, and that ended up in his getting a court-martial and later being kicked out of the Navy. Oh, yes, they do. If you loan them out without getting a signature or you misplace somewhere a confidential publication--it's very important that accurate records be kept on all classified publications, and you have to submit your inventory quarterly.

And, boy, if you ever had a mistake, it was too bad, because that was a court-martial offense at that time, to lose a classified publication. This was all part of the training of making people responsible.

But I did really consider that, boy, it wasn't worth it, the way Lammers was operating, but I lived through it. Of course, it was a lot easier when you became a turret officer and didn't have to work with him so closely.

Q: Well, sir, in the fall of 1937 you went on board the USS Salinas. What was she?

Admiral MacDonald: The Salinas was one of the few oil tankers that the Navy had at that time, and her main task was keeping the oil-farm tanks of the Navy filled with fuel for the ships and gasoline for the planes.

Q: The shore-based tanks?

Admiral MacDonald: Yes, shore-based tanks, and we plied basically up and down the East Coast all the time. It was a very regular, routine arrangement. We'd go down to Houston, Texas, to the refineries, load up fuel, then take it to a dock, a fuel farm, at Guantanamo or up to Yorktown. We even made trips to many other places, Norfolk and so forth.

Q: What kind of supplies did they keep at these various bases? I mean, how much oil?

Admiral MacDonald: They kept considerable bunker fuel oil for all our ships that were burning fuel oil and also gasoline for the planes that were flying around.

Q: High-octane gasoline?

Admiral MacDonald: At that time they were using high-octane gasoline. They weren't using what they call at present JP-4.* We just carried gasoline around. We put in to Key West off and on and filled up the tanks there. Basically, we made two trips a month to the Houston area or the Texas area.

Q: How many gallons of fuel would the _Salinas_ carry?

Admiral MacDonald: She was a fairly large tanker, but I really don't recall the exact amount.

Q: What sort of tonnage was she?

Admiral MacDonald: Fully loaded, I would say only about 18,000

---

*JP-4 is a military aviation fuel, one which is not used in carrier planes.

tons maximum.

Q: For that time, that was large.

Admiral MacDonald: Oh, yes. She was a ship of 500 feet or something like that. You see a lot of the same size tankers cruising around still. She was not one of the enormous tankers that we have now, no.

We stopped in Charleston. Charleston was our shipyard base. I enjoyed that type of duty very much because, still being a bachelor, putting into ports like Charleston, South Carolina, particularly during the holiday season of Christmas and New Year, I seemed to be very popular. Several letters had been written in advance of my coming by friends, and I had a very hectic social schedule.

Q: What was your rank by that time?

Admiral MacDonald: We had just made j.g. by then, and we were very much in demand by the parents of daughters they would like to see marry into the Navy at the time.*

Q: There were a lot of debutante parties?

*J.g.--Lieutenant (junior grade).

Admiral MacDonald: Lots of debutante parties and balls. It was very delightful.

Of course, the trouble with being in a tanker was that you never stayed very long in port. The main job was to go in, load up fuel, then depart. During the summer, I guess it was the early part of 1938, we had several reserve officer training corps people on board, and one was a friend of mine from Washington, D.C. His name was William L. Williams.* He was a bachelor, so when we'd put into Houston during this particular period, we would go ashore together. William L. Williams had a roommate up at Yale whose father was president of Humble Oil. Well, the point was that Texas was dry. They had a sort of bottle club arrangement and, in order to be a member of a bottle club, you had to be recommended and had to sign up.

We had several dates one night, one afternoon, and we felt we'd like to go over and get a cocktail, so we went over with these girls to join this club, and the man took down our names, and I wrote down Donald MacDonald and he wrote down William Williams, and the guy said, "The hell with this, I don't believe you."

So we said, "Well, call up the duty officer at the ship, and you can verify and confirm that those are our names.

So this fellow called up the duty officer, who happened to be

*Lieutenant (junior grade) William L. Williams, USNR.

the chief engineer at the time, a wonderful old fellow who came up through the ranks and was a delightful person. The fellow from the club said, "Do you happen to have two people on board your ship, one by the name of Donald MacDonald and the other William Williams?"

Before he heard anything else, he said, "My God, what have they done now?"

But we finally got into the club. The last time I saw Williams, he was one of the big lawyers in New York with White and Case. He handles all the corporate affairs for them.

It was a lot of fun.

Q: What was your particular duty on board?

Admiral MacDonald: Basically, I was first lieutenant and communications officer. We only had four watch officers. As a matter of fact, many times we were down to only three watch officers. So standing watch was really the main thing. The chief engineer could stand deck watches. We didn't have many officers, and it was really just a watchstanding operation practically all of the time. We were at sea most of the time.

Q: In that time was there any attempt at fueling at sea?

Admiral MacDonald: I don't exactly recall that. I do remember that we used to fuel--even in my destroyer days we attempted to fuel--from alongside ships, big ships, but not under way. They used to go alongside oilers moored to a buoy or something like that.

Q: But not on the open ocean?

Admiral MacDonald: No. I've forgotten when that came along. It was a well-established fact by World War II, though.

Q: So it must have been at this point.

Admiral MacDonald: Oh, yes, it must have been definitely under way. I don't recall too much about that, fueling ships, but working in the _Salinas_ we were really just filling up the tanks. I don't even recall now that we ever got involved in a problem with the fleet. We were almost just a commercial ship, the way we were operating.

Q: And your oil supplies were purchased from commercial outfits?

Admiral MacDonald: From commercial outfits. We used to pump ballast, when we were about 85 miles outside of Houston's main ship canal, and be ready to hit the channel at a certain hour and go up and tie up. They just operate ships in and out of there like trains. They schedule exactly when you have to go to the dock, you fill up within a day or so, and out you go the next day. Turnaround is a big problem in the tanker business, not to lose tides so we could get in or out.

We would be diverted every so often to places like Panama and Guantanamo to fill them up, too. But, as I said, that type of duty is really basically just watchstanding.

Q: Therefore, there was a need for some of these social excursions ashore. It was rather dull otherwise.

Admiral MacDonald: Oh, yes, it was pretty monotonous going. However, when the weather was good and so forth, you enjoyed being at sea. There was no pressure at all, except to make sure that you're navigating well and so forth. We did work on some little problems that the captain was trying to solve in connection with trying to find the axis of the Strait of Florida. He didn't know that you get the biggest push going north if you can get close to the axis and, of course, we had to also discover that the least current against you, going down, was close to the beach, so we'd get in just about as close as we could along the beach running along the coast of Florida, because there was only about a 1.5-knot current operating against us. Out in the middle of the stream, people don't realize this, you have about four knots against you.

Q: So, unofficially, you became experts on the Gulf Stream?

Admiral MacDonald: Yes, we were studying it all the time on our trips so we could try to find where the best place was to go, particularly going north, and get the most push. Our maximum speed, I'm sure, wasn't more than about 10 or 11 knots.

Q: Was this knowledge imparted to the Hydrographic Office then?

Admiral MacDonald: I imagine it was. We were turning all kinds of meteorological weather reports in to them and so forth. I think the captain may have written up his findings on the thing. We did find out that during certain moon phases, currents varied quite a bit. Also, that the strait gets awfully rough if there's a wind hitting it head-on. That's why some of these northeast winds really created a very rough strait.

This all sort of came in to help me later on in connection with the Williamsburg, when I had the Williamsburg, this sort of basic knowledge of knowing where to go, because the Williamsburg wasn't very fast and powerful, either, and we used to make two trips a year down to Key West with the Williamsburg and try to find the right way to get the best push and so forth.*

---

*MacDonald commanded the presidential yacht Williamsburg (AGC-369) from 1948 to 1951.

Q: So experience on the Salinas helped.

Admiral MacDonald: Oh, yes. I think all these things help a great deal. They give you a lot of confidence, a lot of navigating, and all that business.

I can't recall any outstanding features of the duty on that, except my own enjoyable social life, because when we were in and I had a chance to get off I always had a good time. I planned it that way.

Q: How long were you in the Salinas?

Admiral MacDonald: One year. That was the usual routine of going up in your indoctrination--one year in auxiliaries. Some people went to oil tankers, some went to minesweepers, some went to other auxiliaries, transports, and so forth. It so happened that my cruise was in the Salinas.

I might as well mention here that there was another interesting aspect of life.

When I reported in on the California, my roommate was a classmate by the name of Robert Heilig, and I stood one number senior to him.* Therefore, I was always senior to Heilig. Now, he also was ordered to the Salinas, and he reported in, so, as

*Lieutenant (junior grade) Robert B. Heilig, USN, graduated number 86 in the class of 1931.

fate would have it, being one number senior to him, I became the senior watch officer to him, my own classmate. If there's any fellow who's been subjected to one-number seniority over a period of four years in the California and one in the Salinas, it was Heilig, poor guy!

Q: You said earlier that maybe class standing had no significance, but it does.

Admiral MacDonald: Well, as far as reaching the top command. By that, I meant that here was Rivero, a four-star admiral who stood at the top, and Jack McCain, a four-star admiral, virtually stood at the bottom. So, from that point of view, yes. But class standing has great impact on the people as they were going up, because the senior one was always the senior one, and it was all based on class standing, supposedly, at that time.

Q: You left the Salinas in April of 1938 and reported back to Washington for duty. What kind of an assignment did you get?

Admiral MacDonald: My first assignment was as a coding room officer. I was a j.g. then, and in the coding room at that time were four of us to handle all the traffic coming in to the Navy Department. It was another watchstanding type basis, a four-watch basis.

At that time, of course, things were happening out in China; there was a great emphasis being placed on intelligence coming in from China, particularly in the beginning, and we were pretty busy.* All the traffic was coming in from our Marine people and Navy people out in the China area.

Q: So you were working very closely with ONI, were you not?**

Admiral MacDonald: Oh, absolutely. We were providing copies every morning for the briefings in ONI. I worked very closely with all the top Navy Department people at the time. Stark was CNO and his administrative aide was Charlie Wellborn and Smedberg was his flag lieutenant at that time.*** Of course, Rear Admiral Ghormley was the Vice CNO.****

Marcel Lehardy was the assistant communications officer handling the basic coding arrangements.***** He was not a watchstander, but he was assistant communications officer. Before too long, probably about a year, Lehardy left and I fleeted up to his job. He went back to sea, so I became

---

*The mainland of China was invaded by the Japanese in July 1937. By October 1938, large areas had been conquered.

**ONI--Office of Naval Intelligence.

***Lieutenant Commander Charles Wellborn, Jr., USN; Lieutenant William R. Smedberg III, USN; Wellborn and Smedberg were assigned to these jobs when Admiral Harold R. Stark, USN, became Chief of Naval Operations in August 1939.

****Rear Admiral Robert L. Ghormley, USN, Assistant Chief of Naval Operations.

*****Lieutenant Louis Marcel Lehardy, USN.

assistant communications officer. At the same time I became an aide at the White House, to Mr. Roosevelt.

Q: Who was DNI in your time there?*

Admiral MacDonald: I haven't refreshed my memory recently on that, but Leigh Noyes was one of them.

Q: He was director of naval communications, wasn't he?

Admiral MacDonald: Oh, the director of naval intelligence?

Q: Yes.

Admiral MacDonald: I should remember that very well because--Struble was a commander at the time in OpNav and was basically one of the persons who was very interested in all of the information coming in from China.** There was a captain over him whose name at the moment I can't recall, who later ran into trouble in command of his ship and committed suicide.

Q: Captain Bode?

---

*DNI--Director of Naval Intelligence; from April 1937 to June 1939 Rear Admiral Ralston S. Holmes, USN, held that position.

**Commander Arthur D. Struble, USN, was assigned to the Central Division of OpNav from 1937 to 1940.

Admiral MacDonald: Bode, Howard Bode.* He was a captain in ONI at the time and Struble was the sort of hotshot intelligence person, later Admiral Struble.

Being assistant communications officer and heading up this cipher division, and the fact that Roosevelt began to communicate with Churchill, and they wouldn't trust the State Department ciphers because they felt that they were all compromised, so Roosevelt insisted upon the Navy handling all the information between the two of them.**

Q: He thought they were compromised by whom, by the potential enemy?

Admiral MacDonald: Yes, Japan and Germany and so forth.

Q: Why didn't the State Department do something about changing their codes, then?

Admiral MacDonald: Well, it takes a long time to get out a new system. At that time they were still using books, and the books probably had been compromised in different ways, stolen or

---

*Captain Howard D. Bode, USN, was commanding officer of the USS _Chicago_ (CA-29) when she was sunk by Japanese aircraft on 29 January 1943. He shot himself 19 April 1943 and died the following day at the naval hospital in Balboa, Panama Canal Zone.

**Winston S. Churchill was then Britain's First Lord of the Admiralty. He became Prime Minister in May 1940.

something.

So this traffic began to build up, and there were only two people. They had special recognition code words for the traffic, and the minute that traffic came in, it was sent only to the communications officer and myself. We then had to do it and, of course, the communications officer at the time being a full captain, I had to do almost all the deciphering myself of these messages from Roosevelt to Churchill.

They stemmed from the point of view that Roosevelt wanted to help the British; there's no doubt about that. He constantly was asking how they could help and working out details of how they could help one another. I must say that at that time Roosevelt, being an invalid and so forth and I having had a little experience as an aide at the White House and getting to know him personally--you could pick up the phone and reach the President direct. He insisted that this be done. The minute something came in, it was to go right to him first. He often said that he wanted to find out about it first from us, rather than through intermediaries, the Secretary of the Navy and CNO, and this is what we used to do.* So many times I talked to the President directly, particularly if I had a message in connection with something like we were going to manufacture airplanes for them and so forth and some of the details of meetings.

---

*CNO--Chief of Naval Operations.

I'd call him, and then he would direct how I'd handle the message, but this was never given to anyone in the Navy. This was just done independently.

Q: Using naval facilities but not . . .

Admiral MacDonald: That's right, definitely so.

Q: This was a two-man correspondence?

Admiral MacDonald: That's right, a two-man correspondence arrangement. Morgenthau, of course, was considered to be very loyal to the President and apparently had some of the same ideas of making sure that England didn't fall to the Germans, so he was ticked off as Roosevelt's right-hand man to handle a lot of this.*

Q: Did Roosevelt indicate in his messages the problems that he had to deal with in terms of public opinion in this country?

Admiral MacDonald: No.

Q: How he had to walk gingerly on various issues?

---

*Henry Morgenthau, Jr., Secretary of the Treasury from 1934 until 1945.

Admiral MacDonald: Not that I recall did he ever mention any difficulty. It just seemed like whatever he wanted to do was going to be done.

Q: He worked out the details himself, I mean as far as the home picture was concerned?

Admiral MacDonald: Well, it wasn't known by anyone, so there was no questioning of what he was doing or anything. No one knew about it. No one really knew about it at all. It was just one of those things. This started definitely right after the war started in 1939.

Q: What was the general tenor of Churchill's communications?

Admiral MacDonald: Very buoyant at first and so forth, because everything was stalemated. Sort of optimistic and maybe something might be worked out. This was long before the Battle of Britain started in 1940. It was a long period of stalemating.

Q: The phony war!

Admiral MacDonald: The phony war period. When the Germans moved into Poland, England committed itself, of course, and everything sort of stopped for a long period of time.

Q: And Churchill was so buoyant in his messages?

Admiral MacDonald: Yes, they weren't worried about anything at the moment. At least, I don't recall it, except that they did want us to produce definitely aircraft for them and ammunition, of course, and rifles. We were sending all kinds of things over to them.

Q: Wasn't submarine warfare fairly active?

Admiral MacDonald: Well, they agreed to set up this patrol, 300-mile patrol, where we would notify our ships patrolling off the coast about 300 miles.

Q: This was the neutrality patrol?

Admiral MacDonald: The neutrality patrol, which Roosevelt put into existence, and no one seemed to do anything about stopping that. If we sighted any submarines or anything, we'd let the British know about it and try to keep track of them.

One thing that stands out in my mind is when they wanted to produce their Hurricanes and Spitfires over here.* There was a lot of correspondence in connection with who could manufacture

*Hurricanes and Spitfires were British fighter planes.

them and how they could change the metric system of design to fit our measurement system.

Q: That was a real problem, wasn't it?

Admiral MacDonald: Tooling up for it and so forth, and this never really got worked out.

Those were the type of messages that were coming back and forth, particularly the neutrality patrol and what other help. I'm sure that among the many messages that went back and forth there were some in connection with what news could be released in order to buoy up the people and so forth. I don't remember any discussions or anything. As a matter of fact, I never was involved in the discussions. I was just in between, decoding messages and recoding messages going back and forth.

Q: Did the destroyer deal enter into that?

Admiral MacDonald: That was much later, no.*

Q: Yes, but the beginnings for that?

---

*In July 1940, agreement was reached in principle for the United States to trade 50 old four-stack destroyers to Britain for sites for naval, military, and air bases in the Bahamas, Jamaica, Antigua, St. Lucia, Trinidad, and British Guiana.

Admiral MacDonald: No, that wasn't even thought of at that time. Apparently, the British did realize that the German Air Force was really strong and building up, and this is what they wanted. At that time the British fleet was considered invincible, you know. Germany didn't have much of a fleet. It only had a few ships, pocket battleships. Food and other things were beginning to be discussed, but there was no shortage of anything until late in 1941.

Q: During this period the President was trying mightily to build up the U.S. Navy. Did he indicate this in his messages to Churchill?

Admiral MacDonald: Well, you know, Doctor, I just can't recall the contents of a lot of those things. I really don't remember the contents of them, but I do know that some of the things that sort of struck me, I mean personally, was the fact that I was the only one who could decode these messages, and wherever I went in Washington I had to leave my number. I was called from a couple of dinner parties and so forth and told that so-and-so flash had just come in and I'd have to dash down, leave the dinner party, and go down and decode it.

Q: Without explanation!

Admiral MacDonald: That's right. I never could explain to anyone what we were doing.

Q: How frequently did these messages come and go?

Admiral MacDonald: I would say on an average there was some period when there was maybe a message a day back and forth, some sort of note.

Q: Did this mean that when the President went to Shangri-La or places like that you had to go, too?*

Admiral MacDonald: Shangri-La wasn't even built then.

Q: But he had its counterparts?

Admiral MacDonald: He went up to Hyde Park at that time. Shangri-La, we built that for him later. That was built during World War II. Ben Moreell built that for him.** Basically, it was on the old CCC campgrounds.***

I do know that my duties at the White House as an aide were

---

*Shangri-La (known as Camp David since the Eisenhower Administration) was the Presidential retreat constructed in the Catoctin Mountains of western Maryland. Its construction was completed in July 1942.

**Rear Admiral Ben Moreell, CEC, USN, Chief of the Bureau of Yards and Docks and Chief of Civil Engineers from 1937 to 1945.

***CCC--Civilian Conservation Corps.

most interesting, because at that time, the aides were recognized as people of some sort of position over there. We were always available for all kinds of things.

Q: You had to have the social graces, too!

Admiral MacDonald: We used to have wonderful little ceremonies when ambassadors would present their credentials, and we were invited to all of the dinner parties usually. We took turns on that.

Q: How many of you were there?

Admiral MacDonald: There were six from the Navy contingent, two of whom were Marines, and I think there were about six from the Army. Three or four of them were from the cavalry troop that was stationed over at Fort Myer, and two were engineers from Fort Belvoir.

Q: And all these men were bachelors?

Admiral MacDonald: They all had to be bachelors; they all had to be very presentable in the social graces, supposedly, and, of course, from being down there so much because any reception or anything we were always there, all of us, we were socially accepted around here to the extent that my social life was very busy in the evenings. I was always invited out to dinner and affairs in the embassy area crowd, which was not the same size as it is now. As I recall, we only had not more than 20 ambassadors and we had even fewer ministers in those days.

Q: Yes.

Admiral MacDonald: Very few embassies had more than a dozen people in them, so it was sort of a close--I won't say family arrangement--but a sort of close arrangement.

Q: That assignment came before you had the coding . . .?

Admiral MacDonald: No, that was along with the coding job.

Q: With the Navy Department coding job?

Admiral MacDonald: Yes.

Q: But before you got involved with the White House in sending messages?

Admiral MacDonald: No, they went hand in hand, they worked together. I had a dual function. In other words, I was assistant communications officer for coding arrangements and also an aide at the White House. I had a dual function, so I kept pretty busy.

Q: What are some of your recollections of serving as an aide?

Admiral MacDonald: Most interesting, because the Roosevelt family were awfully nice to me, and, really, I must say that, my father being a Republican who didn't take to Roosevelt at all, they certainly were awfully nice to me. Mrs. Roosevelt, when she was in town, even on Sunday evenings, would give me a call and say, "If you do not have an engagement this evening, would you like to come down and join us for a family dinner?" And I'd come on down.

Q: That was the kind with a chafing dish, wasn't it?

Admiral MacDonald: Oh, yes. They had family dinner in the little family dining room, and invariably they would invite--at least I was invited a number of times and have eaten in that room a number of times.

Very few of the Roosevelt children were ever around. They only seemed to appear when there was some big function, and they never seemed to stay in the White House. They stayed at the

Mayflower or some place like that.*

Q: They didn't stay in the house?

Admiral MacDonald: No. Of course, those were the days when the Secret Service was probably a dozen people and security was nonexistent.

Q: So the family atmosphere could prevail?

Admiral MacDonald: Oh, yes, definitely. Everyone knew everyone. I don't think they even had a dozen people on the Secret Service payroll at that time.

Q: Of course, you were not in uniform?

Admiral MacDonald: We always had to wear uniform to the functions.

Q: But not at the family gatherings?

Admiral MacDonald: No, come as you are.

Now, the other thing that was most interesting along that

---

*The Mayflower has long been one of Washington's prominent hotels.

line is that Mrs. Roosevelt loved to ride horseback, and this is one of the reasons why some of the aides were always cavalry officers. They kept, over at Fort Myer, several horses for her to ride. The aides would have to go over and pick up the horses in the morning, about 7:00 o'clock, bring them over to Memorial Bridge, have them there about 7:30 when Mrs. Roosevelt would arrive, and then they would ride horseback along the Potomac River, down towards Alexandria. At that time, there was nothing there but the agricultural farm, no buildings whatsoever. You could ride the whole way down. They had a sort of bridle path along the river.

Q: She also rode somewhat in Rock Creek Park, didn't she?

Admiral MacDonald: No, not particularly. It was basically on the other side because she was riding from Fort Myer. I had always ridden a horse in my early days, so then I used to ride over there, too, to keep up with the arrangement. The Fort Myer people, General Patton--then it was Colonel Patton--was the commanding officer of Fort Myer, and he had several daughters who used to entertain a lot over there.* But the point of this was that the Army--if you would ride one of their cavalry horses at least so many times a week, then they would assign you the same

*Colonel George S. Patton, Jr., USA, Commander 3rd Cavalry Division from 1938 to 1940.

horse, which I tried to do because I found one that I liked, so I'd have it assigned. And I used to ride with the people occasionally on horseback. This made it very nice at that time.

There are two people who are always aides at the White House and, at that time, the commanding officer of the Presidential yacht, which then was the Potomac, was always the senior White House aide.

Q: He had full duty, did he not?

Admiral MacDonald: Well, he had full duty as commanding officer of the Potomac, but his main function at the White House was senior aide at the White House. He wasn't the naval aide; he was the senior White House aide. Dayton Clark was the first one and Count Austin was his exec, but Count, being a married man, was not an aide at the White House.* He was relieved by a fellow called Walter Jones.** Walter liked to ride and he maintained his horse at Fort Myer. He used to do a lot of riding with Mrs. Roosevelt. She really liked to exercise by riding in the morning.

They were so pleasant to the aides, it was unbelievable. It was a wonderful life. We were there so frequently that they

---

*Lieutenant Commander Augustus Dayton Clark, USN; Lieutenant Bernard L. Austin, USN.

**Lieutenant Commander Walter R. Jones, USN.

almost got to know us like their own children. We were invited to lots of parties. I even attended a party when the King and Queen of England were there. I was seated at the far end of the table, but I was there, which was very nice. When they gave balls for nieces or something like that, we used to be invited and dance with them. The Roosevelts were very thoughtful in connection with parties. They gave lots of wonderful formal parties at the White House. They were constantly entertaining.

Q: How did he manage at parties?

Admiral MacDonald: Oh, he arrived and he would be moved around sometimes in his wheelchair, but many times he'd get up and he always would stand up and click his knee brace and so forth and hang onto his naval aide. That's one of the reasons why the naval aide at that time always had to be such a big, powerful man--Pa Watson was the military aide then.* Roosevelt placed great confidence in Pa Watson.

Q: He was an older man, was he not?

Admiral MacDonald: He was an older person, and he didn't do any of this sort of helping Roosevelt around himself. His naval aide

---

*Brigadier General Edwin M. Watson, USA.

did. The naval aide was younger and powerfully built and so forth and was quite able to do everything that Roosevelt demanded. Dan Callaghan, then a captain, was the naval aide.*

Many times Roosevelt would come down in the elevator, he'd walk with his aide to wherever he was going to be in the receiving line, or he'd go into the ballroom, or reception room. Otherwise, he usually went around in a wheelchair. There were a lot of things later, Shangri-La and everything, how he had to construct it just because of his incapacity.

I remember very vividly going in the Potomac a number of times, and they had a little elevator built in a false stack for him to raise him up from the main deck to a higher level. Also all the equipment around the bathtub, toilets and everything. He had to have special fittings, solidly built and powerful, so that he could go to the shower, go to the bathroom, and everything himself. He had very powerful arms. Roosevelt had developed shoulder and arm muscles fantastically.

Q: He swam a lot, did he not?

Admiral MacDonald: Yes, he used to swim a lot.

---

*Captain Daniel J. Callaghan, USN. Later, as commander of a fire support task force, Rear Admiral Callaghan was killed on board his flagship, USS San Francisco (CA-38), during Guadalcanal action in November 1942.

Q: Did he have a pool in the White House?

Admiral MacDonald: Yes, he did. That's when they built the pool. Of course, the White House has been renovated since then. I know that they had a pool in the White House at the time.

Q: Did they entertain on the *Potomac* very much?

Admiral MacDonald: No, the President didn't entertain, but he loved to go on the *Potomac*. As a matter of fact, he would go down to the *Potomac* at the drop of a hat. He just loved to be at sea. The *Potomac* was kept quite busy, going up and down the river with the President. Of course, later on--well, even in my duty at the time, although I wasn't involved in any of it--any time they made an arrangement where the President was going to some ship or other, they always had to ascertain that there would be funds available to do the things that had to be done for Roosevelt.

Q: He went on the *Tuscaloosa* several times.

Admiral MacDonald: He went fishing off of several of the cruisers. Once they'd equipped a ship for him, he usually tried to find the same ship because the ship invariably knew he was going to do something, go on a trip somewhere. Even during the war, later on, you know, when he went in the Iowa and a few others crossing the Atlantic, they'd have to do the same thing, put in special equipment so he could pull himself around.

Q: Felix Johnson told me he was the skipper of the Lang, a new destroyer that went on two fishing expeditions with the Tuscaloosa and even the Lang had to be fitted. The toilets had to be changed and so forth and the shower for just the brief time the President was on board.*

Admiral MacDonald: That's right. They went to all of that trouble, the Navy did. The difficulty in the whole thing was picking a ship in advance, getting the money, and then sending it into the yard before the trip so that they'd have it all ready.

Q: So these fishing expeditions had to be planned well in advance?

Admiral MacDonald: They had to be planned in advance because of the special type of equipment that he required--little elevators and reinforced everything in connection with bathrooms, a mirror for when he shaved, sitting in a wheelchair. At that time they

---

*Lieutenant Commander Felix L. Johnson, USN, whose memoirs are contained in the Naval Institute's oral history collection. USS Lang (DD-399) was commissioned 30 March 1939.

had nickel rods, those big, powerful rods that were bolted into the sides of buildings, and the same things we had to do they did up at Shangri-La, his bedroom and so forth was all special. And big doors, very wide, so that he could get his wheelchair out from the ramp.

Q: Was he not sensitive about appearing in public in a wheelchair?

Admiral MacDonald: I don't think so. He had a wonderful smile that was very disarming to a lot of people, possibly ones who didn't like him, and, of course, that voice of his will always be remembered from listening to him on the air.

Well, I can only be most grateful for my experience with the Roosevelt family, and by that I mean Mr. and Mrs. Roosevelt only, because the boys, I never really got to know them at all.

Q: Did you get to know Louis Howe?* And Harry Hopkins?**

Admiral MacDonald: Oh, yes, I did. I knew them but never well until Harry Hopkins came into my life in London. He was on a mission to Moscow. That's when I really got to know Hopkins.

*Louis McH. Howe, FDR's campaign manager and advisor.
**Harry L. Hopkins, Secretary of Commerce from 1938 to 1940.

Q: When you were an aide at the White House, Louis Howe was still very much in evidence.

Admiral MacDonald: Yes, I remember him, but he worked basically with the chief usher of the White House. There were only a couple of them and the secretaries. They handled all the social and diplomatic functions. But at that time the chief of protocol was one of the top officers in connection with the social life at the White House.

Q: You mean the chief of protocol in the State Department?

Admiral MacDonald: That's right. He was the one who was always responsible for sending out the invitations and announcing people, also the seating arrangements, and all that business.

Q: Who was that?

Admiral MacDonald: Summerlin was the chief of protocol at the time, and his assistant, Stanley Woodward, who later was very prominent in the Truman Administration, relieved him.*

Q: Since you were in the White House so very often on social

---

*George T. Summerlin.

occasions, was your identity as a coding officer kept strictly apart from this other activity as far as the President was concerned?

Admiral MacDonald: Yes, definitely. I would say the same was true for all the aides at the White House, except the ones who were in a cavalry troop and, of course, they did riding. But otherwise what they were doing was never really brought up at the White House.

Q: Did Miss LeHand come on the scene ever?*

Admiral MacDonald: If she did, I don't recall her at all. The two chief ushers definitely we used to communicate with a lot, because they were the ones who always called us and told us that So-and-So was going to do this or that and the President would like to have three or four of the aides present.

Q: Why didn't the children stay at the White House? I should have thought they might have wanted to.

Admiral MacDonald: Some of them were away at school; others were married and had their own lives to lead. They were all older

---

*Miss Marguerite "Missy" LeHand, Roosevelt's longtime private secretary.

than we were, and they just never did. I don't think that some of their habits were what the Roosevelts would like to have had pointed out in the White House, anyway. They may have moved in after I left in 1940, when the President had Jimmy come as one of his first secretaries or something like that.* They may have lived there, but they weren't living there when I was there.

That type of life continued until spring of 1940.

Q: That must have been, in its way, very, very strenuous, since you did have duties in the Navy Department which demanded detailed attention.

Admiral MacDonald: It was strenuous from the fact that you had lots of invitations, you had to answer them, you had to go there and have everything ready, but I was very fortunate. I lived with Lieutenant Stuart Blue.** He and I had an apartment on 15th Street, just off Meridian Park. It was a very lovely studio apartment--I've forgotten the name. It's still there. This apartment was a three-floor arrangement. Stuart was then flag lieutenant to Admiral Richardson, who was then Chief of the Bureau of Naval Personnel, so, being in that capacity, whenever, say, some mess attendant or cook was going to leave the Navy, he

---

*James Roosevelt, the President's oldest son, served as a personal secretary and aide for his father on several inspection tours and at conferences prior to U.S. entry into the war.

**Lieutenant John Stuart Blue, USN.

was retiring, Stuart was in a good position to ask him if he wanted to work for us.* We hired a retired cook and a retired steward, who lived in our third-floor studio apartment. This made it very nice. All we had to do was call the cook and tell him that we were entertaining or we were going someplace at a certain hour and he'd lay out our uniforms. We lived very well. We had a parking spot in the back.

Q: You almost needed that kind of backing up, didn't you?

Admiral MacDonald: That's right. We couldn't have done it. Of course, Stuart was at one time an aide at the White House, so he knew all about it. He was older than I was, but it was certainly very helpful to me to room with Stuart Blue, and I did this until he married. Then I moved in with Mr. Robert Waggaman, down on R Street, in his father's house, and took my stewards down with me, so that I could always get the proper attention in connection with . . .

Q: That was Toggie, wasn't it? Wasn't he called Toggie?

Admiral MacDonald: You mean Doggie. No, this was a first

---

*Rear Admiral James O. Richardson, USN, was Chief of the Bureau of Navigation from 1938 to 1939. In 1942 BuNav was changed to the Bureau of Naval Personnel.

cousin, Floyd Waggaman, one of the old families around Washington. Robert was about my age and he still lives here.

We maintained his father's house because his father did an awful lot of traveling, and it made life very easy as far as living was concerned, because not only did I have my steward to look out for me, but Mr. Waggaman had a chauffeur, a cook, and maids, so we were all set. Of course, we had no idea how easy life was and how pleasant it was then in comparison with today.

Q: Yes, prewar Washington!

Admiral MacDonald: Prewar Washington was just a very delightful place. There just wasn't enough time if you wanted to do everything, but it was pleasant.

This all sort of continued until the spring of 1940, when Admiral Ghormley was going to be ordered out as the commander of Cruiser Division Nine, I think it was, based in Hawaii, and he then asked Count Austin to be his administrative flag secretary, and he asked me if I'd go as his flag lieutenant.* Of course, I was thrilled. Ghormley was a very pleasant, delightful person, and I'd had lots of contact with him while I was at the Navy Department.

---

*Cruiser Division Nine was then commanded by Rear Admiral Husband E. Kimmel, USN, who remained in that billet until he became Commander in Chief Pacific Fleet in February 1941.

We were all set to go and making all these plans, and all of a sudden President Roosevelt called Ghormley over to see him one day, I think it was pretty close to May. Originally we were to leave in June. He told Ghormley that he wanted to send him over to London. Ghormley then returned to the Navy Department and called Austin and myself in and said he was terribly sorry, but he was going to have to release us; he wouldn't be able to go out and take the cruiser division. At that time, all he said was that Roosevelt wanted him to do something else.

This was quite a blow. I don't recall exactly how depressed I was, but I was looking forward to the other assignment, and I just thought in my own mind, well, maybe he might take us anyway. So, lo and behold, a couple of days later he called us in and said, "The President says I can take anyone I want with me. Do you want to go with me?"

I said yes, so I was ticked off to handle the communications aspect of this thing.

Q: Of the SPENAVO mission?*

Admiral MacDonald: Yes, to go to London. SPENAVO was something that came up later, when we tried to work out a codeword for it. Originally, he was going over as the naval attache and we were

---

*SPENAVO--Special Naval Observer--a codeword used for correspondence with Vice Admiral Ghormley.

going over as assistant naval attaches.

Q: He was going to supplant the man who was there?

Admiral MacDonald: Well, he wasn't supposed to supplant, but he was supposed to put Kirk, who was the naval attache over there at the time, into a subordinate job while he fleeted up.*

It wasn't long before Kirk was complaining bitterly that he wanted to be reassigned if Ghormley was going to come in there as naval attache. But it was all set that we were going, and my original passport was as assistant attache. At that time it was easy to call up Mrs. Shipley down at the State Department--the President can get anything--and all we had to do was pick them up.**

Q: No waiting for that!

Admiral MacDonald: No waiting for that.

Then, instead of his being detached in June to go to the cruiser division, we were going to go to London, but the Battle of Dunkirk and all this evacuation and everything happened, so then we were put on ice to wait until it would be an opportune

---

*Captain Alan G. Kirk, USN. Kirk's oral history is in the Columbia University collection.

**Ruth B. Shipley, Chief of the Passport Division, Department of State.

time to go over there. At that time, even messages coming in from Churchill indicated, my God, the situation is so serious he didn't know whether England was going to be able to stand up to anything.

Q: You were still decoding those messages, then?

Admiral MacDonald: Yes.

Q: A note of alarm crept into Churchill's messages?

Admiral MacDonald: It finally did. Really, there was a period of a couple of months there when they didn't know whether the Germans would invade right away or whether Britain would be able to stand up.

Q: How did Roosevelt react to this?

Admiral MacDonald: I personally don't know. I'm sure he was worried.

Q: But wasn't it reflected in his messages?

Admiral MacDonald: Yes, it was. It was reflected in the immediate buildup arrangements of our providing them with military equipment. The British were sending ships over, and we were just loading them down with military equipment, even aircraft, our own aircraft, which we'd been building up fantastically. Even when we went over in the Britannic, there was nothing but airplanes on deck and they were American airplanes. We never were able to solve that problem of building Spitfires and Hurricanes over here.

Q: So we had to send all the spare parts along?

Admiral MacDonald: Our own stuff, and, of course, ammunition and rifles. You see, the British, when they evacuated, left everything, all the military equipment, on the beaches, and then they had practically nothing on the other side. There was a tremendous buildup then of sending equipment over to help stem the tide.

We were sitting around here on ice for a couple of months, until they finally worked out when we'd go over. They worked out with the British that we'd go over on the Britannic, which was in New York loading up.

Q: By that time it was fairly certain there would be a London to go to?

Admiral MacDonald: Yes, at least it was still there. The

indications were that any of the barges that the troops had come over on, the British discovered they had been bombed a little, and they didn't have enough to do anything anyway. The war quieted down, because the Germans had no way to get across the Channel and no way to return home.

Q: Reflecting on those dispatches, it's often been said, and it's been proved true, that Churchill dreamed up various ideas for conducting aspects of the war. Did any of them show in the dispatches?

Admiral MacDonald: Not on the ones I handled, because this was long before we got into the war completely.

Q: You know what I refer to?

Admiral MacDonald: Yes, I know, and I'm sure of that because just the association with Churchill in London, he was a great strategist himself. He would just take pepper and salt shakers on the table and, you know, sort of draw diagrams of tactical maneuvers and so forth. He loved things like that.

To get back to this thing, Roosevelt used to write a lot of things that would come in to me and be coded and sent over there in longhand. I was just thinking, in our files--I don't know where they could possibly be--there was a special file that had all these messages.* Now, where the Sam Hill that is, I don't know.

Q: Whether it was preserved?

Admiral MacDonald: Right, whether it was preserved or destroyed or what. A lot of these things were written in longhand by Roosevelt himself. He loved this communicating with Churchill; he really loved it. The special cipher business, as far as the Navy handling it and all this, we had special ciphers for this.

Q: Developed for this alone?

Admiral MacDonald: Yes, and the cipher section produced some wonderful arrangements, special cipher arrangements, which I had all ciphered, microfilmed and everything. They fixed me up with all these things to go in my watch and they were one-shot arrangements, so there was never any compromise. According to the day, you went into the one it was going to be. I had a watch where you could get into the back, and all of this was put inside of it.

---

*For the substance of the interchanges between the two men between 1933 and 1945, see Churchill and Roosevelt: Their Complete Correspondence (Princeton, New Jersey: Princeton University Press, 1984), three volumes edited and with commentary by Warren F. Kimball.

Q: In the case?

Admiral MacDonald: In the case in microfilm, and I had to look at it with one of those jeweler's microscopes.

Q: When you were decoding?

Admiral MacDonald: On the other side. I was taking it over on the other side.

Q: I see.

Admiral MacDonald: I had to use it all the time on the other side, when sending messages back.

Q: Oh, you continued that?

Admiral MacDonald: Oh, yes, because the only go-between between Churchill and the President was my boss, Ghormley. I then had to handle all this myself.

Q: This was a factor, I suppose, in getting Ghormley to take you over there, was it?

Admiral MacDonald: That was part of it, to be his communications officer.

Q: And Ghormley hadn't realized it when he discovered he wasn't going to the cruiser division?

Admiral MacDonald: No, he hadn't thought of it until later, but he immediately thought of it the moment Roosevelt said he could take anyone else he wanted to.

Q: At that point, Ghormley didn't know that you were doing this job, though?

Admiral MacDonald: Oh, Ghormley knew where I was. He knew I was in decoding and assistant communications officer, and I think that was one of the reasons why he wanted me to go with him in the first place, yes. Oh, he knew all about that aspect of it, yes. But he didn't know how valuable our services would be, particularly when we got over there, because one of the things that unfortunately caused hurt feelings in Kirk and so forth was that Ghormley never cut anyone else in to what was going on. Kirk, being the naval attache, because by that time they had changed our names to naval observers, and there was no sort of conflict then that Kirk would be a subordinate attache. But Kirk was never brought into the meetings. Information was flowing in both directions after we got over there.

Q: I'm sure he didn't react very well to that.

Admiral MacDonald: No, he didn't like it, but then he lived up to it and enjoyed his tennis and a few things. He had to take it in stride, there was no doubt about it. Ghormley would cut him in occasionally, but he never really was brought into the picture. Count Austin would go with Ghormley to these meetings. He was the flag secretary, and if it was going to appear in writing, why, then Count would prepare that. If it was going to go in a message, then I'd take care of it. That was after we got over there.

But we did sail on the *Britannic* out of New York.

Q: Now, who took over your job for Roosevelt's messages when you left Washington?

Admiral MacDonald: Well, the communications officer was still the same one.

Q: You mean the captain?

Admiral MacDonald: The captain was still the same one and, as far as I know, he was the one who was still doing it and then probably passed it on to someone else, but I don't know who he passed it on to. By the time we left for London, the thing was opening up a lot more. It was just during that period of '39 until the spring of '40 when it was really held very closely.

Q: That was because the situation was so delicate on this side?

Admiral MacDonald: Yes.

Q: Did they, a little later on, develop an intercontinental telephonic communication?

Admiral MacDonald: Yes, much later. I hate to go so fast ahead, but that was developed much later, when we found out that the British had scramblers. You'd pick up a telephone and they had a machine like a sort of transformer arrangement that would transform and scramble voice communication and then, if you set it on the same code on the other side, the other guy--it would unravel just the way it mixed it up, so that any transmission through the air or anything got nothing but mumbo jumbo.

The British had scramblers, just like they had radar. I think I mentioned to you once before that before we left for London, we were brought in and were briefed, and we were told that we could tell the British about a lot of thing, but there was one subject that we couldn't even discuss, and that was radar. We were just beginning to discover what radar was here. We had this equipment down at the research lab on the Potomac

River and they had discovered that by sending a beam on a certain frequency, if it was interrupted, there was some contact out there. They were just working this thing up and had equipment that would fill a couple of rooms just for this one thing. We were told we couldn't even discuss it, and we got over there, and, wow.

Q: We seem to have been in a dream world and thought the rest of the world didn't know anything about this!

Admiral MacDonald: That's right.

As to the radar, my God, we landed just with the Battle of Britain starting--we saw all these towers on some of our inspection trips and asked some questions. They were radar towers.

Q: Did the British have the same attitude of secrecy toward their radar that we had?

Admiral MacDonald: Yes. It was some time before they began to let us in on how everything was operated. The minute they did open the door, our people just rushed over there to get it and bring it back.

Q: Then we were great pals!

Admiral MacDonald: Oh, yes.

I was just saying about the scrambler. That did come in, but it came in after we discovered the British had scramblers. They were the first ones to give us scramblers that we could use on the Presidential conversations, the telephone lines. It was British equipment that came over here and, to show you exactly what little progress was made, when I was commanding Truman's yacht--I realized it because Truman used to get up in the transmitter room and telephone communications to different people. Right off the bat, it dawned on me, I've got to get sort of a security system, and I recalled those British scramblers. So I went to the Navy Department, electronics people, communications people, and said, "Look, don't we have any scramblers over here that we can use for the President, to keep his conversations off the air, because every darned little boat could be recording all of this?"

We didn't. We had not developed a scrambler in our whole setup, but they told me I could work with American Telephone or Western Electric and maybe develop one for the President. So I called those people down and said, "Look, we've got to get some sort of scrambler." And, do you know, they didn't even know much about how the thing operated.

Q: They didn't know the principles of it?

Admiral MacDonald: Well, they did sort of. I told them the principle is that you talk into this thing, it's all jumbled and scrambled up. Then that scrambling is received at the other end and, if you put the setting as the scrambler on the unscrambler, it comes out. The only thing you had to do when you were talking to a guy was say, "Let's scramble on A." So you both press A and scramble, then you start talking, and it's coming out just the way you're speaking in. But in the meantime, no one who records it knows what you're saying.

This was one of the funny things. I never was able to get a scrambler. They told me at the time, after many discussions with the telephone company people--our people were just out of it. They'd never done anything on it. It would cost too much money. They did come up with a great big box of sorts that was completely inadequate. It wouldn't work because you couldn't carry it around in airplanes; it was too heavy.

Q: But you did say that later on in Roosevelt's time there was one developed for his use?

Admiral MacDonald: But it wasn't developed by us. Churchill gave him a scrambler. This is the point.

Q: So it was in use?

Admiral MacDonald: It was in use, yes. It was in use definitely by the time the war got started.

Q: I'm surprised that it wasn't of such an interest to our people that we then went ahead and developed our own.

Admiral MacDonald: It doesn't make sense to me that we had, by 1948, not gotten involved in scramblers. This period I'm talking about and getting it for Truman was 1948 when I took over command.

Q: Yes.

Admiral MacDonald: The British provided them for us in our own offices in London. They were circulated around to just certain people. Churchill had them, the First Sea Lord, and a few other top-ranking people had scramblers.

Q: Do you think there was real merit in the emphasis on secrecy? Going back to the radar illustration and the fact that we, in secret, developed our radar haltingly, and the British at the same time developing theirs in secret, is there logic in maintaining a policy of secrecy?

Q: Oh, yes, there certainly was. We were helped greatly after the battle of the Graf Spee, when our people took pictures of all her antennas and everything. All of a sudden, there was an antenna that people said they wanted to measure the frequency arrangement and so forth. They sent a special team to go to the Graf Spee and get all the dimensions and pictures and everything else.*

That was the first indication that even the Germans had radar, and we were way behind on it. But this helped us in connection with getting the frequency arrangement.

Q: My point is that the Americans and the British were allies, prior to our involvement in the war, allies in secret, as you indicate by the communications between the President and the Prime Minister. If we had not had such an obdurate policy of utter secrecy on these things, our progress would have been greater and faster, would it not, between the two nations?

Admiral MacDonald: Well, it was just technological--obtaining this was a technological breakthrough that people had discovered. This was one of the secret military items.

But, getting back to the other thing that you were talking about, public reaction. Now that I think back a little bit,

---

*The German pocket battleship Admiral Graf Spee was scuttled by her commanding officer off the coast of Uruguay on 17 December 1939.

Roosevelt had to walk a very thin line in connection with it. There was a lot of isolationism in this country and Lindbergh was involved in a lot of it.* A lot of people felt strongly that we should back the Germans instead of the English. I don't think that if Roosevelt had given any of this information out to the press or anything like that--he might have had a very rough time of it because support for Britain was on a thin line.

Q: That's why I asked whether there was any of that situation reflected in his communications with Churchill, because I know that he had to deal with this.

Admiral MacDonald: I'd say no, and the reason for it is that he was going to take all of them blind. He definitely felt that he wanted to back the British. I think it was a very strong personal thing, too. I don't know why he would have had great hatred against the Germans, except that Morgenthau, being one of his close and intimate friends, just hated the Germans. This is one of the reasons Morgenthau was ticked off on a lot of these things to try to help. He worked with corporation heads and so forth and companies that provided equipment.

---

*Charles A. Lindbergh. Before the war, Lindbergh had toured German aircraft factories and was highly impressed with that country's potential for air power. After the European war began, he became an outspoken opponent of U.S. involvement, viewing the war as a foreign quarrel.

I think that the general public was certainly lukewarm to pitching in with the British at the time, but the President never told them that he was doing it. He wasn't getting into any sort of fighting arrangement at that time.

Q: Do you recall the attitude in the higher echelons in the Navy at that time?

Admiral MacDonald: We always felt that we had to back the British. The Navy's whole policy, our whole basic policy, was that we back the British, and that's probably because from way back we have always--so many of our traditions and everything and customs and so forth all stem from the British.

Q: So the President wasn't actually espousing this policy alone?

Admiral MacDonald: No. The Navy's planning had always been that we'd never fight England; we'd always team up with her. There's no doubt about that. That may have stemmed from way back, World War I days, too. I mean, we fought with the British in World War I and it just carried right on. We were going to fight with the British again.

Q: That's why I raised that question of the secrecy on radar and so forth. When we did have that tradition as a navy, why there couldn't have been a little relaxation as far as the British was concerned.

Admiral MacDonald: Well, of course, there's always great competition in these navies, you know. The Royal Navy was always known as the most powerful fleet afloat, and even in the treaty of 1925 when it became a 1:1:3:3:5:5 arrangement, who headed up the talks? The British and ourselves. The other thing is we've always tried to work unilaterally in the development of weapons. Their characteristics of how they do things are so different from ours and their whole industrial setup. They have the metric system and we have the other. We've never worked together on any of these things. They didn't do anything in connection with the exchange until after World War II. This policy of dealing with them did change when the nuclear submarine came along. That policy did change. We did give the British our technical knowledge, reports and research, and even provided them with one, and this caused great difficulty later because the French wanted to be considered in the deal.

As far as I know, we have never helped any other nation on the development of nuclear power, except England, but we have turned everything over to them on that.

So that point of yours doesn't apparently hold today, but it did before World War II, when we weren't telling them anything.

Q: As far as the nuclear power goes, that was largely a personal thing that Mountbatten engineered, wasn't it?*

Admiral MacDonald: It could have been. That's another phase of my Navy life, in my antisubmarine warfare position, when nuclear-powered submarines were just coming along. I think Mountbatten made several trips over here at the time. He was a great personality, no doubt about it, but what influence he had, I don't know.

I don't think we'd be so fast to help the British today as, say, 10 or 15 years ago, when nuclear power was coming along, because other nations than Britain are having their own problems, to survive, as a matter of fact. You get other nations popping up.

Just to go back to some of the things just before we went to London in 1940. Admiral Ghormley had asked me--because he had a better idea maybe of what his directive was, while he didn't convey too much to us, I mean Austin and myself--but he did say that I should go down and look up the Sims Report, congressional investigations that resulted after Sims . . .

---

*Admiral of the Fleet Lord Louis Mountbatten. As First Sea Lord in the late 1950s, Mountbatten was largely responsible for the accession and construction of nuclear-powered Polaris submarines for the Royal Navy, a role he later regretted. Towards the end of his life he became an outspoken proponent of nuclear disarmament.

Q: This was Admiral Sims from World War I?*

Admiral MacDonald: Yes, Admiral Sims of World War I, who went over on a similar job in World War I. When he came back, he wrote a letter, or letters, to congressmen saying that if the CNO had given him the ships and so forth that he had requested in the beginning, it would have shortened the war and would have saved many lives and saved many dollars, and so forth.

Anyway, this investigation that got started in about 1921, according to the report--and I told you the other day that there are two thick volumes on this thing--everything the Navy Department did from about 1916 was questioned. The CNO was on the spot, and everyone else. Even though the Americans won the war, Congress was on the spot.

Q: How not to do it again!

Admiral MacDonald: And this was one of the things. Look at this report and see that we don't duplicate the mistakes that Sims made. I was particularly interested in how he set up the headquarters and so forth over there and what he did, just as a matter of information, so if we had to do it, we had to do it.

---

*Admiral William S. Sims, USN, Commander U.S. Naval Forces Operating in European Waters from May 1917 to March 1919. In March 1917, as a rear admiral, he was put on a special assignment to carry dispatches to England.

That was a very interesting report which, really, you thought that no one had done a good job at all after that report came out. It was a terrible thing--the Navy was inefficient, ineffective, and everything else. Well, this wasn't true, and that report brought all this out.

Well, as far as I know, I hope we avoided . . .

Q: Did you read the two volumes of the report?

Admiral MacDonald: Oh, yes, and red-penciled the items that I thought the admiral would like to see, just to get some clue when he set up his own setup.

Q: Did Ghormley read it, or did he rely on you to ferret out the . . .

Admiral MacDonald: No, I don't think he really paid much attention to it. He probably recalled some of it.

Q: Did Austin read it?

Admiral MacDonald: No. They got involved immediately in connection with details about helping convoy ships.

Q: Yes, once they got there, there were immediate problems, but in preparation, this is what you did particularly to prepare for your job?

Admiral MacDonald: That and the cipher, and, of course, one of the things that we had to do right away was work up a common code arrangement which would be mutual for all of us. That was one of the things I had to do right off the bat.

Interview Number 2 with Rear Admiral Donald J. MacDonald,
U.S. Navy (Retired)

Place: Admiral MacDonald's residence in Washington, D.C.

Date: Tuesday afternoon, 23 July 1974

Subject: Biography

Interviewer: John T. Mason, Jr.

Q: It's good to see you today. Last time, when you broke off, you were deep in preparation for your position on the staff of Admiral Ghormley as he went as a special representative of President Roosevelt to London before we got into the war.* You told me that you had gone over the two volumes of the Sims Report in preparation. I assume there were other preparations you had to make as well as in regard to the code situation you were employed in?

Admiral MacDonald: We were ordered to sail on a British ship in early June. However, the evacuation of Dunkirk started in the first week, as I recall, of June, and, therefore, our departure was delayed.**

*Rear Admiral Robert L. Ghormley, USN, who went to Britain with the title of special naval observer. He was later promoted to vice admiral during the course of the tour.

**Between 26 May and 4 June 1940, a total of 338,226 British, French, and Belgian soldiers were evacuated to Britain from the French seaport of Dunkirk.

Q: Rather precarious, anyway, to go on a British ship, wasn't it, at that time?

Admiral MacDonald: Well, about the only way we could get over there was on a British ship. At that time, there was no air transportation going over. Prior to my leaving, I was being briefed as to how to handle the communications aspect of what we might be confronted with in London. They provided me with special secret codes and ciphers on microfilm, which were a sort of one-day business, so after being used once they were destroyed.

Q: You must have had quite a supply of codes, then?

Admiral MacDonald: On microfilm they had it condensed down where you could only see what it was all about with a very high-powered magnifying optical instrument.

Finally, they did make arrangements for us to sail. In the meantime we had obtained State Department passports and visas as diplomats. Admiral Ghormley was going originally as naval observer plus naval attache, and we were all going as assistant naval attaches, but that all was changed later on.

We sailed on the Britannic for England. I don't recall the exact date, but it seems to me it was in August of 1940, and on the same ship the Army was represented by General Strong and the air corps of the Army was represented by General Emmons.*

Q: They were going as special representatives?

Admiral MacDonald: They were going as sort of conferees, because there was no doubt our first meetings were to be with the military people of the British Army and Navy in order to discuss various military aspects of what might come out in the future.

Q: What was your understanding of the nature of Admiral Ghormley's mission at that point?

Admiral MacDonald: At that point it seemed to me definitely that they wanted to have Admiral Ghormley over there because it looked like we were going to get involved in the war and then he would end up being the commander of the U.S. naval forces in that area. It seemed to be obvious that that was what was in mind, not only for President Roosevelt to have a top military man in London at the time, but also to have one ready if things should all of a sudden break fast.

We were not allowed at any time to disclose where we were going or anything else. This was quite a hardship in connection with dealing with my family. I couldn't tell them exactly where

*Major General George V. Strong, USA; Major General Delos C. Emmons, USA.

I was going or why.

Q: Whether you were going east, west, north, or south!

Admiral MacDonald: Yes. It wasn't clarified for some time afterwards. We've already talked of Count Austin, and he had children and a wife and he had to more or less really make arrangements.*

My getting ready was fairly simple. I had to sell an automobile and vacate my quarters.

Q: Was the _Britannic_ escorted?

Admiral MacDonald: No, the _Britannic_ was not escorted, because at that time they didn't escort anything that could travel as fast as the _Britannic_.

Q: And her speed was what?

Admiral MacDonald: I think she probably made 17 or 18 knots all the way. At that time they were only convoying ships that made less than probably 10 knots.

---

*Lieutenant Commander Bernard L. Austin, USN, whose oral history is in the Naval Institute collection.

Q: But she did zigzag?

Admiral MacDonald: Not that I recall, but she was loaded down with military equipment, airplanes, ammunition, and everything else, and had some passengers on board. Of course, the trip over, as far as the passengers were concerned, was really delightful. We had awfully good food, we had all of the servants and stewards and everything that made for very good cruising.

When we finally landed in Liverpool, why, we had had a very uneventful passage.

Q: Did Captain Kirk, who was then our naval attache over there, have knowledge of the mission?*

Admiral MacDonald: Not particularly. He didn't know too much about it and was very anxious to find out what his status was when Admiral Ghormley arrived. He had made arrangements for us to stay at the Dorchester Hotel in a suite of rooms with two bedrooms and a sitting room on the top floor of the Dorchester.

Q: That was a dubious honor, was it not, the top floor of the Dorchester Hotel in a raid?

---

*Captain Alan G. Kirk, USN, whose oral history is in the Columbia University collection.

Admiral MacDonald: That's where the story begins. We had no sooner arrived than the Battle of Britain started. In the very beginning, we could go up on the roof and watch the bombing down by the docks. The original bombing by the Germans was the dock area, where they set off warehouse fires, ship fires, and everything, and they were burning furiously for weeks. That's where it all started.

Q: But they weren't concentrating on the city itself?

Admiral MacDonald: No, they were not concentrating on the city. That came much later. They were trying to hit specific targets at that time. Later, they shifted their specific targets to the roadways and the railroad stations. But, due to the British defense, particularly their wonderful fighters, all this bombing was in the evening, at night, quite late at night, so that our stay at the Dorchester was quite an experience because practically every night there were air-raid sirens, so we had no sleep. We used to go up on the roof when the air-raid sirens sounded to see what was going on, where most of the people were supposed to go into the shelters down below. They had air-raid shelters in the basement of the hotel.

Of course, everything was all blacked out, so we couldn't turn on any lights.

Q: Did you ever go down there?

Admiral MacDonald: No, I never went down into that shelter. Most of the people never did go into the shelter. They went down to the ground floor, in the dining room and lounges and so forth, and stayed there.

The air raids didn't last too long in the very beginning. Just sort of solitary bombers coming over and unloading.

The thing that I admired after we were there for a while were the air-raid wardens who, the minute a siren sounded, would have to go out and patrol the streets and everything in the pitch-dark, make sure there were no lights. They were pretty courageous people, and a lot of them were women. I certainly admired them.

What we were doing after we got over there, there were a lot of meetings set up, which later were given the name the ABC papers meetings.*

Q: What did that stand for?

Admiral MacDonald: I'm sorry you didn't ask Count Austin that. He used to sit in on all of those meetings with the admiral, and I just would work on the communications aspect, working to

*ABC--American, British, Canadian Plans.

prepare a mutual codebook that the British and American navies could use in the event hostilities involved us. The ABC was more or less what we would do in the event that we got into the war, what help would we give the British, and dividing up sectors of control and responsibility, command responsibilities, and so forth. This was more or less what ABC papers were all about, getting all set to do certain things on each side and who would be responsible.

Q: And Ghormley had the authority to go ahead and do this?

Admiral MacDonald: Well, he went ahead. He was a very brilliant tactician and strategist, well known in the Navy for those qualities. He worked with the British and then, of course, after drafts were prepared he sent them back to the United States in order to get comment from back here whether they were going in the right direction and whether this was satisfactory. He was just sort of the intermediary in all of these dealings but also in on the preparation of the original draft.

Emmons and Strong, who were representing the military, sat in just for a couple of days, but then they realized there was not much for them to do, because General Strong indicated that even if we got into the war it would be three years before the Army could really do anything. So he saw no point in working like this at this present time and at this distance, and Emmons more or less said about the same thing.

Q: It was only the Navy that could really get into it?

Admiral MacDonald: It was only the Navy because the Navy was already somewhat involved in our patrolling of the Atlantic about 200 miles off our coast, and if we saw any contacts we'd report them to the British--I mean German submarine contacts. And we also knew that if we ever got into the war we'd have to immediately do something, and we had to be ready to do it. So decisions were made to patrol convoys to, say, Iceland, where we were then relieved, and this was done even before the war.

Q: Is it not true that Admiral Stark, as CNO, had been working in this direction to gear our Navy to a wartime standard?*

Admiral MacDonald: Yes, but at that time there's no doubt about it in my mind, and I'm sure it was very prevalent as far as the Navy concept was concerned that we were always going to be allies to the British. We would have to support the British, and all of our plans and everything were drawn up on the basis that the British would be our allies and that we would join the British. That's one of the things that was around as a permanent thing all

*Admiral Harold R. Stark, USN, Chief of Naval Operations from August 1939 to March 1942.

the time. So our working with the British and drawing up plans was sort of a natural thing.

Q: Did Ghormley draw on the resources of the naval attache's office in doing this? Obviously, the naval attache, having been there, had the contacts.

Admiral MacDonald: The naval attache had the contacts, and he set up the original meetings, but upon Ghormley's arrival, he had to tell Kirk that Kirk would handle the administrative side of the naval attache's office and that he would not be involved in any of the discussions. So Kirk was left out, and this was one reason why Kirk was a little upset and disturbed that he was not going to participate as an active member of this group. I think then he requested that he be sent home.

Our passports were then changed. Admiral Ghormley became a special naval observer only, and Count Austin and I became special naval observers also, and we were no longer assistant naval attaches.

Q: What we knew over here as SPENAVO?

Admiral MacDonald: That was the codeword that I recommended that we use for Admiral Ghormley, special naval observer, SPENAVO. That was accepted back here, and from then on everything was sent back and forth to that address.

Q: Oh, I remember those messages.

Admiral MacDonald: That was one that I produced and recommended.

Now, getting back to Kirk, this was a disturbing thing, that he wasn't going to participate. Although I played tennis with him and so forth and on the surface he didn't really show it, but deep down he was most anxious to be relieved because he was unhappy that he was no longer the top Navy guy over there.

Q: He was a very proud man.

Admiral MacDonald: Oh, yes, and very able, very personable, and he'd done a good job as naval attache, but he did stay on for a while. Eventually he was relieved by Admiral Lockwood.* He wanted to be the special naval observer from the very beginning, but this wasn't to be, and Ghormley had to tell him that he was over there for a purpose and that was it. I don't think Kirk ever accepted the fact that we were getting ready to get involved in a big way. He was just looking at the day-to-day picture of his own sort of standing.

*Captain Charles A. Lockwood, Jr., USN, naval attache in London from January to March 1942. Lockwood is best known as Commander Submarines Pacific Fleet from 1943 to 1945.

But I will say that prior to our arrival he did have dealings with Sir Dudley Pound, the First Sea Lord, and he was on a friendly basis with them. So he really had set up some good contacts, but the doors just opened when we arrived.

Q: Kirk had also a number of men sent over on special missions.

Admiral MacDonald: They were naval observers, and they started a flow of that coming, of which an awful lot of them I could mention did go over as naval observers. Kirk then would set up a program for them. They'd either go out on a carrier or in submarines or out on destroyer escorting duty and so forth to observe how the British were doing it. Then they'd come back and write up a report. Very few of them stayed very long. They were not on permanent assignment; they were on very temporary assignment, and quite a few of them flowed through there during the next two years, until we got into the war. Some of them gained great experience. Joe Wellings happened to be in the Rodney when she got into the battle with the Bismarck.* They got great experience.

*Lieutenant Commander Joseph H. Wellings, USN. The German battleship Bismarck was engaged by British warships on 27 May 1941 and was destroyed. See Wellings's On His Majesty's Service, edited by John B. Hattendorf (Newport: Naval War College Press, 1983).

Q: They were all, in a sense, specialists?

Admiral MacDonald: Oh, yes, Jack Opie and . . .*

Q: Muddy Waters?**

Admiral MacDonald: Muddy Waters came over for a different purpose. He came over to go through their school for mine warfare and deactivation of mines and so forth. This was a big problem even when we arrived over there. They hadn't solved the magnetic mine that the Germans were using, planting around the beaches, in the Channel, and so forth. This was one of Hitler's secret weapons, the magnetic mine. It was activated by a ship passing over it, with an electrical current being sent through the water.

Q: Pretty devastating!

Admiral MacDonald: It was very devastating, and the British didn't know how to sweep it without causing all kinds of trouble to themselves. One was washed up on the beach, and finally some of their brave people went down and found out how it worked.

---

*Lieutenant Commander John N. Opie III, USN.

**Lieutenant Odale D. Waters, Jr., USN. Waters's memoir is in the Naval Institute oral history collection.

That's when all of our degaussing programs got under way. Once we found out how the thing worked and found a solution to it, all ships were then immediately sent into the yards to have degaussing cables and all necessary equipment put on them.

So Muddy Waters went over there for a specific purpose. Some of these naval observers were sent over there for a specific function, knowing that eventually we were going to have to set up similar organizations. And, along that line, I think that was one of the missions Muddy Waters and another officer came over for.

Q: There were two of them.

Admiral MacDonald: Yes. They were to go back and set up a school here, get a school organized, and this was very true in a lot of other aspects.

Q: That's precisely what they did.

Admiral MacDonald: Yes. We had people doing this in other aspects, particularly involving the photographic area. Bob Quackenbush came over as an observer to find out how the reconnaissance planes were seeing what damage was done, sort of reconnoitering all the beaches on the other side, photographing them, and his purpose in life was to set up a Navy photographic setup.*

This type of person we even requested, once we found out that they were doing certain things a certain way, someone to come over there. Admiral Ghormley requested them to come over there and go into this whole thing so that someone would be familiar with every aspect.

Q: And that's where the SPENAVO and the naval attache meshed, in a way, isn't it?

Admiral MacDonald: Well, they never really did mesh. Kirk was administrative in a way. He was keeping track of intelligence, and a lot of this was intelligence, so these reports didn't go through us. These reports went to Kirk, and he was sending them back here, naval intelligence and so forth.

Ghormley's job was really getting ready for us to participate in the war, along a planning stage of what we would do and when and how, how much we could give right away, and all that. Kirk handled all that other aspect, and it finally got so that there was so much new information coming in, and new equipment, particularly radar, sonar, and everything that they sent over a group of which Lee and Libby and a few others--this was a

---

*Lieutenant Robert S. Quackenbush, Jr., USN, who was assigned to the Bureau of Aeronautics.

materiel group.* They then took over working on all of the new sort of different weapon systems, electronics and so forth. This really came under Kirk but on the same level because they had their own boss, who was a commodore.

All of our top materiel people, sort of engineering types, started coming over, ones that were later chiefs of the Bureau of Engineering and materiel, all of those got their start, really, in a way, over in London at that time.

Q: I remember the flood of reports, and I recall now they weren't all addressed to ONI. Copies came to ONI.**

Admiral MacDonald: Yes. Well, there's no doubt about it, that probably was broken down as soon as they got organized in the materiel department over there, of sending the reports directly back to the specific bureau in the Navy Department plus copies to ONI, because ONI would have been swamped with intelligence . . .

Q: They were, anyway!

Admiral MacDonald: . . . of which the materiel bureaus here were

---

*Commander Paul F. Lee, USN; Lieutenant Commander Ruthven E. Libby, USN. Libby's memoir is included in the Naval Institute oral history collection.

**ONI--Office of Naval Intelligence.

most interested in getting ahead with our designing and manufacturing of equipment that was going to be used, probably, and very definitely the new landing craft usage and all that business. They had to get working on that right away and couldn't get bogged down in ONI passing it on to someone else.

No, Ghormley didn't get involved in that type of thing. He was on a much higher level, and it was all political and planning.

Q: He had an opposite number in the person of Admiral Bailey?

Admiral MacDonald: Yes. He was ticked off when we first got there to be the liaison for Admiral Ghormley, the one who could make all the arrangements for him--Admiral Sir Sidney Bailey.* He was sort of liaison. He set up the meetings with the different levels in the Admiralty that Ghormley might talk with. They had five sea lords, and they were all like our chiefs of bureaus back here.

Bailey did sit on all the meetings in the beginning and was responsible for making sure that Admiral Ghormley talked to the right people at all times. Basically, the people who worked with Ghormley were people you would call planners and the operations side. Michael Goodenough was one of the planners, and his boss

*Vice Admiral Sir Sidney R. Bailey, RN.

was--they always called him Tom Thumb. He was just a short fellow and was later killed in the _Repulse_ off the coast of Indochina.*

Q: Phillips?

Admiral MacDonald: Phillips, yes, Tom Phillips, Sir Tom Phillips.** He was sort of heading up the planning operation and was one of the key members in all of these meetings.

The meetings went on, and, of course, the bombing started getting more expansive over there and, after the bombing got so intensive at night, where for weeks the British would not allow their different artillery barrages to open up with their antiaircraft fire. The bombing just got so bad that people said they've got to fight back, do something to retaliate. They just can't let the Germans come in and bomb without doing anything.

Q: Why didn't they retaliate?

Admiral MacDonald: Because they thought the shells that they'd put up in the air would do more damage probably than the bombs. That's basically what they had in mind at the time, at the beginning.

---

*Commander Michael G. Goodenough, RN.

**Rear Admiral Sir Tom S. Phillips, RN, who was lost in HMS _Repulse_ on 10 December 1941.

Q: Shells falling on . . .

Admiral MacDonald: The shells falling all over the houses and everything else would do more damage, all these shells going up and coming down, particularly in the city of London. I will say that all of the parks had these balloons. That's another thing that we discovered. They had these high balloons secured by winches to the ground, which they could lower and raise. They'd keep them down fairly low in the daytime. Then at night, after it got dark, they'd stick them up quite high so that if any bomber came in low, he'd run into the cables of these balloons. All the parks had these winches and barrage balloon arrangements. They were in effect when we arrived.

Q: Were they effective?

Admiral MacDonald: Yes, they were effective to keep the German planes up above a certain altitude. There's no doubt about it; the Germans knew that they were there, just about the altitude that they were arriving. So it did keep them above and definitely handicapped them in pinpointing targets when they would come in on a night raid. But once they started this bombing and our living in the Dorchester, facing Hyde Park, we used to keep the windows open. And the gunfire drove us just about crazy, because they'd be firing all night, and with those batteries going off just outside the window, we weren't getting much sleep.

That, coupled with the fact that when they started bombing London generally, communications stations, railroad stations, the highways and powerhouses, the people who were living in the Dorchester and enjoying it and so forth all started moving out because they wouldn't allow them to use the elevators once the air-raid siren sounded. The people didn't want to have to walk up, and we had to walk up to the top floor.

Q: That being what floor?

Admiral MacDonald: I think it was the ninth floor or the eighth floor. That's how high it was. But that was enough, having to walk up there, no elevator, and the noise. So the admiral decided to move out into the country, and we did go out to Wentworth. We were paying guests of Lady Smiley.

Q: It was her home, was it?

Admiral MacDonald: It was her home, and she took us in as boarders. She still had some servants, so that we had our meals, and we rented the garage for the chauffeur and the admiral's car. So then we lived out there for a while.

Q: How far out from London was this?

Admiral MacDonald: It was about half an hour's drive, Wentworth Estate. The place beyond Wentworth was Sunningdale, and there was a place where we rented some houses for the materiel people later called Virginia Waters. A lot of them lived in Virginia Waters. We rented a couple of houses there.

Q: Some of our naval people are still out there.

Admiral MacDonald: Yes, as a matter of fact, the commander in chief, as far as I know, still had a house out in Virginia Waters. He maintained that house.

We moved out, but it then became a little difficult. Austin and I were standing watches at night and later we decided, when the bombing eased up considerably--I guess we were out there for a number of months--and we finally got a place for the admiral--but this was much later--in town. Then Count got an apartment of his own, and I moved into the Connaught Hotel and lived there for a little over a year.

Q: You left Lady Smiley, then, did you?

Admiral MacDonald: We left Lady Smiley because after the bombing eased a little bit it was too time-consuming to go back and forth all the time. Particularly the admiral used to go out so early and some of us had lots of work to do later.

Q: You say that you and Count were standing . . .

Admiral MacDonald: Watches, yes, at the embassy. The embassy, at that time, was at 3 Grosvenor Square. I don't know exactly the time phase of this, but while we were there it was a very crowded area, the original chancellery building, 3 Grosvenor Square. The embassy really was at 14 Princes Gate, that's where Joe Kennedy was.* When Winant relieved him, why, then Winant decided he didn't want to live in Princes Gate, so he rented a flat in the building next door to 3 Grosvenor Square, so he could be close to the chancellery or embassy all the time.**

I got a directive, and it must have come from Ghormley, to look around for a possible headquarters arrangement in the vicinity.

Q: A naval headquarters?

Admiral MacDonald: Naval headquarters originally because it looked like we'd have to expand pretty fast eventually. There

---

*Joseph P. Kennedy, U.S. ambassador to Great Britain from 1937 to 1940.

**John G. Winant, U.S. ambassador to Great Britain from 1941 to 1946.

was an apartment building at 18-20 Grosvenor Square, which was a very nice building with flats in it. Bill Ammon, I know, had an apartment there and I stayed with him a couple of times.* So we went to the British in connection with this, and they requisitioned the building for us. When we finally moved in there, we had all kinds of additional space, so then they decided to turn a lot of it over to the Army, too, and this is where Eisenhower's first headquarters was, at 18-20 Grosvenor Square, although the Navy maintains it at the present time because we were the ones instrumental in getting it requisitioned.**

Next to 18-20 Grosvenor Square were several bombed-out houses, but there was another one still standing at 15 Grosvenor Square. So we requisitioned that, too, and then they built a sort of walkway from 15 to the 18-20 building. I've been mentioning materiel, but I really meant technical people. The technical people then moved into 15 Grosvenor Square.

There's a funny story about this. Just about three or four years ago--the U.S. Navy still has the headquarters and the British have been trying to get it back. They'd been putting a lot of pressure on the State Department, and the State Department didn't know how the Navy got it in the first place. So they

---

*Lieutenant Commander William B. Ammon, USN.

**Major General Dwight D. Eisenhower, USA, appointed as Commander United States Military Forces in Europe, arrived in London on 24 June 1942 to take charge of the military buildup and planning.

finally tracked down that I might have been instrumental in it, and they called me and asked me if I could write up a little memorandum in connection with the acquisition of 18-20 Grosvenor Square, because the British wanted to get it back and give it back to the owner!

Q: I'd think after all these years he might want some rent from you.

Admiral MacDonald: Yes! We were paying rent. That later was worked out. We paid the rent, there's no doubt about their getting money for it, but they wanted to get it back into civilian hands. No one knew how it had been done, and all I could help them on was the fact that I just went down to the British requisitioning office and they requisitioned the building for us. It was up to them. I mean, they could take it away from us, too.

Q: They had a right of eminent domain, didn't they?

Admiral MacDonald: Yes. Well, this is still the headquarters of the Commander in Chief, U.S. Naval Forces, Europe. The same spot. It hasn't been given back yet.

During this period we were there, a lot of things were going on. We were certainly being briefed on everything the British were doing.

Q: Was there any hesitancy in this area at first, when you went over, any hesitancy on the part of the British?

Admiral MacDonald: They were very slow to tell us a lot of things. It was some time before they let us in on radar. They were very quick to want to turn over all of their progress along the lines of sonar and so forth, but radar was one thing that they were very slow about. They also were very slow about telling us any of their operational plans. They weren't telling us that.

However, when an operation like some of these battles, the Cape Matapan battle, the British fleet going in the Mediterranean against the Italians, when those things were going on, Sir Dudley Pound would invite the admiral to go down to the operations room and watch what was going on.* The same thing in connection with the Bismarck battle, we were invited in to watch the flow of traffic coming in and to watch the event. Particularly interesting at the time was when the Bismarck had escaped and for about four or five days no one knew where she was. They couldn't locate her. Watching this thing develop, which later developed

---

*During the Battle of Cape Matapan, on 28 March 1941, the Royal Navy sank three cruisers and two destroyers of the Italian Navy.

into the battle that sank the Bismarck, was very interesting.*

As far as their operational setup was concerned, they had their own operation rooms where they kept track of the movements of all shipping and all this business. The convoys--you could go down there to one of the offices and there'd be big charts for Sir Dudley Pound, changing them all the time and showing the movements of ships and convoys and all that. Those Sir Dudley Pound wanted to see all the time, where they'd located German submarines and so forth. That type of thing they revealed, but they never revealed the sort of advance operations in many aspects in the beginning.

The relationship built up to where they treated us almost like British, to the point that they weren't leaving Admiral Ghormley out of the picture on anything, and he was able to convey some of these things to Roosevelt.

Q: This had to be a personal relationship, didn't it?

Admiral MacDonald: Yes. It was such, for Ghormley, that Churchill, who used to communicate with President Roosevelt through Kirk, then started doing all his operations--his messages to the President--through Admiral Ghormley.

---

*The German battleship Bismarck was sunk by the British on 27 May 1941.

Q: And you were the communicator?

Admiral MacDonald: That's right. Either Austin or myself handled those messages.

Admiral Ghormley used to go down to some of the dinner meetings with Churchill when they were talking about certain things, so obviously he was being cut in a little bit on what they had in mind, too, in the way of strategy at the time. It wasn't held back, the fact that the British were in desperate straits and needed a lot of things. These were some of the things that we had to send back, too, in connection with the needs of the British in order to sustain them and in order to make sure that they didn't fall.

During some of these early meetings, before the ABC papers reached their conclusion and stood as future plans, President Roosevelt sent Hap Arnold over there to look at the picture.* He was the head of the Army Air Corps at the time. It wasn't the Air Force yet. He wasn't of any help at all because Ghormley took him down to one of the meetings, and he more or less told the British, "Just give me 50,000 planes and I'll bomb Germany out of the war if we get into it." And this is the word he brought back to President Roosevelt:

"Give me 50,000 bombers and you won't even have to use a

---

*Major General Henry H. Arnold, USA, Chief of the Army Air Forces from 1941 to 1946.

soldier. I'll just knock them out."

This was off on the wrong track.

Q: The British knew better than that!

Admiral MacDonald: You still had to occupy the land, take over, and hold it, secure it, and so forth, and this was going to require troops.

The person who really stood up for the Army was a naval officer, and that was Admiral Ghormley. I don't know whether he said it to Arnold's face, but he certainly conveyed it to the rest of us, that Arnold is dumb, stupid. Even if he knocked them all out, someone has to move in, and you could only do this by the Navy getting the Army on land and so forth.

Well, anyway, this is just one of those things that happened, but it was a little silly at the time.

Q: Let me ask you a question with regard to the Churchill messages to Roosevelt and your knowledge of what Ghormley was acquiring through his contacts and committees and so forth in London. Was there ever a time when some of the Churchill messages conveyed information that had not been available to Ghormley?

Admiral MacDonald: Yes, I'm sure there was, but the

communications, particularly the rapid communications, the Navy was the only way of getting them back, other than by ship, and there weren't very many planes or other means. I think the British were probably communicating with their own people here, conveying something, by special courier. These special couriers were still operating as far as the United States and Great Britain were concerned. I could tell you more about that later, because that's the way I came back, as a special courier, via the Pan American out of Lisbon and British Overseas down to Lisbon. Those planes were still flying.

Q: That's the way Count Austin came back.

Admiral MacDonald: Yes. BOAC was still operating planes down to Lisbon and then Pan Am was still flying in to Lisbon.*

Q: And that was one of the most hazardous routes possible, wasn't it?

Admiral MacDonald: It was, and they had to change the route depending on the seasons.

But, getting back to Churchill, a lot of the things did definitely go through Ghormley; there's no doubt about it, but a

*BOAC--British Overseas Airways Corporation.

lot of this information was conveyed in special letters. Ghormley never told anyone else but dictated the letter and sent it back. He wrote an almost daily letter to Admiral Stark in connection with the situation.*

Q: Those were sent by hand?

Admiral MacDonald: They were sent by courier, yes. There were so many naval observers going back and forth at the time, they were being sent that way, too. I'm just not too sure whether all the observers were being flown over from New York to Lisbon or exactly how they were all getting there, but they were getting there somehow.

Q: There was another route, to Prestwick, wasn't there?

Admiral MacDonald: Later, we started flying bombers over to Prestwick, and that's when it really opened up.

Q: But most of the stories I've been hearing have been the route from Lisbon to the Azores to Bermuda.

Admiral MacDonald: That's the way I came back, yes. I think

---

*Admiral Harold R. Stark, USN, Chief of Naval Operations from 1939 to 1942.

Count left before we got into the war, but I left after we'd gotten into the war, and then I had to be ticked off with papers to be a State Department courier.

Q: To get a priority?

Admiral MacDonald: No, because they would have interned me in Lisbon, being a military man. We were at war, too. That was one of the complications of my getting back, that I had diplomatic courier service status, so my passport didn't indicate I was a military man. I was a State Department courier carrying State Department documents.

Q: The Gestapo probably knew in London, though, who you were!

Admiral MacDonald: Well, it's a strange thing. The British were flying their planes into Lisbon, the Germans were flying in, the Italians were flying in. They were all landing on the same field, and there were different offices right across the corner from one another. You'd see these people coming in from Berlin or Rome and I was there, coming in, but they never talked. They were coming in from different areas. Lisbon was neutral, so they were observing neutrality, but if there were military people going through there, they could have interned them, if they knew it.

The Battle of Britain was really something. On one occasion when we were first over there, Mr. Churchill invited Admiral Ghormley, Austin, and myself to go down on an inspection trip to Dover. What he wanted to do was observe the fighting over the Channel. This was rather early in our stay. So we were told to be at a certain station at a certain time. We went down there, and, lo and behold, there was Churchill, his secretary, and a few other people arrived and in a special train we went to Dover. Certainly his main purpose was an inspection of the military operations around Dover and to look across the Channel. Through high-powered binoculars, he could see what the Germans were doing, and they were building gun emplacements and everything else on the other side. He could watch all of this going on.

In the meantime, the Germans would send fighter planes over the Channel and pick a scrap with the British, and dogfights were going on the whole day we were down there. You could observe these fighter planes dogfighting overhead and, now and then, one would crash into the Channel.

The commander in chief at Dover at the time was Sir Ramsay.* His quarters were built into the chalk cliffs; they were down quite a way in the chalk cliffs of Dover. It was like being in a tunnel. It was well-lighted, well below any bombing difficulty, but he had an opening arrangement he could watch what the Germans

---

*Admiral Sir Bertram H. Ramsay, RN.

were doing on the other side. It happened to be a clear day the day we were down there, and poor Churchill was very curious, because they had moved some old guns from British battleships down there on railroad tracks and the British were all ready to fire them. Churchill wanted to test out the Germans, and he more or less asked whether they could fire over there and see what happened. Of course, Ramsay said, "Please don't do that, because we did that once before, fired over there, just to get the range or something and, my God, the Germans fired back ten times as many shells right into the city of Dover. We don't want that any more."

Anyway, Churchill did ask them to fire a shot, and, sure enough, the Germans opened up with ten times as many shells! It only lasted a few minutes; then they both stopped.

This was one of the interesting things. While we were there, Ramsay was talking to us about the convoys coming up. The British, you know, were trying to get their merchant-ship convoys into the Thames, close to London. They would plan an operation where the convoys would be passing on the darkest of nights, up the Channel on a dark, dark night about midnight, passing Dover, passing the German fortifications on the other side. He said it was just unbelievable. The Germans had some sort of detection arrangement that they'd attack these ships. Now, the British at that time didn't know whether they had radar or a heat-seeking detection device or what, but they knew that they had something like that, because when they'd open up on these convoys they were straddling these ships right off the bat. It almost got unsafe to run these convoys at night, because the Germans would open up and they hit some of them. They just couldn't figure it out, but this was when the British were first feeling their way on radar. Of course, later on it was a well-known fact that those guns over there had radar fire-control equipment.

As I mentioned earlier, when we were briefed before we went to London, this was one of the things we couldn't even talk about, radar. The British did have radar aboard ship but they never had it tied in with gun control, and that's where we stepped up. I think I mentioned this before. With our know-how and everything, we put the radar into gun control. Later, our ships came out with fire control equipment that was radar-assisted right off the bat.*

This was one of their conclusions right off. They realized that the Germans probably had radar, too, at the time, but we had no idea that they had made such great advances.

Q: They must, because, as I recall, Sir Robert Watson-Watt, who was instrumental in developing British radar for the coastal areas, had traveled in Germany prior to the war, and was

*For a discussion of the technical interchange between the two nations, see James R. Leutze, "Technology and Bargaining in Anglo-American Naval Relations," U.S. Naval Institute Proceedings, June 1977, pages 50-61.

knowledgeable in what the Germans were doing. He had an idea that they were coming along with it.

Q: Yes. In connection with the conversation we had with Ramsay at that time, during some of the conversations, because we saw him several times after that, he mentioned that after the evacuation from Dunkirk, the Germans were not very smart in the way they were bombing the beaches, because every available little boat was evacuating troops from the beaches of Normandy and so forth for the British. They all had to converge on about two different landing places and, he said, instead of strafing the beaches and having bombers bomb the beaches over a 100-mile front, if they'd only pinpointed their bombing 22 miles across the Channel, they'd have hit where the people were coming in and they could have wiped them all out. But what they were hitting was abandoned equipment and stuff. They weren't trying to sink all these little boats, because they could never have really hit all those, but Ramsay specifically said if they'd only concentrated on where they were all being landed on the other side, and there were only several places where they could land.

Q: Wasn't it fortunate?

Admiral MacDonald: Oh, yes.

Well, when we arrived there, England was in desperate

straits, there's no doubt about it, and this was when Churchill came on the air with his "blood, sweat, and tears" speech. We'd only been there about a week when he came on the air with that one. They were desperate. They had no way of defending themselves, really, because the military equipment, as far as the Army was concerned, was virtually all left on the beaches of Normandy in the Dunkirk arrangement. It was all left over there, so the only thing they had were the volunteers who were called up to bring their shotguns and a few things like that to stand by. England had a terrible time.

Actually, one of the great needs immediately then was for rifles and ammunition.

Q: Small arms.

Admiral MacDonald: And, of course, planes. The British were manufacturing planes, but their production lines were very slow. But they needed planes long before that. I think in my previous conversation, when I was talking about the White House and the messages coming from Churchill to Roosevelt, we were trying to build up a production plant for duplication of Spitfires and Hurricanes. This started way back in late 1939. But we were never able to help them along that line. They had to then take our American production, our own planes, and this is what we were sending them, our own Bostons.*

They had some awfully good planes, but they were just not able to produce them fast enough because of the attrition from operations and also accidental attrition.

Q: Did you at any time see any of the coastal installations, the radar towers?

Admiral MacDonald: Oh, yes. The whole coastline, as far as the east and the south and way up north, was lined with radar towers, as a matter of fact. This was the first thing that caught our attention that they had radar, but, of course, we got brought into the picture of radar controlling their airplanes over there when they started trying to solve the night bombing. They started putting guns on night fighters, and then it was a matter of controlling the night fighters within range of the bombers. They were working on this all the time. Basically, it was done by radar and ground control using radar. It became desperate to get night fighters up every time the bombers were coming. That was much later, maybe when we'd been there a year or so when they were perfecting that. Later, when the Germans first started firing the V-1s, particularly if they were firing in the daytime,

*Boston was the British designation for the U.S. Army Air Corps A-20 bomber. The American version was known as the Havoc; Douglas Aircraft was the manufacturer.

they would send up fighter planes to try to shoot them down before they got very far and try to shoot them down in the Channel before they reached land.

Hitler, no doubt, had wonderful secret weapons, and when he thought that he could really conquer the world, he was relying on advancements in technology that was so far ahead of the rest of us. There's no doubt about that. His mining techniques, his V-1s and V-2s, jet-propelled planes.* The only mistake he made was after the British evacuated Dunkirk, not setting up an amphibious landing force and landing. This is the same type of thinking that Hap Arnold had at the time. No follow-through, no way of winning. They had the planes, the Stuka bombers.** They even had missiles that they were firing from these bombers that were riding a beam, beam-rider missiles. All this stuff we didn't have. We never had any of this stuff. The Germans had it.

Q: But they were planning for many years of war.

Admiral MacDonald: That's right. For instance, when we landed in Normandy--of course, I wasn't there, but Kirk was there--their bombers were firing bombs, trying to ride a beam down. The

*V-1s and V-2s were long-range weapons launched from Germany to deliver explosives on Great Britain. The V-1 was a jet-powered flying bomb, and the V-2 was a rocket.

**The Junkers JU 87 dive-bomber was known as the Stuka.

minute we found out about it, of course, the thing to do was develop a way of defense against it, and we started jamming the beam. But this was not new to the British, either, because originally when they would come over at night on the bombing raids--the British had no way of fighting the bombers in the beginning. They were coming over unmolested, because, on a dark night, they could get them by radar that they were taking off and so forth, but at that time radar didn't give you altitude. There wasn't much they could do about the altitude but try to do the timing and so forth, try to figure out what the altitude was. Of course, their antiaircraft fire wasn't tied in with the radar, and it was very ineffective. All these things were ineffective.

The Germans were using for targeting, where the plane was supposed to drop its bombs, beams. One they would send over from Norway and another one, say, from northern France, and they would so beam this thing that whenever the intersection was, that was the point where the plane was supposed to drop the bomb.

Well, the British finally found out how they were coming in and targeting these things by finally tuning in on the frequency and so forth, and they learned to jam it, or twist it. They did do this on several occasions.

Q: Was this when they dropped those metal things?

Admiral MacDonald: No. This was when the Germans dropped some bombs in between Ireland and England because the British had twisted the beam. Most of the planes were riding a beam coming over, and the minute they got the other beam, at the intersection, he let go. This is how they were originally doing it, a beam-riding type of thing.

The British were working hard on all kinds of aspects to solve these problems, but I think the most serious problem, which almost licked them in the beginning, was that mining problem. They could sweep and all this business, but it didn't seem to do any good because these mines were not sweepable. They'd sit at the bottom, or sit down below, and they wouldn't be activated exactly when a steel hull went over them. Then, of course, they had pressure mines. Until they found out what they were, the British were almost on their backs as far as getting ships and equipment and everything over to the British Isles was concerned.

I must say there's always a solution, once you find out how the other guy is doing it.

The Germans were way ahead because the V-1 was a unique thing. It was a beam-rider and this was one of the things where the British--they'd fire the V-1 beam low. The Germans knew the British had radar, there's no doubt about it. That's why the V-1 would fly so low it wouldn't be detected by the radar until it was very, very close to the radar. The V-1s were coming in low, below the horizon where you couldn't pick them up with radar. Then, of course, when the British solved that problem, the

Germans shifted to the V-2, a trajectory type of missile.

The Germans were so far ahead, because even after the war and years and years afterwards, we hadn't even worked up our Regulus, which was a missile, what they call an air-breather. They were something like an airplane engine but with unmanned airplanes.

There were a lot of things going on all the time over there.

I would just like to explain one thing about the aluminum foils that were dropped. Once the Germans knew that the British were detecting their planes by radar coming over, in order to baffle them the Germans threw out aluminum foil, strips of aluminum, which would indicate to any radar receiver that there were hundreds of planes coming instead of maybe just one. This was just a deceptive type of thing, which could cause consternation in any military organization.

Q: It did for a brief moment, didn't it?

Admiral MacDonald: Yes, it did. In other words, they thought massive forces were coming when only one aircraft was coming. It's the same thing as sort of jamming your electronic frequencies in a deceptive way.

Of course, the Germans lost out early in the war when they didn't invade Britain, but their bombing, which was very effective, really had London at a standstill for days and weeks, when these bombs would come down, crash into these buildings, scatter glass and everything all over the place, and the people had to stay underground. It was so bad that people would go into the air raid shelters, which at that time all subway systems were converted into air raid shelters. People would start going into them about 5:00 o'clock in the evening and stay in there until daylight the next day when it felt safe to come out. This was going on all the time.

But the Germans realized, apparently, that the bombing wasn't doing enough damage to really create too much havoc, so they shifted their attention rather from high-powered bombs to incendiary bombs, where a plane might carry over several hundred incendiary bombs. They had in London, during the period that I was there, about four tremendous incendiary raids. These incendiary bombs sometimes would start fires that would burn for days and days and days. On several occasions--I was in London at the time--they must have had over--well, as a matter of fact, I went down and visited the top man responsible for all the fire equipment and so forth in London a couple of days after one of the big raids, and he said they had something like 2,500 fires all burning at the same time, all over London. He said it was just impossible to put them out and they just had to let them burn out.

Q: You said it was impossible to traverse the streets.

Admiral MacDonald: Oh, it was dark. All these incendiary bombings would start at night, and once they'd set off a lot of fires, the Germans would just pour over with more, including some high-powered bombs. This was a real target area. It gave them a real beacon as to where they could go. It was really hectic, but they only launched these every so often and, as far as I can recall, during the bombing period there were not more than about four big fire-raid nights. Four, but that was plenty.

Q: Four nights of hell!

Admiral MacDonald: Four nights of hell, there's no doubt about that. The whole area around Grosvenor Square was hit by incendiaries. Although people had been warned, after the first one, to keep buckets of water handy where they could throw them on their roofs in case a bomb landed, and they landed all over the place because the planes could carry so many of them and they just spread them around. The fire people couldn't handle the situation.

Q: What did it do to people who were working at important jobs, if they had to spend every night in an underground place where they couldn't sleep too well? Their efficiency must have gone down considerably.

Admiral MacDonald: There's no doubt about that. Their efficiency had gone down; their morale had gone down to almost the cracking point at that time. Fortunately it stopped. I guess the British got better control of the situation, with their night fighters and so forth.

British morale was at low ebb several times, and the worst time was when I went back to London in 1944, when the V-2s were being fired and they couldn't do anything about it. They almost cracked again. It's not easy to have to go to an air raid shelter every night and live that type of a life, and then produce. There's no doubt about it. The efficiency and effectiveness of the people went way down. People who were required to be on the spot more or less lived right in their offices. This is how they did in most of the headquarters. People had bunks and, if they went to an air raid shelter, it was in the same building. They just virtually holed up in the building where they worked, if they had to work and the job required them. Occasionally, they'd get out during the daytime and maybe get a little relaxation and change, but it was a very strenuous period for all hands, I'll tell you that. Even for the Navy, for us, it was very strenuous because we used to have to spend nights in a shelter.

But, there again, the curiosity of the Americans is something. I remember when Winant first came over there and, as I mentioned, he rented an apartment next door, and Jack Beam was first secretary, and when I'd have the duty at the embassy and the air raid siren would sound, who would go up on the roof and watch all of this but Mr. Winant, Jake Beam, and myself.* Several times we were up there and incendiaries were hitting all around Grosvenor Square.

There's only one thing I can tell you about the existence that they had to endure, and I don't know whether they all react the same way; you get very fatalistic. You just say, "Well, I'm dead tired, and if a bomb has my number of it, so what? I might as well be asleep and never know about it. I just can't worry about being hit by a bomb."

This is one of the things that developed. You just are so numb to what the pressures have been and so forth that you just felt that if it's going to be, then it's going to be, and that's the way we were able to get a little sleep. And I want to say that that particular education helped me a great deal later, when I came back to the United States and had to go out to the Pacific.

Q: Yes, indeed, it must have.

Admiral MacDonald: It gave me what you might call great ability

*Jacob D. Beam, former foreign service officer who was secretary, U.S. Embassy Berlin, 1934-1949; secretary, U.S. Embassy London, 1941-1945; acting head, U.S. Embassy Moscow, 1952-1953.

to take things in stride and not try to get too worried about what was going to happen, because if it's going to happen, it's going to happen.

Q: Apparently, Mr. Winant didn't accept that philosophy entirely, did he, because he eventually cracked up?*

Admiral MacDonald: Exactly what philosophy do you have in mind?

Q: The fatalistic one.

Admiral MacDonald: Oh! No, I'm not saying that he developed it. He was a person who was not aloof, but he just stayed by himself. He was very quiet and serious-minded. He made no effort to get involved. He just seemed to be there, and how he was reacting inside to all of this, I don't know. Surely, he was pleasant and friendly when you talked with him or when you were with him, but he never really gave anything. Maybe it was because this was all a new experience for him, too. He also did know that the reason he was there was that Churchill had asked the President to remove Mr. Kennedy.

Q: Kennedy didn't get along with the British, did he?

---

*Winant committed suicide in 1947.

Admiral MacDonald: No, Kennedy didn't get along with the British.* They didn't trust him; they didn't tell him anything. He didn't know what was going on, and they weren't about to tell him. They didn't trust him at all. The association, the relationship, was very strained. Yet, Kennedy loved London, he loved his life over there, particularly he loved to entertain. And this was the first time, because we all had offices in the same building when I first arrived there, and I found out that he had his own personal public relations people there. He always had his picture taken at the right time. They released them; they never went through the State Department. Anything in connection with publicity for him that they wanted to release, they released it on their own. They never cleared it through anyone. Their main objective was to keep him in the limelight and build up his popularity, apparently, by publicity.

Q: Did this work in the opposite direction? Is this what annoyed the British, or what?

Admiral MacDonald: No. The thing that annoyed the British in connection with Mr. Kennedy apparently happened before we ever arrived, and that was that he felt that the British weren't strong enough. He didn't have enough confidence in the British

---

*Joseph P. Kennedy, father of President John F. Kennedy, was U.S. ambassador to Great Britain from 1937 to November 1940.

to defeat the Germans. He felt that the Germans were going to lick the British right from the start. This is why he never seemed to get in behind the British and push them along, because he felt they were going to be beaten. And I think that was his attitude. He felt they were going to be beaten by the Germans, for whom he had great admiration because of their military power and their whole attitude about pushing ahead. I think Kennedy was maybe a little disturbed when he went over there about the way the British took things so easily, so slowly, and muddled through this and muddled through that, while the Germans were dynamic and ambitious.

Q: He wasn't a part of the team, then?

Admiral MacDonald: He wasn't a part of the team, and he was bypassed all the time. As I mentioned earlier, they bypassed Kennedy completely. Churchill went directly to the President. He was out; he wasn't informed. So when Winant got over there, the picture had been set up in a different direction. He wasn't exactly in the mainstream, either, because the military had taken over by that time.

Q: I doubt that any ambassador would have been.

Admiral MacDonald: He was sort of a figurehead over there, as far as the ambassador was concerned, handling the social aspects. At that time, with the Battle of Britain going on, there were damned few social aspects, and he decided to stay in town, where Kennedy had a property outside and he couldn't wait until about Thursday to go out there and not come back until about Tuesday. He was safe, where Winant stayed in town and went through a lot of this business, bombing and the dangers of being in town, and it was dangerous at the time. You never knew when the house next to you--even the house next to 3 Grosvenor was hit by a big bomb. Also, later on, incendiaries were dropping all over the place, all over Grosvenor Square, and every now and again, coming around the square about every second or third house was knocked down by bombs. All the debris was out on the streets. It was just a critical period over there.

Winant was sent over there to appease Churchill, and he really, as far as I know, didn't have any real objective or mission given to him to do anything. As far as I know, he was just to keep the situation stabilized.

When he arrived, you see, England had taken all of those occupied nations, so that you had the Poles, and you had the Norwegians, and you had the Dutch.

Q: And the Free French.

Admiral MacDonald: The Free French, and all of this business had moved in, and particularly if there was any leading person, he was headquartered over there.

Q: Including Mr. de Gaulle!*

Admiral MacDonald: Well, I'll tell you about Mr. de Gaulle.

But, due to the ambassadors all coming in, it was later during Winant's regime over there, and I was still there, when Tony Biddle was then sent over to be ambassador to the occupied nations and he set up a separate headquarters.** That relieved Winant of having to worry about the Poles and all the other people who were there, and there were a lot of them in the London area.

Of course, de Gaulle was there. When I moved into the Connaught Hotel, my room was right next to his suite. He was there, and we used to see one another quite frequently in what they called the lift, the elevator. We'd always exchange greetings and so forth, but this guy stayed very aloof, but his aide de camp was a very close friend of mine. A young fellow, we were very friendly and we'd have meals together and so forth.

De Gaulle had a chip on his shoulder. The only top-ranking officers that he could find to bring back to set up a puppet

---

*General Charles A. de Gaulle, Chief of Free French and President of French National Committee, London.

**Anthony J.D. Biddle, Jr., named ambassador to the Netherlands, Norway, Yugoslavia, and Czechoslovakia in 1941.

arrangement in the event that they went back into France, and he was told to try to build up a Free French setup and so forth, and he did. He worked at that all right, but on the other hand, he was not cut in on anything that was going on, and this bothered him. It really hurt him that he wasn't told anything. He just found out like the rest of the people on the street, and this is why he had a big chip on his shoulder always.

Q: It hurt his pride.

Admiral MacDonald: Oh, yes.

While we were there, Ghormley had other assignments. For instance, at that time the President had sent Harry Hopkins over to Russia to talk to the Russians, and Churchill and Roosevelt had agreed that, in order to take the pressure off England--this was all before they landed in Normandy--they had to open up another front in the East. So missions were sent over. Actually, the planes were flying to Prestwick and, say, our own American bombers were being delivered and then British war planes would take them, fly them, over the North Cape in to Archangel.

Hopkins was the first one who went over there to talk to Stalin and find out maybe what they needed to open up a second front, and then there were also commitments in connection with giving the Russians what they required. I can remember when Hopkins came back from his meeting with Stalin, he called up a few people close to the top there in London and briefed them.* He told them about his trip and he said, "You know, it's a funny thing, when I asked Stalin what he needed, because we wanted to help him, he said, 'Listen, give me a million rifles and all the ammunition you can right away.'"

And Hopkins said, "Don't you want anything else?"

He said, "No, this is what I need right away. I have 17 million troops, but we only have so many rifles. We have them in waves. If we have a million rifles, we'll have the front wave with a million rifles. If they get knocked down, the second wave will come up, pick up the rifles, and so forth."

As Hopkins pointed out, this man had no idea about human life at all. It was just a mass movement, expendable life going on.

This is what they asked for at first. Of course, after Hopkins's trip, there were some other people. Harriman came over.** Then they started asking for other equipment, tanks and so forth, and this is when we started running convoys around the North Cape.

Q: To Murmansk?

Admiral MacDonald: To Murmansk, and the Germans started trying

---

*Joseph Stalin, Soviet Premier, 1941-1953.

**William Averell Harriman, special representative of President Roosevelt to Great Britain in 1941, ambassador to Russia 1943 to 1946.

to intercept the convoys. These ships were loaded up with American equipment, but the British had to convoy them and they got into some battles up there, the British Navy.

Q: Some of those convoys were almost wiped out.

Admiral MacDonald: Right. Well, see, the Germans sent some ships up there, the Scharnhorst and others, to try to wipe out some of them.

Q: Isn't it true that one summer the convoys were stopped because the damage had been so great?

Admiral MacDonald: I don't recall too many of the specifics, but this could be.

What I was trying to build up to is that after these conversations with Russia started and we almost got a commitment out of Stalin at the time that if he got the equipment and so forth he would attack the Germans in the East, even though he had talked to the Germans and said he wouldn't attack. This was a political thing that Churchill and Roosevelt knew, that Stalin had more or less said that he'd open up a second front and this was quite something.

Based on that assumption, the Russians then sent different missions to London and the top navy people were sent over, too.

Ghormley then started conversations, and I had to do all the arranging and appointment work and even work with the aide to the Russian admiral. They were talking about what help we could give and how we could give it, what they needed and so forth, and the thing that developed from these conversations was that the Russians did nothing but listen. We would ask them things and so forth, and they would listen and say, "Well, we'll give you an answer." They wouldn't answer anything without saying, "You'll have to wait, we have to refer this back to Moscow, or Stalin." They even mentioned him by name, "We have to refer this to Stalin and then we'll let you know."

So these conversations with the Russians were the slowest process possible of ever getting anything accomplished, because they just wouldn't tell you anything.

Q: They weren't authorized!

Admiral MacDonald: They would take our questions or queries and so forth, but they weren't authorized to do a damned thing except listen. They were sort of intermediary between us and Stalin. Every time, when something important would come up, didn't they need help along certain lines, aircraft and so forth, they'd say, "Well, we'll have to wait," and it would be two or three days before they'd get an answer to questions that should have been answered the day before. It was a tortuous thing, trying to deal with the Russians over there.

Q: It's still pretty much the same, isn't it?

Admiral MacDonald: I think it is. I haven't had any dealings with them since World War II, although they were in Frankfurt when I was there, sort of on the fringes of Eisenhower's staff. I'll bring that up later.

It was terrible, trying to find out what the Russians wanted. What I think was the problem at that time was the navy people were somewhat ashamed that their navy was so inferior and forgotten. They just didn't have a navy at that time.

That was one of the things that Ghormley did and, of course, he had to work a little bit with de Gaulle on several occasions because we wanted to make sure those French ships, the ones that had escaped . . .

Q: The ones in Dakar and in North Africa?

Admiral MacDonald: Yes. Well, the ones that ended up in the island down in the Caribbean.

Q: Admiral Robert's?*

---

*Rear Admiral Georges Robert, French Navy.

Admiral MacDonald: Yes. He had a carrier and a couple of other ships and we wanted to make sure that those ships never got into the wrong hands.

In trying to deal with General de Gaulle on this, we wanted to make sure that those ships were not moved at any time and particularly after the British went into Oran and shot up the French ships.* This was another sad point. The French Navy then took a very dim view of the British, when they went in there and sank these ships because they wouldn't surrender.

This all happened while we were there. These things were going on all the time. It's hard to place them in the right time frame right now. But messages were conveyed through de Gaulle to the admiral to try to get some definite statement that those ships would not go to anyone else. We weren't going to interfere with his command down there as long as he kept them there. But if he ever moved them out of there, we were going to do something about it. We also knew that he'd carried a hell of a lot of gold out of France in those ships.

Q: This was in Martinique?

---

*On 3 July 1940, a force of British naval vessels bombarded French ships at Mers-el-Kebir, a naval base near Oran, Algeria, in North Africa. The attack against the former British ally is described in Warren Tute, The Deadly Stroke (New York: Coward, McCann & Geoghegan, Inc., 1973).

Admiral MacDonald: Yes, Martinique.

Q: Was Robert under the aegis of de Gaulle?

Admiral MacDonald: No, no one was under one another at all. They all operated separately. The one de Gaulle was close to, and he was sent over there by the British, on this French island off Canada, and then, all of a sudden, he revolted and took over the island.

Q: St. Pierre and Miquelon?

Admiral MacDonald: Yes. I've forgotten the name of the admiral.* He was sent there by the British, and he was the counterpart of de Gaulle. While de Gaulle was the army, this guy was the navy. He was sent down and, all of a sudden, he revolted. But he and de Gaulle were communicating back and forth a little bit somehow. I don't know exactly how, but they were. The fact that de Gaulle couldn't influence him had quite a lot of bearing on how much information he was going to get, because he couldn't control the admiral up there. But they never interfered with the one down there as far as pinning him under anyone. He

---

*On 24 December 1941, a Free French naval force under the command of Vice Admiral Emile Muselier took control of St. Pierre and Miquelon from the Vichy governors. Muselier outranked de Gaulle but was pushed from power because of intense conflict between the two.

was his own boss, but they just wanted an assurance.

Q: How did Ghormley get along with de Gaulle?

Admiral MacDonald: Actually, he had very little contact with him. I think probably most of the contact was through the aides, myself and his aide. De Gaulle lived next to me, and his aide lived out in town someplace, but we used to see one another all the time. I think an awful lot of the information was conveyed back and forth this way.

Ghormley may have had one session with him, but de Gaulle was only interested in the British. He wasn't interested in us. Of course, the British were the ones who brought him over there, took care of him, and all that. I don't know what happened later on, when Eisenhower was over there and the whole thing was shaping up. That's something else. I don't know about that. I'm sure he was told something of what was going on and warned to get his Free French people into position or something, but I don't think they told him a thing about the landings until after they had landed.

Q: Were they not afraid of the precedent?

Admiral MacDonald: Well, he had communications with the Free French in France, there's no doubt about that, so they had some communication channels, probably through the British. He was supposed to keep the Free French informed. Of course, there was Vichy France and there was also occupied France. That's another long, different story. We had Admiral Leahy over there as our ambassador to Vichy France.* That's when the difficulty at Oran happened, when the British went in there, and, of course, our position was just untenable after the British shot up their fleet. The reason they shot them up was that they wouldn't surrender.

Q: Was there any credible intelligence coming in to your headquarters from western Europe? Did you derive, at this point, any knowledge of what new developments the Germans might be under way with?

Admiral MacDonald: It's quite possible that some of our people, particularly the technical people, were informed about some of these things, because I think by this time, after a year, the British were quite open with us and, as they found out things, they would reveal them to us. But it didn't filter through our headquarters, because there was so much material being filtered through, anyway. Admiral Ghormley stayed on a level above a lot of that. He certainly was invited to go down to the daily

---

*Admiral William D. Leahy, USN (Ret.), ambassador to Vichy France from November 1940 until July 1942.

briefings that they had in their operations room with the admiral, if he wanted to. But they were all these sort of, not monotonous, but I mean just routine types of things of convoys and speeds and attacks, submarines and convoys, and so forth. So he only really went down on several occasions when special things were sort of going on in the operations room.

Q: Did you go to any of the RAF command posts?*

Admiral MacDonald: Yes. This is another thing. Any time the admiral wanted to do something, arrangements were made very easily for him to do it.

We went to a number of RAF fields, fighter fields, and watched the fighters take off and attack the Germans. We had several meals with them and I was impressed. An awful lot of these RAF pilots were very, very young. Some of their top people were not even 26 years of age and were fighter pilots of renown by then.

When we started getting involved in setting up the communications headquarters for navy traffic and so forth, we visited Coastal Command of the RAF, where they flew these big Sunderlands and everything patrolling off the coast, and visited their headquarters in connection with how they patrolled Ireland,

---

*RAF--Royal Air Force.

the west coast, and the Atlantic approaches.*

In addition to being the aide to the admiral and seeing that everything went well, all his appointments were kept, and always being there when he was there, I had these other tasks to perform. We were getting involved in setting up a communications station. We were going to build some radar stations and were looking over sites. We did have a couple of technical people come over, and I went with them. We toured Northern Ireland and finally decided to set up our radio station outside of Londonderry, because that was going to be one of the ports where convoy ships and escort ships would put in on their visits in that area.

We looked over the situation up near Greenock, the Clyde, and so forth for submarine headquartering. We had to make arrangements for all these things, you know. You have to get the land and you have to get a requisition, make sure that you could build the proper power requirements into the station so that you could transmit all the messages and everything. This took up quite a bit of time, too, traveling around, but we did. I even went up on one trip, a British battleship coming in from Canada, which had on board one of our communicators carrying some special equipment, coding equipment. I was sent up to the British base in Scapa Flow. I flew in there, went aboard the battleship, got

---

*The Sunderland was a British long-range flying boat patrol craft.

the equipment, and we then had to put it on a special cruiser to bring it down to London. I'd known the commanding officer of the cruiser before. He was a wonderful guy, and we left Scapa Flow. I had to wait up there for several days until the ship got in, but it got in all right, and that's the place where the German submarine, the famous German commander, Prien, got into Scapa Flow and sank a battleship.*

Q: He got through the boom?

Admiral MacDonald: He got through the boom. Well, they were very sensitive about it up there. It's a cold, barren place. We waited for this battleship to get in and then we transported the equipment to the cruiser and took off for London. We were going down the east coast at night. They had mine-swept channels along the coast, very dimly lighted. Going down was uneventful, except we were constantly passing convoys and intercepting them, going in both directions. There was an awful lot of traffic moving up and down that east coast at night. Barges and everything were moving things around that way at night in these swept channels.

Next morning, it was just about daylight and I happened to be up on deck when, all of a sudden, wham, wham, the general alarm

---

*In a daring raid on the night of 13-14 October 1939, Gunther Prien, commanding officer of U-47, entered Scapa Flow in the Orkney Islands and sank the British battleship Royal Oak.

went. Here was a German Stuka and he dropped two bombs, but they straddled the ship. The Germans were patrolling that whole North Sea area all the time, out just far enough so that the RAF wouldn't be out there to intercept them, except in the early morning they'd come in low and that's what this guy did. He came in low just at daylight and everyone in the ship--we weren't even at general quarters or anything, weren't alert at all--and he damned nearly sank this cruiser!

Q: With all that valuable . . .

Admiral MacDonald: With all our brand-new American communications equipment! Fortunately, we weren't sunk.

After that fellow pulled that one, of course, they were on the alert. I think another guy at a distance was hovering around, but he never really came in to attack. The minute this fellow attacked, we sent out word to the RAF to try to get out there and clear the area a little bit. The Germans were out there. They were patrolling that area pretty well and, not that I know anything about it, but they must have caused a lot of difficulty for some of the convoys by sneaking in low at night.

Well, we got in and unloaded the equipment, then set it up and operated on a much bigger scale.

Q: Austin said that one phase of the ABC conference was held in

Washington in 1941.

Admiral MacDonald: That's right.

Q: Did you go back for that?

Admiral MacDonald: No, no one went back, except Ghormley, and that was one of the things that bothered Count Austin, that he wasn't invited to go. Ghormley was invited, and only Ghormley.

Q: Ghormley flew back, did he, or how did he go?

Admiral MacDonald: He came back with Churchill in a British ship. He was the only one invited to come back.* It was one of the new British battleships that had just been commissioned and they sent it out and had a speed run out to this country. Churchill came with it.

Q: He said that one thing they did discuss was the turning over of 50 destroyers.

---

*The Joint U.S.-British strategic conferences began in Washington on 29 January 1941. See Samuel Eliot Morison, _The Battle of the Atlantic_, Volume I of _History of United States Naval Operations in World War II_ (Boston: Little, Brown and Company, 1947), pages 45-49. Churchill's trip to America in the new battleship _Prince of Wales_ took place in the summer of 1941 so he could join President Roosevelt at Argentia, Newfoundland, for the Atlantic Charter meetings of 10-15 August.

Admiral MacDonald: This is the type of thing that they were discussing. I cannot shed specific light on that. Count probably could to a great extent, because he sat in on most of the meetings. I was not invited to sit in on them because I was, as I mentioned before, given different types of tasks to perform. Whatever he said, he would know because he was there.

Q: He said, as a result of it, U.S. officials wanted all sorts of data from England as to her ability to stand up under this because they were afraid the destroyers might get to the Germans.

Admiral MacDonald: I don't know anything about that, except when they finally decided to go along with this, the arrangements were all made back here about how to turn the ships over. Our personnel took them up to Canada and turned them over to the British up there. That was a British deal. The destroyer deal came along much earlier than the base deal. The base deal was then coming up and, all of a sudden, the government here sent some of our legal people over there, because it was going to be what you might call a real legal agreement with certain terms involved.

Q: A treaty agreement?

Admiral MacDonald: It had to be a legal treaty, you might say, because moving in and taking over another person's territory, there had to be legal wording to make sure that they followed through correctly. They did send some lawyers over to work on that, one of whom I don't think ever did any work. He was drunk about all the time he was over there. I don't know how the hell they ever sent him over there. That was true of a lot of people. He was a poor representative, but he was involved in that base deal.

They had to draw up the real fine points of the agreement as to what we would get and . . .

Q: For how long we had them?

Admiral MacDonald: How long and so forth, and, of course, the agreement was based on our giving them 50 destroyers as part of the payment. The British would have given us anything at that time just to hold out. They were so desperate.

Q: Austin also said that, at the outset of your mission, Admiral Stark said that it might possibly last only six weeks. Does this indicate that the nature of the mission changed, or what?

Admiral MacDonald: Well, I think when we went over there, we really didn't have too much of an idea how long it would last. When he said that, there was a feeling back here that maybe

England wouldn't hold out. I wasn't present when he made that remark, but I will say that the atmosphere at the time was that maybe England wouldn't be able to hold out, so we might not be over there too long. But basically, from what Ghormley told me in connection with getting ready to go over there, I assumed that if everything went all right, we would be over there for a long time, and, as it turned out, Ghormley was over there for about two years. So what Stark had in mind when he told Count that, I'm not sure, but I do know that we were held up well over a month before we were able to go, after we were ready the first time because of the situation, the evacuation, and so forth. This could have prompted Stark to make a statement like that, not knowing what the future held as far as England was concerned.

I certainly didn't go over there with the idea of being back six weeks on a temporary assignment. I didn't, and if Count had that idea, I'm sure his mind got changed very quickly over there, because we became pretty darned involved, even after we'd been there a couple of months, that this thing was going to drag on in making all these plans for a long time, as long as the British were still holding out. I know the first two or three months we were over there, it was touch and go as far as the British were concerned.

The British had these reconnaissance planes going over, taking pictures, and so forth, and there was a lot of building going on up around Holland in connection with barges and so forth. It looked like maybe the Germans were getting ready for an amphibious operation of sorts. This is one of the reasons why Churchill ordered them to go over there and bomb these barges. They even dropped fire bombs on them and so forth to try to prevent this thing. Well, that particular thing never got off the ground.

I think at the time the Bremen was in one of those ports in Holland, and they were watching that one, too.

That just doesn't ring a bell with me. At least it wasn't my feeling. Ghormley may have indicated that he didn't know how long he'd be there, but he certainly didn't put a short period on it.

Q: Speaking of people over there, was Paul Hammond of any use to you?*

Admiral MacDonald: Paul Hammond was a great gentleman. Lady Astor was a close friend of his.** He said Mountbatten was a distant cousin of his. Paul had spent so much time in the British Isles, he knew quite a few people, knew what they liked and so forth, but as far as being a navy help, no. I think Paul

---

*Commander Paul L. Hammond, USNR, a prominent New York banker.

**Lady Astor (Nancy Langhorne Astor), born in America, succeeded her husband in House of Commons to become first woman to sit in British Parliament.

was just a wonderful guy to have around. He entertained people like Sir Dudley Pound in some of the periods when he could get off. Paul, I know, rented a shooting box for a certain period of time, and he used to take some of the top-ranking officers down shooting, just to let them relax. His interest was also helping the British. Paul was just a wonderful person. I probably was as close to him as anyone who was on the staff there at the time because he liked me. I was a bachelor and he liked things like entertaining nicely, and he did.

Q: He was very wealthy, too, wasn't he?

Admiral MacDonald: He was a very wealthy man, yes. Paul offered to put me up for the New York Yacht Club when I was over there and backed me. He was a person who always tried to help the Navy. He was always trying to do things, but as far as pinpointing him to a specific job, I don't think he ever was given a specific job to do. He was just around in his uniform, was always cheerful.

Q: What rank did he have?

Admiral MacDonald: As I recall, he was a commander. Yes, Commander Paul Hammond. He later became a captain in the Naval Reserve. As a matter of fact, I think he's still alive.

Q: Yes, I believe he is.

Admiral MacDonald: But very badly crippled with arthritis. I've talked with him many times when I've gone to New York and I'd drop in and see him. He had a nice office down on Park Avenue, but after his secretary died, he had no feeling about going in the office. So the last time I talked with his wife, he just wasn't interested in anything. He called me about two years ago and asked me if I could set up an appointment with a famous orthopedist here at George Washington University so he could get his arthritis cured. I made the appointment and I talked with him on the telephone.

Somewhere along the line, Mrs. August Belmont, some distant relative or something, had the papers of Commodore Perry, and the Naval Historical Foundation wanted to get these papers. Whether they got them or not, I set up the arrangements through Paul Hammond for the Navy to talk to them. Maybe they're going to get them and maybe they're not, but it was through him. He's always been helpful.

He's the one who got young Chester Nimitz his job as president of Perkin-Elmer.*

---

*Rear Admiral Chester W. Nimitz, Jr., USN (Ret.), retired from the Navy in 1957 and accepted a position with Texas Instruments. In 1961 he joined the Perkin-Elmer Corporation and eventually became president and chairman of the board.

Q: I know that. Admiral Nimitz told me that.

Admiral MacDonald: Paul always admired Admiral Nimitz. There were about four people in the Navy he was very fond of. Nimitz was one and was the tops, there's no doubt about it. And if Paul turned to to try to help someone, he really turned to. He did this in my case when I left the Navy. He picked up the telephone and called Tom Watson of IBM and set up an appointment for me.* He did things like that. But as far as doing a specific job in London, I don't recall he did anything but just be a good public relations person. He was there. He loved London, anyway.

Q: You mentioned his friendship with Lady Astor. Did you have anything to do with the Cliveden set?**

Admiral MacDonald: Admiral Ghormley was invited out there a number of times, and Count and I went out there a number of times. That was when Lord Astor was alive and, of course, his family are _The Times_ people. It was always very pleasant. We had no sooner arrived than we started getting invitations. She,

---

*Thomas J. Watson, Jr., president of International Business Machines (IBM) Corporation from 1952 until 1961 when he became chief executive officer.

**Cliveden is the Astor country estate on the Thames. The Cliveden set was a group of British aristocrats who gathered at the estate in the late 1930s and favored appeasement towards Germany.

being an American, wanted to entertain Americans. She always did; all the top people who came over there, they were always invited out to her place. Her sons would be there, but they were always low-key people, sort of in the background. Later, I think, when Eisenhower was over there, she turned that into a hospital. When I was over there, she was still living there and still was a member of Parliament.

As far as Paul was concerned, he was just a great person, a great sailor, an enthusiastic sailor. That's how he really knew these people. He sailed a lot all around.

I stayed over there doing the usual things for Admiral Ghormley. Count Austin was relieved by--he's now dead--Ken McManes, as flag secretary.* By that time, most of the things had been pretty well organized, and it was just a matter of sitting around waiting. I'm sure that by then we were convoying already to Iceland and the British would pick up any convoys from there and we'd take anything back, and that was before we got into the war. We'd moved out that far.

There were several things that came up in connection with the planning operations when the Army was there. I think it might have even been suggested by the Navy that we try to obtain bases in Ireland. This was one point where Churchill put his foot down. He said, "We will not even consider the thought of you

---

*Lieutenant Commander Kenneth M. McManes, USN.

trying to get bases in Southern Ireland."

We thought maybe we could follow the routine of World War I, and Churchill said, "Absolutely not. You'll have to make plans otherwise."

Q: What was his reasoning?

Admiral MacDonald: His reasoning was that after that brown-shirt rebellion in 1916, the feeling and the attitude were so bad and there was so much difficulty, like now sort of, that they couldn't put up with it--the hard feelings and along that line. He said all of the good Irishmen who want to help Great Britain were already in her service, so why upset the apple cart.

Q: But wasn't there some danger for a period of time that the Nazis might get into Ireland?

Admiral MacDonald: Well, they'd have to invade, and how were they going to get over there? I mean, this is the thing. If they couldn't invade England, how were they going to invade Ireland? They just had to move so fast that they weren't prepared. They hadn't gone that step beyond what happened when they moved through France and so forth; it all happened so quickly that they weren't prepared to go any further. They were working on secret weapons, but, on the other hand, they weren't planning on operations.

The British wouldn't go along with that idea. That's when we had to figure on maybe Iceland and a few other places, particularly Northern Ireland and Scotland.

The headquarters that we'd set up at 18-20 Grosvenor began to fill up with a lot of Army toward the end of 1941. In 1941 the Army had a couple of generals there, sitting around. They were talking, I guess, to the British Army people, but the Navy was the big deal there at the time and our communications system was, as far as I know, the only one. It was being used by everyone there.

Interview Number 3 with Rear Admiral Donald J. MacDonald,
U.S. Navy (Retired)

Place: Admiral MacDonald's residence in Washington, D.C.

Date: Tuesday afternoon, 6 August 1974

Subject: Biography

Interviewer: John T. Mason, Jr.

Q: You told me off tape just a moment ago that in preparation and anticipation for active participation in the war we had done something about the preparation of codebooks.

Admiral MacDonald: One of the main jobs that I had while I was there was to work with the British in order to prepare a manual security code, communications from one another. This was accomplished in the early fall of 1941, and the books were printed in England at the time and distributed to both U.S. forces and Royal Navy forces, so that we would be prepared if, eventually, we became involved in World War II.

Q: Was this done in conjunction with Naval Communications in Washington?

Admiral MacDonald: It was done in conjunction with Naval Communications in Washington in that I had all my background experience in that way--but it was a matter of a directive from

Admiral Ghormley to work it out, and we really didn't work with the United States too much.* We were working on our own, and I had to rely on my own special knowledge of what was required and to try to get our own special signals written into this book so we could mutually understand one another and still have a secure cipher.

Q: Let me ask you also, since you're on communications, did you continue at this time with the dispatch of Churchill's messages to the White House?

Admiral MacDonald: As far as I know--and I think I've covered this point a little bit before--the messages were all going through Admiral Ghormley, as far as the British were concerned, because the Navy obviously was the one involved and we were getting ready to help by convoying British convoys as far as Iceland, which at the time was going to be relieved by the British, which all took place prior to World War II. That decision had been made by the President, possibly at the meeting in the fall of 1941 with Churchill.**

As far as I can remember, the communications and the whole buildup and our participation as far as the Navy was concerned

---

*Vice Admiral Robert L. Ghormley, USN, special naval observer in Britain.

**Roosevelt and Churchill met on board ship at Argentia, Newfoundland, from 10 to 15 August 1941.

was all handled through Ghormley back to the United States.

Q: I was thinking particularly of the personal messages between the Prime Minister and the President.

Admiral MacDonald: Well, right now I cannot recall when there was a big shift of sending them through Navy channels. I can't pinpoint that, but an awful lot of it was going as long as we were flying airplanes back and forth to the United States; an awful lot of it was going in the mail by dictated letters. Of course, we were also giving the British planes. They were picking them up in the United States and flying them to Iceland and Scotland. The courier service by that time, in the late fall, before the war broke out for our side, there was an awful lot of communication going back and forth by airplane and an awful lot of our observers were coming over that way, too, at that time, in our own aircraft. We were delivering them over there.

This condition sort of existed until December the seventh. I personally was not made aware of any impending crisis the way it developed, and I think most people were taken somewhat by surprise, although they did expect that eventually we would get into the war. The last country we were even thinking of trying to help or fight against, particularly in the beginning, was Japan.

I've left out a lot of the sequence here, and history, of course, will record this accurately chronologically. Japan had already declared herself an ally and so had Italy and Germany by that time, so we knew that if we ever got involved with the Germans we'd be fighting the Japs also.

On December the seventh, I happened to be down in the country visiting some people when the word came over the air about the air raid on Pearl Harbor and, of course, immediately went into London. Admiral Ghormley was there in the office, and he was trying to get as much information about what had happened as he could from different reports that were coming in at the time.

Q: Can you recall in some detail the reactions in the Ghormley staff and also in the Admiralty to the Pearl Harbor attack?

Admiral MacDonald: Maybe not in great detail, but I know that the news about the air raid on Pearl Harbor was quite a shock, even though we had been expecting something. The British also were expecting that something would happen. They were shocked at the way it happened, but still expecting something.

Q: Was there any relief that now all the subterfuge was over and we were openly in the conflict?

Admiral MacDonald: I would definitely say yes, there was some relief. Now we knew where we stood. We didn't have to go around and pretend we were doing something else. The doors were more or less wide open to get together with the British and plan with them and so forth. But prior to this time, of course, there was a lot of planning going on as far as the Navy was concerned and even with the Combined Chiefs of Staff. And I think by the time we got into the war, the Army had several generals over there, and they were beginning to be cut in on the Combined Chiefs of Staff discussions, so that they were able to follow what was going on, even though they weren't actively going to participate for a couple of years.

Q: Was there any stepped-up activity in your outfit?

Admiral MacDonald: Yes, there was considerable activity in that we started trying to round up all the American officers who had even reserve commissions who were living in the area. One big example the minute we got into the war was that Draper Kauffman, whose father was Admiral Kauffman, who was in the Royal Navy as a reserve officer and working in their mine disposal outfit, came up to the office, and Admiral Ghormley immediately swore him into the U.S. Navy as a regular officer.* He had been in the class of 1933 but was one of those persons who was not given a commission

*Lieutenant Draper L. Kauffman, USNR, son of Captain James L. Kauffman, USN.

at the time. But in 1941 he was commissioned and, as I recall, his rank was just about comparable to his class.

Q: And he came directly from the Royal Navy?

Admiral MacDonald: He came directly from the Royal Navy.

Q: And prior to that, the French Foreign Legion.*

Admiral MacDonald: Yes. Well, I don't recall what sort of career he had while he was over there, but he ended up in the Royal Navy.

Of course, there were a lot of other military people who were doing things in the various British military services who were being called up into their own services to fight for our country. I'm thinking particularly of the people who were in the Eagle

*Kauffman was forced to resign from the Navy upon graduation in 1933 because of poor eyesight, joined the American Volunteer Ambulance Corps with the French Army in April 1940. In June 1940 he was captured by the Germans and held prisoner for several months. Upon his release, he joined the British Royal Navy Volunteer Reserve, serving as a junior officer doing bomb and mine disposal work from September 1940 to November 1941. His reminiscences are included in the Naval Institute oral history collection.

Squadron and had been over there as free agents.* They finally got tied up, and also some of the people who were working in the Red Cross and a few other things all began to come back and see what they could do in our services. It did crystallize the whole thing as far as a lot of Americans were concerned, being over there and trying to help out and then, all of a sudden, we got involved and they immediately applied to join services with us.

Q: Did this event have anything to do with our liaison with the various foreign governments in exile?

Admiral MacDonald: No. The British handled that completely on their own. They had the different countries' military people kept in certain areas where their own officers were taking care of them, and then they fed into the British scheme of events. We didn't participate in that aspect of it at all or want to.

I'm sorry, I made a slight mistake. The French were an exception. We did try to deal with the French officers, de Gaulle and the top French admiral who was over there and then escaped to the islands off Canada in order to make sure that the

*There were three Eagle Squadrons--Royal Air Force squadrons composed of American pilots--formed between 1940 and 1941. They were active in interception, bomber escort and ground attack, and were credited with 73-1/2 kills (one kill was shared with another unit). On 29 December 1942, the three squadrons were transferred to the U.S. Eighth Air Force. The pilots were commissioned into the U.S. Army, but wore wings for both the RAF and the U.S. on their uniforms.

French forces would not be made available to anyone else. And to that extent, of course, we had prior set up blockades so that the French ships down in the Caribbean would not be able to get out. We were just waiting. Then, on our getting into the war, we asked them if they would join us, the French.

Q: Not the British, but join us?

Admiral MacDonald: Join us Americans, yes. The French admiral who was commanding a small group down in the Caribbean, Martinique, I think it was, said no. He refused to join us, so then we just bottled them up so they couldn't move, and they stayed there throughout the war. And, of course, why he said that he wouldn't join us, the other top senior Free French admiral, who was up in the islands, wanted to take over the whole fleet, and he told the French admiral who was down in the Caribbean, Robert, to come up there, he wanted to take over that fleet. That, of course, was not allowed.

Ghormley did talk with de Gaulle a little bit. They had several meetings, but there was nothing that I can recall very constructive out of them, because no one was telling de Gaulle anything and this, of course, as I mentioned earlier, I think, caused him to have a chip on his shoulder. He felt that he was over there and had no access to what was going on. No one would brief him. No one kept him up to date.

Q: He didn't have that much direct authority over the French forces, anyway.

Admiral MacDonald: No, but he was more or less told in the very beginning, when they brought him into England, that he would be the senior one to try to coordinate the French if they were able to get back on the continent and he should work to that purpose. That's when he set up the Free French channels, liaison, and so forth. He was getting ready to take over, but all of this time he was not exactly informed, and it was very difficult for him, and it created a bad feeling in his mind. Later on in life, when he was President of France, you could see some of his animosity to both the British and the Americans because of the way they handled the situation at the time. I won't say that they treated him badly. They provided him with support and he lived very well and comfortably, but, on the other hand, his feelings were hurt because he wasn't kept up to date on what was happening. I don't know when he eventually was informed about the invasion of Normandy. I don't know when that happened. I wasn't there.

Q: Was the Ghormley mission particularly interested in the British experiments with commando units?

Admiral MacDonald: Yes. As a matter of fact, by the time we got into the war we had built up quite a staff over there. There were different divisions operating, and the commando part was definitely one aspect of what we were following. This sort of separation of the naval attache and the special naval observer made it easier for independent groups to come over there and operate on their own. They didn't have to account to any naval attache, and they were given great freedom of action as far as Admiral Ghormley was concerned, but the top people were all very senior people in our Navy in their specific fields. And they went about getting their information and sending it back to their own departments, which, of course, bypassed the old way of sending everything through ONI.*

Q: A little bit chaotic, though, wasn't it?

Admiral MacDonald: Well, yes. There was no one person who really knew everything that was going on there, but then no one person--it was building up rather rapidly--could keep his finger on everything, really.

Q: It must have been a little confusing to the British, dealing with all these different, independent . . .

Admiral MacDonald: It was, and actually prior to our getting

*ONI--Office of Naval Intelligence in Washington, D.C.

into the war, the naval attache had to clear things with the British whenever someone was going anyplace in advance and get approval. I will say that that was definitely delegated to the naval attache prior to the war. But the naval attache, as far as I know, had no difficulty. Once the green light was given, then people could almost make their own arrangements to do certain things. Also, the stationing of observers on the different ships, to a certain extent, was still left with the naval attache. Of course, when they sent Admiral Lockwood over there, his main interest was submarines, and he was making sure that everything connected with submarine warfare was well taken care of.*

I don't recall in the later part of my stay over there Admiral Ghormley specifically asking for any of the special people by name or anything. We used to cover it by areas, by mentioning, say, photo-reconnaissance, someone could come over and look at that, or the mine thing. These communications were going, in the beginning, from Ghormley to Stark back in CNO. He was passing it on down and ticking someone off and sending them on over.

Q: Will you focus on the area of supplies, which were building

---

*Captain Charles A. Lockwood, Jr., USN, was naval attache in Britain from January 1942 to March 1942; he was promoted to rear admiral in May of that year.

up? Had we established that big base in Exeter?

Admiral MacDonald: No, we had no bases at all. The only thing was just sort of crystallizing, planning. Even for our communications setup in Londonderry we had just requisitioned the land and sent back word, and they were compiling all the equipment. We didn't even get that radio station, as I recall, under way until after Pearl Harbor, although we also had worked with the British. I'd been involved somewhat in that in connection with where the escorts would go. They finally were able to extend on beyond Iceland, and Londonderry was sort of indicated as one of our bases at the time.

While the Navy was working on that part of it, of course the Army Air Corps was working on trying to find out where they could get a base up in Scotland. They were working separately with the Air Corps people for, oh, I'd say the last six months of 1941, and we weren't watching that too much. The only thing we were really interested in at the time was the strong feeling even in our own air arm of the Navy, the sort of impression that our aviators had and also the fact the ambitious ones saw a great opportunity for an aviator if we had a separate arm of the Navy. This is something that was growing up over there which was very disturbing. It was to me at the time. They were sort of interested in trying to get a separate air force, just like the Royal Air Force. After several of the British experiments in connection with lack of air cover as far as the surface ships were concerned and the fact that they were at the mercy of the Japs, particularly the Prince of Wales battle and so forth, it was very definite that the Navy had to maintain a strong air force for the protection of our own ships.* We couldn't rely on another service to do it, and that battle was a very revealing battle as far as coordination between the different services was concerned.

One of the officers who later went out there said when he came back alive--he was chief of staff to Admiral Sir Tom Phillips; he was one of the survivors--that the best thing he could do for the United States was stop the United States from setting up a separate air force so that the Navy could continue to develop its own planes for its own uses. Such things as when the Bismarck was loose, the battleships in the British Navy had no really adequate planes going out and searching for her. They almost had to rely on patrol planes from the Royal Air Force's coast guard people.

Q: They'd gone through the experience of having a fleet air arm and having it be absorbed by the RAF?

---

*On 10 December 1941, while on an ill-advised attempt to prevent the Japanese from attacking British and Dutch possessions in the East Indies, the British ships Prince of Wales and Repulse, without air cover, were sunk by Japanese aircraft.

Admiral MacDonald: That's right, and the fact that the planes on their most modern ships--their battleships and their cruisers had old biplanes--Swordfish--slow and they couldn't do anything. They were just no good at all. They had absolutely neglected the development of naval air, and this was very evident over there in the last year or so, very evident. This was one of the things that was very disturbing, our own air people even advocating it. I could mention a few names. They thought that if they set up a separate air force, they could go away sky high quickly, get away from regular channels.

Q: Did your mission have a close relationship with the Prime Minister?

Admiral MacDonald: I would say not a relationship where you could just pick up the telephone and go down and see him. It was sort of an invitational affair. When he had something important to convey, he might send word that he'd like to see Admiral Ghormley. As a matter of fact, Admiral Ghormley was invited to have dinner on, I would say, a number of occasions with Churchill, at which time he may have revealed some of his strategy and some of his thinking, even with a request or so to send it back to Washington.

Q: Was Ghormley ever invited to sit in on the sessions of the war cabinet?

Admiral MacDonald: I don't recall his ever having sat in on any sessions of the war cabinet, but he definitely had some private sessions--well, not private, but dinner sessions--with Churchill in the evening. And, of course, Churchill dined very late and the meetings went on quite late in the evening. His main meetings, of course, were with the First Sea Lord and his group and with the Combined Chiefs of Staff, to a certain extent. The Combined Chiefs over there, of course, had the Chief of Staff of the Air Force and also the Chief of Staff of the Army.

Generally, Ghormley's mission toward the end was purely with the Navy. By that time, all the channels had been set up in a different way, except our getting ready for the Navy to move in and cooperate with the British Navy.

Q: Do you recall the British Minister of Supply? How effective was that for the British services?

Admiral MacDonald: No, I don't recall that at all. All I know is that there was a tremendous number of ships and convoys and they were all loaded down as far as leaving from the United States was concerned. It wasn't a matter to us of what all was there; it was a matter of getting the ships that were in convoy over safely.

We watched operationally what the situation was on a daily basis and Admiral Ghormley was invited down for briefings. As I mentioned before, he was invited down to watch special operations and monitor the progress being made. Along that line, we were gaining experience. We had several officers who went down there all the time. They had a completely open door to go down and watch operations. They had in mind seeing what was being done and how it was being done. Robert Montgomery was one of them whom the British liked, and he was allowed to go in there.* Of course, when he went back before the war, he was asked by Roosevelt to set up a similar operations room in the White House, which he did. That's the same idea as some of the other observers who went over there, followed through on their own specialities, and then came back and set it up.

But I don't recall anything in connection with supplies at the time. As far as we were concerned, we weren't getting any special supplies. We were virtually living off the British supplies at the time, and almost living just like any British citizen, as far as eating and so forth were concerned.

Q: And that was fairly sparse?

---

*Lieutenant Robert Montgomery, USNR, was a popular American movie actor who had gotten a Naval Reserve commission in 1938 and served in 1941 as an assistant naval attache in London.

Admiral MacDonald: That was very sparse, very little meat, and sometimes you were quite hungry.

After we took over 18-20 Grosvenor Square, they sent over a supply officer who was ordering a lot of supplies, and they did set up a little canteen arrangement with any number of such things as cigarettes, candy, and things like that coming from home. It was sort of a shipboard type of canteen. At that time we also had a disbursing officer assigned because our staff was growing quite large.

Q: I recall Count Austin saying that, in a personal sense, on the subject of food, the American personnel were invited and welcomed in a number of the British clubs in London and sometimes it was better than dining elsewhere.* One did a little better.

Admiral MacDonald: Well, that's true, particularly our group. We were extended invitational membership in a number of British clubs, particularly the service clubs. Particularly when we were working at the Admiralty and so forth, there was no doubt about it. It was close by, and we could go there. The service was much better than probably you could get in a lot of different places around England, and definitely better than you could get in a private British home. How they arranged that, I don't know.

*Lieutenant Commander Bernard L. Austin, USN, whose oral history is in the Naval Institute collection.

I'm sure that the military had their own way of getting supplies, and they were getting a lot more firsthand supplies than the citizens, for instance.

There were definitely shortages of certain things, and people had to make out the best they could. I'm sure Count Austin felt just as I did. Many times there was just no meat available at all, and they just put things together which you ordinarily would never eat in your life, but you had to when you couldn't get anything. I don't recall having lacked any kind of liquor, except bourbon. There was plenty of gin and Scotch.

Q: British-type liquors?

Admiral MacDonald: That's right. There was plenty of that. At all the British messes, it flowed very freely. I used to go to some of the British messes, and there was absolutely no shortage of drinks beforehand. I won't say that British food was always the best, but the drinks did flow.

Q: You left after . . .

Admiral MacDonald: No, I was over there after we got involved in Pearl Harbor. By that time, of course, Count Austin had gone back. He'd been relieved by Ken McManes.* I guess Count left in the middle of 1941 and I stayed on. Ken McManes took Count's job but he wasn't the same type as Count Austin. Ken's background was as a lawyer and his job was flag secretary. I don't know that Ghormley put the same amount of reliance on McManes as far as his intelligent grasp of what was going on and how to do it as he did on Austin. He relied greatly on Austin, who was a very clear thinker and a very able, meticulous person. But McManes did operate as flag secretary and I stayed on. We got along very well, there's no doubt about that.

After Pearl Harbor, things began to build up, of course, in connection with our trying to get everything operating smoothly with the British, and it was already a going concern, except we extended from just convoying to Iceland. We were able then to convoy farther, and that relieved the British a great deal. They didn't have to go out so far. I don't know, but everything just seemed to be going along the same way as it had been.

I got a cablegram from Smedberg saying that my father was seriously ill and wanting to know whether I could be ordered back.** Ghormley talked with the ambassador. That was in February. The only way they could work out to get me back was for me to be a State Department courier, and I left in February

---

*Lieutenant Commander Kenmore M. McManes, USN.

**Lieutenant Commander William R. Smedberg III, USN, aide to the Chief of Naval Operations. His oral history is in the Naval Institute collection.

of 1942 and tried to get back in time to see my father. We flew to Lisbon, and I was supposed to take a Pan American flight out of Lisbon back to the United States. Flying from London to Lisbon, of course, the planes had to fly out beyond the patrol areas of the Germans, who were patrolling the Bay of Biscay.

Q: An extremely dangerous flight!

Admiral MacDonald: They'd shoot down any plane they could. Everything was in a war condition, but we were fortunate enough to get into Lisbon all right. I think I even mentioned to you before that when we landed in Lisbon, planes were coming in from Berlin and also Rome, and the air company offices were all in the same corridor--BOAC, Lufthansa, Italia--and we could see these fellows coming in, but no one talked with anyone.

Well, the Pan American flight that I was scheduled to take, due to bad weather in the Atlantic and everything, was delayed. It was originally scheduled to go to the Azores, so I had to stay in Lisbon for about three days. I went out to Estoril, got settled, and waited for information when I could get on. We were then diverted down to Africa, then over to South America, and up to Trinidad. Of course, by that time the 50-destroyer base deal had already been contracted and our people were moving in to try to get started. It was just a stormy season over the Atlantic, and planes were delayed all the time. Every place we went we were delayed and had to hole up for a day or two. During my stay in Trinidad, I got a cab driver and asked him to drive me all around the island and, as we were passing all these banana plantations, I asked him why they didn't pick the bananas. He said, "Oh, they're just going to sit there and rot because all the people who used to pick them for 25 cents or 75 cents a week are now working for the U.S. Government, building docks and a base, and they're getting three times that much in one day. The worst part about it is they work one day, they get so much money, they're not used to it, then they go and drink for the next two days."

This same type of thing I ran into later, too, but this was really a shocker. The whole economy of Trinidad had been completely upset by that base deal. Here they were, building a base for us and all that, and the working people left. Where they had lived, the different plantations were just going to pot and ruin.

Q: That's the kind of an observation that happened throughout the world. Isn't that a part of our current problems?

Admiral MacDonald: Yes. I have an excellent story along that line in the Pacific, which I'll mention later. Bora Bora, it was unbelievable.

Anyway, we finally left Trinidad and the best we could do was

Bermuda.

Q: It was pleasant for you, wasn't it?

Admiral MacDonald: It was very pleasant. Of course, Bermuda had been on a war footing since 1939, so it was a very austere arrangement in Bermuda at that time. The hotels would ordinarily be filled, and I was practically the only one staying in this one hotel. We eventually got to New York and home. I saw my father just before he died. I was most grateful to Stark for sending the message indicating that, if at all possible, I be sent back.

After that, it was a matter of knowing that I wanted to go to sea, contacting some of my friends, and they lined up a job for me as executive officer of a new ship to be commissioned in Bath, Maine.

Q: Did you have any leave before you went to Bath?

Admiral MacDonald: I'm sure that I was granted leave at the time, after my father's death, but not for very long.

Going as executive officer, which was just in the category of a few of my classmates at the time, of a new ship was very appealing and very attractive to me.

Q: Was she of a new class?

Admiral MacDonald: Yes, a 2,100-ton Fletcher class, the O'Bannon, which was the second one produced by Bath, Maine.

Before I got my orders I checked out--I knew the commanding officer, Ed Wilkinson--and I called him and asked if he'd mind if I were his exec, and he said he was delighted, so I was very happy about that.*

At that time, with a little time to spare because these ships were still building, I went down to the ASW school at Key West, and one of my classmates whom I remembered very well, Smedberg, was going in this particular class, which was composed mainly of prospective commanding officers and prospective executive officers.** It was basically an antisubmarine warfare type of class. We learned all about sonar, at least the sonar we had, and how to attack submarines.

Q: So current wartime experience was being funneled into the ASW school?

Admiral MacDonald: Oh, yes, it was, definitely. Our people in the latter part of 1941 in London, in service over there, went on the British ships and watched how they were doing it, and then

*Commander Edwin R. Wilkinson, USN.

**ASW--Antisubmarine warfare. Lieutenant Commander William R. Smedberg III, USN, became the first commanding officer of the USS Lansdowne (DD-486), which was commissioned 29 April 1942.

came back, and this was part of the basis of setting up this school and instructing the commanding officers in attacks and so forth.

After completing that course--all the prospective commanding officers at that time were funneled through this school--because that was the biggest thing on the horizon at that time, antisubmarine warfare . . .

Q: Was it a six-week course?

Admiral MacDonald: I think it was about that, yes. We didn't have to qualify and all this business.

Then I went up to Bath, Maine, to get the ship ready and, of course, worked with the captain in getting the organization all set, the personnel.

Q: What stage of completion was the O'Bannon in?

Admiral MacDonald: I think I got up there in the latter part of March, and we were commissioned in June of 1942. Of course, there was nothing but classes being conducted in the daytime for the crews that we had. An awful lot of them were very inexperienced in everything.

Q: Reservists, were they?

Admiral MacDonald: A lot of them. Well, volunteers, more or less, because we were in a war then and they volunteered to go in the Navy rather than be drafted into the Army. We did have a couple of experienced people in the different divisions and they had to train them. There was an awful lot of training going on during the month of April and in May. It never stopped, really, the training part. After what they called trials--before acceptance by the Navy, the Navy required the yard to take the ships out and run them through certain speed requirements and so forth, in order to find out whether they were acceptable. After we were accepted, we went down to Boston to load up supplies and to Newport to load up torpedoes and all that business.

As I recall, we were commissioned somewhere around June, as far as being a Navy ship was concerned.

Q: What sort of modern damage control features were installed in the ship? Do you remember?

Admiral MacDonald: I don't know that any real special damage control features were installed. I mean, the same old thing of watertight doors, getting your charts and everything, so that the people who were in various job categories that would have to carry out fire control missions could learn where the equipment was and how to operate it.

An awful lot of my job was drawing up ship's plans and

organizational arrangements, as far as handling personnel assignments to different divisions as they came aboard was concerned.

Q: If she was still building, did the skipper and some of the senior officers have a voice in any proposed changes in what they were installing? Did the chief engineer have any voice?

Admiral MacDonald: Yes, the commanding officer did in a way, to see that the job--I mean, the yard that was building her did it right. Of course, all yards have naval inspectors right on the spot. We couldn't tell the yard directly, but we certainly had a lot of meetings with the yard in connection with arrangements for where certain things were going and whether they were the way they should be, and the naval inspector's office was in the middle of that. We told him we were not happy with certain things, and he would then have to make sure that, if it was in the specifications, the yard complied. This is just sort of normal with the shipyards, except in a navy yard, where the captain has a lot more to say about certain things. But basically, civilian yards have their specifications and drawings already provided for them. They carry them out, and if it's a matter of alteration or something, it has to go back to the bureau to be approved. But a lot of things are done without going through that long channel, which is a very slow process to get something changed. It's done on the spot, just by the courtesy of the yard.

I would say that basically the ships come out the same, but there are slight little idiosyncrasies of the commanding officer and some of the other officers and heads of departments who want things a little bit different, and the yard probably can comply very easily.

Q: Where did you live in Bath while the ship was in the yard?

Admiral MacDonald: Captain Wilkinson, who was then a commander, and his wife, and the commanding officer of the _Nicholas_ and his wife, and another couple, the engineering officer in the _Nicholas_, and his wife, six of them, rented a house. When I came along, I was not the first one up there by any manner. They were already there, and they allowed me to join them, so I stayed with them in this house. It was very nice. I contributed my share of the money for the support of the house, although I won't say that I did much in the way of cooking. It was a very congenial arrangement. The evenings were very pleasant. We played poker and all that sort of thing, and it was a lot of fun.

Q: I was thinking that Bath, being a somewhat small place . . .

Admiral MacDonald: Yes, but we rented a house.

Q: And in the middle of winter, not very . . .

Admiral MacDonald: A five-bedroom house, which, of course, was quite adequate for the seven of us.

Well, it was getting on into spring when we were commissioned up there.

After going to Boston and loading up and getting all our equipment, the rest of our troops and everything, we went down to Guantanamo on what's called a shakedown cruise.

Q: Did you also include some spare parts?

Admiral MacDonald: Oh, yes, whatever spare parts the yard had to supply. We picked up all the spares that were on the required list.

Q: Did you take any extras for destroyers out in the South Pacific?

Admiral MacDonald: No, this was a shakedown cruise first. We would go down and start firing our guns, running trials, and so forth. We went to Guantanamo in July.

Q: There was something of a submarine menace in those waters?

Admiral MacDonald: At that time we got very little opportunity to work the kinks out of our crew on our own, because in the middle of the night we were being called out because one convoy or another was being sunk by submarines, and we were going out to try to sink the sub or try to rescue the people.

This is what happened during our stay down there. One convoy was attacked shortly after we got there, and we had to go out and see what we could do. We couldn't find the sub, but we found a lot of debris, and we searched around for a long time but found nothing.

Back home, at least they knew that German subs were in the area, but we weren't getting those daily reports of submarine locations. We were then ordered to help another convoy up north of Cuba, headed towards Florida, on the north side of Cuba. We got involved there with a convoy operation in which some of the convoy ships were just small craft. It was a very difficult setup, because it's sort of shallow water there, and the submarine was probably just sitting there, and he sank a couple of ships. Our task was to try to find him and see that there weren't more. Well, about two submarines attacked that convoy before it got to Florida. As far as I know, we never got any of the subs. Airplanes were out trying to find them, too.

Q: Were you under the temporary command of Caribbean Sea Frontier?

Admiral MacDonald: No. We were obviously under the command of the Training Command Atlantic, at that time, but, of course, if the commander of the Atlantic needed some help in going out to help convoys, he could go over to the commander of the training command and ask if ships couldn't be designated and, of course, we were designated.

As far as I can recall, we never were able to spend too many days just working on our own to build up our crews in all aspects of fighting the ship, but we worked hard at it and, eventually, when we got back we were ordered into Norfolk to pick up a battleship, to escort the Alabama up to Casco Bay. We were the convoy for the battleship.

Q: She was going to Scapa Flow?

Admiral MacDonald: Yes. She was going up there to get shaken down a little bit, and we had to escort her to Casco Bay, then, of course, back to Boston to get more supplies.

Q: That must have proved to be the best kind of shakedown?

Admiral MacDonald: Oh, we were right in the war! It was a fantastic shakedown. Some funny experiences happened in that type of an experience. After some of our crew saw ships being sunk, this alarmed some of them. At night, some of them wouldn't go to their bunks. They just stayed up on deck, wearing life jackets, expecting they would be torpedoed! But they survived it. With only one exception did we lose any personnel.

Then we got up to Boston and got ready to go to the Pacific.

Q: What was the one exception?

Admiral MacDonald: There was one black boy who was scared to death all the time and wouldn't go to his battle station when we had drills at night. I called him up and talked to him and told him none of us liked this war, none of us really wanted to fight, but this was our job and we had to get on with it. He didn't like that. He wanted to be put ashore. He happened to end up being one of the sentries and, of course, sentries at that time were all armed. When I came back to the ship one morning, I found out that he had shot himself in the foot. Of course, he was sent to the hospital, and this was his way of getting out of fighting the war, shooting himself to the point where he ended up being somewhat invalided, physically retired from the service. But he was still alive.

Q: That's a form of malingering, isn't it?

Admiral MacDonald: Oh, yes, there's no doubt about it.

Others didn't want to go back to sea, particularly when we

finally received orders to go out and really go to war. I'm sure they felt very badly, too, and would have liked to stay ashore. There were a lot of cases later, but that was the only one case of a guy, and he took a way out that I never even dreamed of, shooting himself to the point that he would not have to come back to sea!

My experiences in London, of course, held me in pretty good stead, because by that time I was very fatalistic. I felt that if it's going to come. But the rest of them had no indoctrination in anything as far as war was concerned except that experience in the Caribbean and down off the coasts of Cuba and Florida.

Q: As the war progressed and you had experience with naval personnel, would you say that the fatalistic attitude is one that gripped most people?

Admiral MacDonald: I can't answer for all of them, but it certainly was helpful to me. I think that it did come on after we'd been out fighting for about a year and an awful lot of the crew were the same. I think that that did come on definitely, and when it didn't later on, I found out certain people tried other means of getting away. I'm getting ahead of my story a little bit now.

We were ordered out with the Radford. The Nicholas had been

commissioned just ahead of us, and she was ordered out to escort one of the battleships out to Noumea, and we were ordered out with the Radford to report to Commander South Pacific. The exact date we left, I'm not sure, but I think it was in late July, after three of us, all new destroyers, were sent out there, a few more followed, but the rest were all earmarked for the African landings. Commander in Chief King refused to let any more ships go to the South Pacific, so we eventually ended up out there with only four 2,100-tonners.*

Q: You just got under the line, didn't you?

Admiral MacDonald: Yes, we were ordered out first.

We went different ways. Of course, we went to the Panama Canal, and by that time all of these different ports were being pretty well mined. Before leaving Boston, I tried to get port information and mining information, and it wasn't available anyplace. No one seemed to have a sort of master chart of what mining had been going on. This all, later on, was a very important factor, because we lost a lot of our own ships to our own mines; they ran into our own minefields.

Q: Lack of coordination.

---

*Admiral Ernest J. King, USN, Commander in Chief U.S. Fleet.

Admiral MacDonald: Lack of coordination and promulgation of what they'd done. It was a local operation.

Anyway, we got through the canal and went to Bora Bora and, of course, there was nothing there then, except just one officer stationed in one of the few hut houses in the area. We were then to await information as to where we were going from there. I checked in with the officer who was there, particularly after we found out where we were going, and tried to find out if he had any plans of the entrance to the different ports, when we got there, how we were going to get in safely. Just like no one showed us how to get into Bora Bora and the lagoon that they have there. You have to go in between these coral reefs. It was a very tricky arrangement.

While we were there in Bora Bora, we anchored while we were waiting for instructions, and we saw all these natives out in canoes fishing. I had gotten a lot of fishing gear in Boston just for rest and relaxation for the crew, and when we saw that, I took a few of the crew and went over and joined the fishermen, to get some fresh fish. We went over with our brand-new equipment and hooks, and I'd got some frozen shrimp from the icebox. We went over there with our little launch and we sat right in the middle of all these canoes. They were yanking out fish, looking over at us, and we'd been fishing there for an hour and not getting anything with our brand-new equipment. All they had was string, pins, and there they were hooking all these fish!

Of course, they didn't speak English.

Finally, I asked the coxswain to go over near one of the natives and maybe we could buy some fish, and also to ask them how they were catching all these fish. He said, "Oh, sure, I'll sell you some fish. All I want is some good fish hooks."

We asked them how they were doing this, and he said, "Oh, we have chum bags." They had little sacks, and every time they jerked one up it threw out some of this garbage. Then the fish come to eat the garbage and they just snag them. All they were doing was snagging the fish. We were trying to catch them on a hook! They were snagging them, hauling them in like mad.

Why I'm revealing this story is because it was quiet, the natives were all on the beach; there wasn't a sound. It was a very quiet place in 1942. And in the last week of December 1943, when we came back to Bora Bora, by that time we had an oil dock there, we had an oil tank, we had an airstrip, and everything else. When I finally tied up at the oil dock to fuel, I told my commissary officer to see if he couldn't get the natives to go out and do some fishing for us. The natives in their little canoes now were bumboats, and they came alongside with all these trinkets, shells, and so forth, and all they wanted to do was sell you a sort of a trinket of shells for five dollars. I said, "Well, how about if we give you five dollars and you go out and catch us some fish?"

"Oh, no, we don't fish anymore."

I said, "What do you mean, you don't fish anymore? How do you eat?"

"Oh, we have a canteen up here. We can go up to the canteen and buy all the food we want."

"With all that money, what do you do?"

"We buy all this food and we bury it in the ground."

Everything was five dollars. The whole economy, just like Trinidad, was turned upside down. It was most amusing.

Q: Now most of them want to be independent nations and join the United Nations!

Admiral MacDonald: It was a unique experience, to go back there.

Anyway, after we got our orders, we went to Noumea. There was no one there. There was no small craft outside to try to lead us in or anything, and we were very leery. I was the exec/navigator at the time; Wilkinson was still commanding officer. We were leery about how to get into this place. Fortunately, we saw another ship heading in a certain hole, so we started in there and that part was all right. But, all of a sudden, you have to make several sharp turns and we weren't making the right turns and, if it hadn't been for some other destroyer watching us, a small destroyer just coming in from ASW patrol, we would have run right into a minefield. He screamed over the TB, "Change course immediately! You're running into a minefield!" That was a difficulty in those days.*

We got in all right, but even after we got in, I couldn't get any diagram of where the mines were, except they had planted a couple of buoys that the local people knew about, and these were the landmarks, or trees on the beach. Of course, later on, when we finally went up to the Hebrides, well, we lost one transport on its maiden voyage. It went right into the minefield and was sunk, a brand-new ship, big transport. All the Marines were saved, but everything else was lost. And down at the other end, a destroyer, one of those 1,500-tonners, ran into a minefield. The water was so clear you could see the destroyer down below.

Q: How soon did that situation change?

Admiral MacDonald: I don't know that it ever really changed to where anyone was really telling anyone, except back in the headquarters, exactly what to do, but they were putting out small escort boats, eventually, when they knew certain ships were going to arrive off the point. They were sending out small escort boats with maybe just a naval officer, but he knew the landmarks and could tell the captain what landmarks to steer for. As far as I know, it never really did change an awful lot as far as promulgation of minefields, and maybe there was a reason for it,

*TB[S]--Talk Between Ships--voice-powered radio.

except that we were losing our own ships from lack of proper information.

But they began to get escort vessels when they knew some ships were going to arrive out there, just to meet you, with either a native or an officer who knew something about the entrance, to try to help you get in.

The minefields weren't the only problem. The charts were all about 40 or 50 years of age, and things weren't too accurate. We did have a charting ship sent out there quickly, which could set up the mapping of the area to do some charts on its own, right off the bat. So, after a while we were getting our own charts which our people had produced, but originally we had old British and old German charts. And although they were quite accurate, sometimes the contours and everything had changed a little bit, particularly the channels through the coral reefs, and this is where the danger was, getting through the reefs and the channels into a port.

we did get into Noumea. By that time admiral Ghormley had been made Commander in Chief South Pacific. He had his flagship tied up in the harbor at Noumea. His chief of staff was Dan Callaghan, who was a naval aide when I was a White House aide, and the communications officer was Marcel Lehardy, whom I had relieved in the Navy Department.* The minute we arrived,

*Rear Admiral Daniel J. Callaghan, USN; Lieutenant Commander Louis Marcel Lehardy, USN.

Wilkinson, of course, made his normal official calls, but as soon as Ghormley knew I was there, he invited me over to lunch.

By then, the action reports were coming in because we had made our landings on Guadalcanal and were trying to protect that foothold, and the action was building up to prevent the Japs from reinforcing their own positions.

I don't recall at this stage, but I suppose if people looked through our historical logs or something, they'd get the exact chronology of all this.

We were sitting around in Noumea for a little bit and definitely were there when the cruiser action took place in October.* I had been invited for lunch on board Admiral Ghormley's flagship Argonne at Noumea. Admiral Callaghan, the chief of staff, was present. Admiral Ghormley treated me like a son, since I had been with him for two years in London. We had a nice lunch, and we talked about what was going on. Ghormley wasn't exactly depressed, but he just thought he was trying to hold the line with very little strength. He said he wasn't getting enough support, having to fight on a shoestring. The

---

*This refers to the Battle of Cape Esperance, 11-12 October 1942, in which the cruisers Salt Lake City (CA-25) and Boise (CL-47) were damaged.

thinking back home was toward the European war. He said, "You know, Donald, I don't have any fighting admirals out here." While I was there, they brought in a communication about our cruisers being damaged. The next time I was with Admiral Callaghan, he was the task group commander of the battle group to protect Admiral Turner's force at Guadalcanal.

Q: What were the circumstances under which he accepted that command? Did he think he was going to have more units?

Admiral MacDonald: The circumstances, I think, were just developing just before I left London. Roosevelt wanted to shift Stark out of CNO, and Stark felt that the best job he wanted was Ghormley's job. Then it was a matter of what job to find for Ghormley. At the time, which was probably February or March 1942, I'm not quite sure when, but I don't think Ghormley went there until March. They had to find a job for Ghormley, and he was an able officer; there was no doubt about it. I didn't realize until we actually got out there that he was Commander South Pacific, but I do know that Stark wanted to relieve him. I didn't know that Ghormley had been assigned this job. Admiral King definitely was in command at that time.

Well, as a matter of fact, one of the things that grew up in London was the priority list, how we would fight, and top priority was given to knocking the Germans off first. There's no doubt about that, and then we'd go after the Japs. That was the way the priority was set up and, of course, after a few ships were ordered out there, that was a token force and then nothing else was forthcoming because they had the African invasion getting lined up. Everything that was being commissioned after we left was being held back for the African invasion, and this is what bothered Ghormley. He was trying to hold off the Jap fleet with a very small fraction of a force, and they were getting knocked off all the time. The Coral Sea Battle had happened and on the 26th of October a couple of carriers got damaged and the *South Dakota* got banged up. She was out of commission. She came into Noumea while we were there, having been hit getting ready to go back to the States.* The *Washington* and the *Enterprise* were the only two big ships in Noumea at the time, and the *Enterprise* had been in an action. They were afraid to let the *Washington* even go outside the harbor because she might be sunk, the only big ship we had at the time.

Another battleship did come in, but as far as the escorts and destroyers were concerned, they were being held for the invasion.

---

*The *South Dakota*'s superstructure was heavily damaged by Japanese gunfire in a battle near Savo Island on the night of 14-15 November 1942. She had earlier been hit by a Japanese bomb in the Battle of Santa Cruz Islands on 26 October.

I guess the Royal Navy could handle anything they might expect as far as big-ship actions against the French. As a matter of fact, that had already taken place before the African invasion.

Q: That was in November.

Admiral MacDonald: We were in the port until we were ordered out.

Q: One of the charges against poor Ghormley was that he wasn't aggressive enough.

Admiral MacDonald: Well, he didn't have direct control. He was sitting in Noumea, and everything was communicated via air to the different groups that were roaming around, trying to get them placed in the right spot, with all the information about the Jap fleet building up in Truk and elsewhere and moving down. They could get down there in about 48 hours from Truk.

But that cruiser action on November 30th was a very disheartening blow, I tell you that. But we had scheduled this big convoy operation to support Kelly Turner, who was the commander in chief for operations, and they had to get escorts to get the Marine divisions that were going to land up there.*

*Rear Admiral Richmond Kelly Turner, USN, Commander Amphibious Force South Pacific from July 1942 to July 1943.

Kelly Turner had been out there for the original landings.

Q: On Guadalcanal?

Admiral MacDonald: Yes. They had to hold that line, because if the Japs got into Guadalcanal, it's just a stone's throw to Australia, and there was nothing to stop them.

I don't know exactly how we got involved, but we were ordered to convoy the Marine division up with the escorts that were then provided, the Atlanta and the Reno and the San Francisco and the Helena, and there were two of the 2,100-ton destroyers involved in that operation. The rest were all older destroyers.

Q: And this was to provide reinforcement for Guadalcanal?

Admiral MacDonald: Yes, and also for the air, bombs, and everything. The convoy was loaded down.

Q: This was in November.

Admiral MacDonald: Yes. We landed them on the 12th of November. We got up there all right, safely, and we were protecting the ships unloading off the beaches there at Guadalcanal, and the Japs were not too far up on the point in the area.

Q: Lobbing shells down?

Admiral MacDonald: Yes. They couldn't quite reach us there, but they could reach the airfield occasionally. We were just off Lunga Point, midway on Guadalcanal, just inside the Skylark Channel. We all had to go up through Skylark Channel in single file, it's so narrow.

On the afternoon of the twelfth, with Kelly Turner in command, we'd arrived there early in the morning and started unloading troops and equipment and everything else, and about mid-day we got a report of an air raid warning that about 100 Jap Bettys were coming down to attack this force.* Of course, the Marine fighter pilots all took off who could, but about 25-30 of the Japs came in from all directions, very low. Kelly Turner, of course, had us all under way by that time, and we were making 90-degree turns, going right and left, going around in circles, because the ships were all being attacked by these Bettys. Thank God, the fighters from Guadalcanal knocked down quite a few of them so they didn't have to get in, but they were coming in so low our radars weren't picking them up. They were coming in between the islands, just skimming over the water.

Q: They were torpedo planes, weren't they?

---

*The Betty was a land-based Japanese aircraft capable of dropping bombs or torpedoes.

Admiral MacDonald: Yes, Betty torpedo planes, and they fired a lot of torpedoes, and we shot down quite a few of them. The only real casualty was in the San Francisco; one of the planes half-crashed into the mast of the ship. There were no serious casualties as far as we were concerned. We did shoot down maybe ten of the Bettys, but the fighters shot down quite a few of them.

Well, that was only the first wave; then a smaller wave came down, and there was constant getting ready to shoot the airplanes. But we had no further real difficulty, because they went off and we got under way, started maneuvering and zigzagging, so that the torpedo planes couldn't really line up on anyone and they couldn't get close enough. We were ringing the convoy, and they couldn't really get close enough or they'd be shot down.

Just before dark, when we more or less had got everything just loaded on the beach, we were told to withdraw, and we covered the flank while they went down the channel. We were still covering the flank, just about dark, Kelly Turner sent Dan Callaghan a signal and told him to go back and intercept the Japs. Intelligence information was that they were coming down, and their mission was to bombard newly-landed troops and all the equipment.

We were very happy when that day was over, thinking we were going back to port to sort of relax a little bit, and then we were turned around and ordered back. Dan Callaghan at that time was commander of our task group.* As I said, just about a month before, he was chief of staff to Ghormley, but they had no other admiral to take it, apparently, and he got involved here, so he was in command of the task force, and he put us in the column and all that business going through Skylark Channel, and that's when the Battle of Guadalcanal really got under way. All single file, going through there just a little after midnight so the battle was really fought November 13th, and we had 13 ships--four destroyers ahead, four destroyers astern, and five cruisers, of which the Atlanta was the lead cruiser, then the San Francisco, the Helena, one other ship, and the Juneau. Of the three destroyers ahead of us, the first was the Cushing, of which Butch Parker was the commanding officer.** We were the fourth destroyer and just ahead of the cruisers and we were the only ship that had a radar. At that time, the radar was nothing but the pip system; there were no repeaters or anything, and that was all in a dark room.

Well, the captain had worked up such a deal that I always had the conn on the bridge and he was in there to watch for contacts on radar. Then he would tell the guns when to fire, but I was

---

*Callaghan was Commander Task Group 67.4 in Turner's Task Force 67. He had been Ghormley's chief of staff until October. Ghormley was relieved by Vice Admiral William F. Halsey, Jr., on 18 October.

**Lieutenant Commander Edward N. Parker, USN, whose oral history is in the Naval Institute collection.

conning the ship when we were coming through there, and we were getting the pips on the radar, but we didn't have any intelligence information. That went only to the top commands, so we didn't know exactly what it was and we were conveying to the San Francisco, which didn't have a radar, that we had radar contacts. Dan Callaghan had never worked with radar; neither had his staff, and the San Francisco didn't have any radar.* Our guns were on radar. By that time we had radar gun control.

So we were passing this word on to the San Francisco. The Atlanta had radar gun control, and they were passing this information on, so that they knew in the San Francisco, but here we were confined in a narrow channel coming right up through Skylark Channel. We couldn't deviate or we'd run aground at night. They couldn't assimilate the information on the San Francisco.

We kept on steaming up there and, all of a sudden, there were a number of ships around. Then Callaghan gave a direction for the ships to fire one side and, just before we opened up, they changed the command to the other side. So we were all ready to shoot to starboard and all of a sudden the firing got all messed up and they said shift the other way. By that time the Japs were coming down that side and we were running right into them. That was a real close-range battle if there ever was one. The Japs

*The San Francisco (CA-38) was Admiral Callaghan's flagship during this battle.

had two battleships there and some cruisers and destroyers, and they capped our T, there's no doubt about it.* As we were coming out of the channel, they were coming down the sides.

Q: And you really couldn't see them, either?

Admiral MacDonald: Oh, no, it was very, very dark. There was no indication until searchlights went on. The Japs turned on some searchlights. Right then we were told to put on our battle lights or something. Well, the minute you put on a light, you're a real target, there's no doubt about it. Later we never used battle lights, which were designed so that when you went into battle you could identify friend from foe, but they're only targets and, boy, you don't want that to happen.

There's no doubt about it, we made a couple of radical turns, but I'm not sure that the stern end of our formation had even cleared the channel. The Cushing ran right into some of these ships. Then it was a matter of some radical turns and they started shooting. Just before we opened up, Callaghan changed the order. By that time the Japs were shooting. Just as we were changing, the Japs opened up, which resulted in our being second

---

*Capping the T refers to two columns of opposing ships steaming on perpendicular courses. Those in the cap, the Japanese, had the advantage because all their guns would bear on the Americans; only the forward guns of the American ships could be used against the Japanese.

to open up, and by that time they were hitting us very hard, and the battle was well under way. We were in so close to the battleships you could almost hear the bullets go overhead and in between the masts. It was the most terrible experience that I've ever endured.

Right in front of me, while I was trying to stay in column and not hit anyone, the Sterett, which was right in front of me, was virtually blown out of the water, and the other two ships ahead were both torpedoed. So we ended up being at the head of the column and heading right for one of the Jap battleships. But we were firing by that time, just pouring it on to the battleship, and I don't know whether he could depress low enough to hit us. Anyway, he didn't hit us.

At the same time we were shooting, we were supposed to shoot on that side, and I could see Jap destroyers going down the other side and we weren't supposed to shoot at them. So they just had a field day torpedoing our ships at the end of the column. We did fire three torpedoes, which I think were the main vulnerable hits that the Hiei received that night, which put her out of commission completely. Later, the next day, she was sunk, dead in the water, just off Savo Island by some of our bombers. I don't know whether she was sunk by the bombs or whether she was scuttled, but anyway she was dead in the water and she was such a target and she did go down. There's some question about whether she was scuttled then.

After about 15 or 20 minutes of this fantastic shooting and noise and racket and explosions--when a ship like the Sterett went down and everything, the depth charges having been set, they were going off, and they were going off underneath us. It was a terrible mess. Finally, it quieted down; then it was a matter of finding out where you were and who was the enemy and who was friend still alive.

By that time, with Wilkinson back in the radar shack, trying to find out where the contacts were, we pointed out some. He thought then they were still enemy and wanted to get ready to shoot some more, when I on the outside could see that the ship he was more or less indicating was one of our own, the San Francisco. So we didn't shoot, and we finally went in towards the beach and sort of drifted along there trying to find our way out.

You can't imagine a close-range battle action like that with all the ships firing guns and torpedoes.

Q: Utter chaos!

Admiral MacDonald: It was. It was utter chaos. That's the only word for it. We did have an explosion go off underneath that knocked out our sonar. At that time, the ships all had the battle ports hanging from the top. Well, when that explosion happened, I was looking out of the port, trying to conn our ship, keep clear and head in the right direction, and the battle port came down on my head. It should have knocked me out, but it didn't. That was one of my recommendations--that they change the battle ports from hanging on the top to lifting them up so they'd fall down, instead of on top of people.

Anyway, we finally eased out and just at daylight began to communicate with some of our ships that had been easing out, too. We found out that the upperworks of the San Francisco had been blown off, probably hit by Japanese shells, and the reason why they didn't sink these cruisers, the Jap battleships didn't sink them, was probably that their mission was to bombard, and I'm sure they had the ammunition all ready to bombard when they ran into us. So they were using bombardment ammunition rather than armor-piercing, which they had to use because they couldn't shift that fast, running into us like that.

At least the success of that was that they didn't bombard our newly-landed troops and supplies. From then on, it was a pretty safe hold. The Japs had tried to knock us out and, if they had knocked us out that night, they would have had Guadalcanal.

Q: So the Navy had stood in between?

Admiral MacDonald: Stood in between all right, there's no doubt about that.

The next morning, when we began to get communications a

little bit, we realized that Callaghan's whole staff, commanding officer and all, were wiped out.

As far as what ship hit what, this would be such a confused thing to try to solve, except as I recall, it did note that some of the fragments that hit the San Francisco definitely were from the battleship bombardment shells.

Q: From the Japanese?

Admiral MacDonald: The Japanese battleships.

That was an experience where it was so confused that it's quite possible that friend was shooting at friend. There's no doubt about it. It was at night, and all they had to do was see something and they would shoot. This is the disadvantage of inexperienced fighting and, later on, it was so true that I personally, when I was a commanding officer, in a lot of these engagements only hoped that any new ship that joined up and hadn't been in one of these battles could control itself to the point of not shooting some of its own friends, also at some of its own friendly aircraft. This is one of the things that you gain by experience and experience only, because the great tendency is to be trigger-happy once you start opening fire.

Well, we assembled the remnants of the force.

Q: What other ships survived?

Admiral MacDonald: The Juneau was still there, the Helena was there. We were damaged as far as sonar was concerned, but we seemed to be all right otherwise. A couple of destroyers that had been on the tail end of the action were still all right.

There was one other cruiser, I can't remember which it was. The senior officer, I think, was on the Helena then, for the whole task force, and he got them formed up into a little formation and told the destroyers to try to escort them back to the Hebrides.

We hadn't even gotten started; we'd just cleared the Lunga Channel, when we were ordered, after they'd assessed the damage, to go up 50 miles to the north. The Juneau definitely was still alive, but she had been damaged. We were to go north and send a message. We were to act as a decoy, to decoy anything that might be coming after the cripples, and send a message to Commander South Pacific on what the situation was the next morning.

So we steamed off to the north, about 50 miles, while the rest of the cripples were all trying to make their way back to the Hebrides. We drafted and coded a message and sent it off, and all the time we were very alert to the fact that Jap airplanes were coming around, trying to spot us and all that business. We saw a couple of them, but they never came in for an attack.

Our instructions were that after we'd sent the message we were to join up with the other force, so we turned around and started back to join the other force. The distance between us, of course, was 100 miles or so, and they were still making a little mileage.

Q: But considerably slowed because of the . . .

Admiral MacDonald: Because of damage, but most of the damage really was topside damage, not so much down below, because they either were sunk by torpedoes or the gun damage was on the surface. So most of them were able to maneuver around on their own steam, except the San Francisco, whose whole bridge structure was out, so it was all auxiliary steering. She was the main cripple they were trying to get back.

We went to join up with the rest of them, and that afternoon, a long distance off, we saw--it was still daylight--black towers of smoke dead ahead of us. I was on the bridge more or less all the time when Wilkinson was commanding officer, because for some reason or other his specialty was engineering, and he liked to play around with the radars. We saw this smoke, and the question came up, should we go over and investigate, or should we carry out our instructions to join up. We finally decided we should join up because they weren't well-protected. Instead of going down to where this black smoke was coming up well over the horizon, we went off to join up.

The next morning at daylight when we joined up, we saw that

the Juneau was missing, and we signaled over to the senior officer to ask him, and he wouldn't tell us anything. No message came back. So we sent a message over to one of our sister ships, a destroyer, and said the Juneau is missing. They said, "Yes, she was sunk yesterday." I'm only bringing this up because when she was sunk by a Jap torpedo the day after the Battle of Guadalcanal, they thought that all the survivors had been lost, so rather than letting some ship stay there, the commanding officer, assuming that the way she blew up all personnel were lost, kept on going.

Q: This was Captain Hoover?*

Admiral MacDonald: Captain Hoover in the Helena.

We then found out the next day that what we had probably seen was the Juneau. Then we asked about survivors and they said there were none. This bothered us a lot. Then, some time later, as you know, there were 75 survivors in the water, a few of whom were picked up six or seven days later.** Seventy-five in the water right after the explosion, and I think this was held against Hoover, too.

---

*Captain Gilbert C. Hoover, USN.

**On 13 November 1942, while limping back with the San Francisco from Guadalcanal action, the Juneau was fired upon by the Japanese submarine I-26. One of the three torpedoes launched hit the Juneau--breaking her in two--and she sank within 20 seconds. Ten crew members survived.

Q: Yes, he never made flag rank.

Admiral MacDonald: It was held against him for not trying to look out and see if there were any survivors.

Anyway, if we had gone over there we might have been able to find a lot of them, because apparently from the few who were picked up a week or so later, there were a couple or three or something like that, and they said that originally there were 75 of them in the water. They were rescued by a seaplane. That obviously is what we saw at that time.

Well, that was just the beginning of the real battle of Guadalcanal. The Japs sent down some more forces which Admiral Lee--with the battleship Washington and another battleship--was always flying off as a decoy.* Everything was set up as a decoy with Lee and his two battleships and a few destroyers and escorts sitting off, just waiting to draw them out, to go in and attack them, so that they could get in there within two days and run into these other two battleships, the Jap battleships and destroyers, and lost all four destroyers.

There's another thing where they could have wiped all the Japs out, but the battleships got separated and were afraid to shoot because they thought they'd shoot at one another. They got

---

*Rear Admiral Willis A. Lee, Jr., Commander Task Force 64, which comprised the battleships Washington (BB-56) and South Dakota (BB-57) and destroyers Benham (DD-397), Gwin (DD-433), Preston (DD-379), and Walke (DD-416).

separated in the dark. They could have wiped out the Japs completely. Most all the action in that period out there was at night.

Q: That was a fairly new experience for most of our ships?

Admiral MacDonald: Oh, yes.

Q: Up to that point, had the Japs used their flares and illuminations?

Admiral MacDonald: No, that came on later, much later, although they used their searchlights. They continued using searchlights until June or July of 1943. The minute they turned those searchlights on, God, those ships of ours would just aim right for the searchlights as a fantastic target. There was no problem. We had them on radar and everything, but as soon as the lights went on, you knew damned well where the target was. As long as we had radar later, no one ever turned on a light. But that all came along much later than this Guadalcanal thing.

We went back and, of course, all the ships were more or less out of commission, except the Helena. We were repaired quickly. The only place where they had any repairs was down at Noumea at that time. There were no repairs in the Hebrides or anything. So we went down there and got our sonar fixed, and we were told we could take a few days down at Sydney, so we went to Sydney, and when we were ordered back I relieved Ed Wilkinson.

Several things came out of that Battle of Guadalcanal that were very evident to me, and I wrote them up in my report. Incidentally, as far as my part in this Pacific war, as far as the chronology and specific actions are concerned, it's all in the reporting library. Due to my line of experience, I realized that certain things would be helpful if you recommended what to do. One of the things I immediately recommended to do, besides the battle port thing, was to have repeater radars out on the bridge so that whoever was conning the ship would know what the hell the score was so he could . . .

Q: Not have it exclusively . . .

Admiral MacDonald: Not have it exclusively in behind a black curtain, to have another repeater where I could look in instead of standing out there just using my eyes and lookouts on each side with binoculars.

Q: That technique has been superseded by the CIC now, hasn't it?*

---

*CIC--Combat Information Center.

Admiral MacDonald: Oh, yes, all that. But at that time this was one of the disadvantages. All the new ships, the 2,100-tonners that were sent out there, had surface radars. We had a surface radar. All the cruisers and battleships out there didn't have them. They didn't have surface radars. They had radars all right--air radars. And the battleships didn't have gun mounts tied into radar, either, so they had to have the target named. The advantages of radar weren't known to a lot of these people, the great advantage of being able to pick up a target. They couldn't assimilate it. That's unfortunately what happened to Dan Callaghan; he didn't know the capabilities of the system at the time. He was getting reports. He was getting some from us and some from the Atlanta.

The Atlanta, of course, accuses us of all jamming up on the knuckle as we went up through the channel, but the trouble was the ships were all being blown up and sunk right in front of him. No wonder he ended up in those tight spots. The ship was sinking right when the battle started. The ship in front was virtually torn off by gunfire, then, of course, it blew up, hit by a torpedo as well. There weren't many survivors from those three leading destroyers. Butch Parker was one, the only one I really know.*

*Lieutenant Commander Edward N. Parker, USN, was commanding officer of the USS Cushing (DD-376), the lead ship in the American column. She was hard hit early in the battle and later sank. About 70 men were lost from the Cushing.

Anyway, we visited Sydney for a little relaxation and then I took over command.

Q: And that was in January?

Admiral MacDonald: December, the latter part of December. Then they formed a group called the Cactus Striking Force.

Q: Of destroyers?

Admiral MacDonald: Four destroyers, the _Nicholas_, the _O'Bannon_--the _Chevalier_, and the _Strong_ came out later--the _Radford_ and the _DeHaven_. The _Strong_ and the _Chevalier_ participated in the African invasion and then came out.

Anyway, then Captain Briscoe was given command of the Cactus Striking Force, and in early January we convoyed some PT boats up to Tulagi.* At that time, no one had ever even put in at Tulagi. We were then to work with the PT boats in intercepting the Tokyo Express. We'd go out at night and let the PT boats--we'd worked out a plan where the PT boats would go sort of north and keep to the west, and we'd stand over there and, if they sighted anything like the Tokyo Express coming in, they'd give us a signal and we would be off to the east. We'd come dashing in and intercept the

---

*Captain Robert P. Briscoe, USN.

Tokyo Express at night. Every night about dusk, we'd all get under way so that the Jap forces on the different islands wouldn't see us; it would be dark when we'd get on station.

We did this a couple of nights and not much happened, except when we were coming in in the morning and there was sort of a fog and so forth, all of a sudden the PT boats came up very close to us, screamed for action, and they wanted to shoot at us. One let go their torpedoes at us. You could hear them screaming, "Enemy ships, enemy ships!"

Well, that day, after this incident and also one that happened on another night when the PT boats got way off to the east, they sighted us and reported us as the enemy. We figured it was too dangerous.

Q: They were too trigger-happy?

Admiral MacDonald: Too trigger-happy. They didn't know where they were. They didn't have control of the situation.

Q: How did you stop them from firing under those circumstances?

Admiral MacDonald: I don't know. I think they even fired. I don't know about that. Jack Kennedy's PT boat was out there at that time, anyway.*

Briscoe met with the people and they decided that it was just too damned dangerous the way it was going. They couldn't stay in position. They didn't have radar to know where the hell they were. Anything they sighted was enemy and they weren't going to help us one bit. So we then worked out a schedule. They'd go out one night and sort of patrol on their own and we'd go out the next night on our own. We depended on intelligence information from the coast-watchers as to whether anything was coming down so we could get ready to go into action.

With all of this Cactus Force type of arrangement, nothing seemed to happen as far as our making contact at that time, except that we were all tying up in Tulagi Harbor, coming in there, and, of course, getting under way. It was a very small harbor, and the only thing we were being subjected to was an occasional air raid over there in Tulagi. But we stopped this nonsense of working with the PT boats.

This went on for some time, but we never got into any action because we never really intercepted them. The Japs apparently knew we were out there, so they were staying away off to the west on the other side, coming in just offshore, letting all their supplies drift down, and I understand that not even a third of

---

*Lieutenant (junior grade) John F. Kennedy, USNR, commanding officer of motor torpedo boat PT-109 from December 1942 until February 1943.

what they dropped over in these floatable kegs reached the beach and the troops would bring it in the next day, so they were losing a lot of stuff, but they were staying out of our reach.

One night we did get a contact and we got all set to go. I was following the Radford, and Briscoe was riding in the Nicholas. All of a sudden we were told to get ready for action, and the next thing I saw was sparks flying up from the Radford's stack and her torpedo mounts were still fore and aft. My God, when I saw all this stuff, I called over to find out what the hell was going on in the Radford and they didn't know anything had happened, but someone, in testing a torpedo, had fired one into their after stack and set up all these sparks and flames. Well, that put the Radford out of commission, but we did get a relief ship.

Q: Wasn't there an explosion?

Admiral MacDonald: No, it didn't go off. It apparently wasn't armed. They were testing firing and they fired the goddamned torpedo, but it didn't go off. But, boy, they were afraid it was going to go off and he was told to get out of there right away! That was a hell of a mess but it happened in one of our night setups over there.

We were then sent out on a number of sort of bombarding missions up north in the Munda area, in the plantation area, and

Kolombangara, bombarding missions at night. We'd leave in the evening, steam at full speed, and go up and bombard some of these places where intelligence indicated they had supply dumps and also troop supplies. This thing was going on, and we were also called upon in the daytime to bombard Jap positions on Guadalcanal, when air raids would be signaled and we'd have to get out in a hurry, get out in the open where we could be free to shoot and free to move.

It was a pretty hectic life.

Q: Would you tell me about the usefulness of the coast-watchers?

Admiral MacDonald: Well, there's no doubt in my mind, although I personally never had any real experience directly with any of them, that they helped a great deal, because a lot of the intelligence information we were receiving came from them originally, for the islands up to the north. When they'd spot the Japs coming down, they'd let our people know. This whole coast-watcher organization was set up by the Australians, and they were the ones who originally had been in the area and knew the people and had set up these people. However, it was a great help to us. On the other hand, I'm sure that the Japs were aided up there by their own coast-watchers, because if you take some of the various battles like Savo Island, after our cruisers had steamed around that island in a square for a couple of days, the coast-watchers definitely had the ships timed to the minute, and when the Japs came down, they knew exactly where they were at a certain hour. So it helped both ways. I'm sure they had them, too, along those islands, who were reporting just like we were getting information. But it was exceedingly helpful. The top people were getting information that wasn't getting down to the commanding officers. We were only told to go out and intercept a possible force. We weren't told exactly what was coming or what; we were told to go out and intercept or attack it in some sort of specific general direction. They were getting information and they helped a great deal in the whole campaign in the Guadalcanal area, the Solomon Islands, and so forth. They were terrific.

Q: You mentioned Tulagi. Had the Seabees landed there and were they at work on Tulagi?

Admiral MacDonald: No, they weren't even in Guadalcanal at the time. It was just the amphibious force and whatever people they had to do that type of work. Tulagi had nothing at the time. They did bring in an oil barge that tied up there. We may have escorted it up with the PT boats. I guess we did. We fueled from that barge every day when we came back in. Nothing else was there. The PT boats made their headquarters there, and there were a couple of shacks that they took over. The natives sort of disappeared at that time.

Later on, when we used that area as a base, we were using Purvis Bay, which is connected with Tulagi, but it's a great big bay and could accommodate all of our ships. But in the very beginning, we were trying to stay in this tight harbor of Tulagi because there were mountains or hills all around it and it wasn't too visible to the air raids that were coming down. Incidentally, there are a lot of little streams coming in to Tulagi and also Purvis Bay, and it was in these little creeks that they were shoving the crippled cruisers until they could get them repaired enough to get them out of there. They were stuck up in these creeks and covered over with bamboo and camouflage so that they couldn't be seen from the air. They did a magnificent job of camouflaging. The Minneapolis and a few others were up in there, having been banged up at Savo Island on 30 November. The vegetation in these creeks was right up to the waterline so they were very well camouflaged.

There were a number of raids while we were there. All the raids weren't centered on Guadalcanal; they were coming over Tulagi, too.

Basically, during the month of January one of the things besides trying to intercept the express at night, was bombarding for the Marines in the daytime, drifting along the coast. We all had Marine spotters and liaison officers on board. We'd pick them up, go over there, and they would then try to get us to pinpoint in on the targets. We did an awful lot of shooting in the way of bombardment for the Marines on Guadalcanal.

Q: Tell me about the order you received to go in great haste to the sinking Chicago. She was damaged at Rennell Island.

Admiral MacDonald: The Chicago and a small task group were under the command of Admiral Giffen, and this force had just come from the Mediterranean area.* They were quite inexperienced in fighting the Japs and this, of course, is one of the reasons they ran into so much trouble. At the time the Chicago was out there and being sent up on the western side of the islands, there's no doubt about it that they were being a decoy for Admiral Lee and his battleships and carriers sitting off to the west. The decoy was to attract the Jap big ships out of Truk, Saipan, or wherever they were, and we were sitting off there, waiting. Obviously, intelligence must have revealed that they were moving or something; otherwise, we probably wouldn't have been out there.

The O'Bannon was one of several escorts for the battleship, and we were steaming around waiting for information as to what to do.

On the night of 29 January, we received a very hectic call from Admiral Giffen on the TBS saying that Japanese planes were dropping red and green flares all around his force and he didn't

*Rear Admiral Robert C. Giffen, USN.

know anything about it, what were they doing, what was it all about.* He was told that this was customary for the Japs, sort of marking courses and so forth, either for air attacks coming in or for surface attacks.

Well, the next thing we heard was that Japanese torpedo planes were attacking the force, then that the Chicago had been torpedoed and he needed help. He needed help to get at the enemy. Basically, what he was asking for was antiaircraft help.

So Admiral Lee ticked the O'Bannon off to go up and help them, and they were 100 and some miles to the north, maybe not quite that much. I put on full speed, worked up to full power, and headed up towards the Chicago to try to help them, one ship ordered out of the task force. After I'd been steaming for three or four hours, about midnight, I picked up on my radar one of our friendly convoys coming down the coast with escorts, and I started trying to communicate with them. I had them on radar and I was calling them on TBS but never heard them answer. I was getting closer and closer, going alongside of them shooting up to the northeast. I kept calling and all of a sudden, when I get alongside of them, I hear over the TBS, "Enemy, enemy, starboard side," the general quarters alarm sounding and everything else.

I recall it vividly, and I think they were even told to open fire, but I finally was able to communicate with them to the

---

*TBS--voice radio.

extent that it was a friend and we were just passing by, and we did pass by, very fast.

At daybreak the next morning, we got up to the Chicago and she was ready to sink. She was going down, and all the survivors were being put on several auxiliary ships that were in the vicinity. The admiral went on board a destroyer and after he got himself and his staff and some of the officers from the Chicago on board a destroyer, they took off for the Hebrides. He sent a signal over to me to take charge and bring the survivors back to port.

Well, nothing ever disturbed me as much as that did, after being out there fighting the way we had for so long and then to have to take some cripples--as I remember there were several cripples there, and we had to escort them back. They had to have water because their condensers had been damaged and a few other things, so we had to go alongside and give them a little water, then start slowly convoying them back to the Hebrides.

Q: Was there any danger from the Japanese?

Admiral MacDonald: Oh, yes, the submarine danger was always very prevalent in that area.

After we got straightened out and were on our way back, I sent a message down to my boss and told him what I had been ordered to do and requested that someone else be ordered out to relieve me of the escort duty. Eventually, this was done, so I didn't have to escort them the whole way, and then I rejoined our force.

But the fact was that Admiral Giffen had his own ships; he could have escorted his own cripples back, but he didn't.

Q: In January 1943 there were a number of night bombardment missions up the Slot to various islands and plantations where the Japs were staging--a staging ground where they were building an airport. Tell me about the overall effect of these missions and tell me a little about the danger involved in them.

Admiral MacDonald: Apparently, this was the time when Admiral Ainsworth had taken over command of this task force, which consisted of about four cruisers and usually seven or eight destroyers, and our task objective was to go and bombard the Japanese positions up in the Munda-Kolombangara area.* As I recall, the first one was on the west side of Munda Island. In this type of operation, we were leaving from the Hebrides to get up there, say, approximately about midnight and bombard on the next day. We had a sufficient force to decoy part of this work off in one direction to deceive the Japs, if they were watching us, and also to support us if we ran into any trouble.

*Rear Admiral Walden L. "Pug" Ainsworth, USN, Commander Task Force 67.

Well, the January operations that we conducted in the area of Munda and Kolombangara, where the Japs were staging some of their supplying of the Munda airfield and some of their other operations, due to our coast-watchers and our plane reconnaissance, we had a pretty good idea where some of the real targets were.

It was a considerable distance, and we had to travel at awfully high speed after it got dark to get up there in time. The object was always to get up there to open up at the exact moment, because we were using Black Cat spotting to help us get on the target and these planes had to be coordinated so they'd take off in time to be up there over the area at a certain hour.* If they got up there too soon, they were liable to run into trouble and be shot down or something, and they couldn't hover around. So the thing was to coordinate all of our bombardment, even at long distance, to very exact timing of getting the spotters there just about the time when we hit the firing line. The operations in January under Admiral Ainsworth were exceedingly successful, and they were fantastic operations. We missed nothing, except quite occasionally Japanese patrol planes would spot us, drop flares, and send us a blinker flashing-light signal to try to get us to identify ourselves. We didn't shoot

*Black Cats were Catalina amphibious planes that were painted black and used pilots specially trained for night work and barge hunting.

and they didn't do anything and we just hoped that nothing else would happen. And in these early operations nothing did.

But when the cruisers got on the firing line and opened up, it was just like watching a hose spraying bullets over there on the target area.* We could hear these Black Cat spotters give us these wonderful comments about right on target and explosions and all this business, so we knew we were doing quite well.

Q: And no effective opposition on the part of the Japs?

Admiral MacDonald: We didn't run into any effective opposition on the part of the Japs, but we did take some precautions. For instance, I remember one period where I went in scouting ahead just to make sure nothing was in there when we headed into the gulf area, no targets of any surface craft or any submarines around. Then the rest of the ships followed right in and opened up when they hit the target line, or the firing line.

These operations were not easy, but they were absolutely fantastic in certain ways, the precision with which we had to operate, and they were well planned. The other thing is while you're shooting and everything, you still had to watch out that

---

*The light cruisers of the Brooklyn (CL-40) class were noted for their high rate of fire. Each ship had five triple 6-inch gun turrets, a total of 15 barrels, and each barrel could shoot approximately ten rounds per minute. The result was a theoretical ship capability to fire 150 rounds per minute of 6-inch projectiles.

something else wasn't coming in and going to hit you on the other side. All these things had to be considered. But those operations were exceedingly successful all around.

Later, instead of bombarding, we did the same type of task force operations. We started running up the Slot for other purposes. That comes along a little bit later than the January bombardments.

It seems to me that several times we were going up later on in January and we were spotted by Jap planes in the afternoon and there was a small raid made on several occasions and planes were shot down. The task force had, of course, to move along, and the O'Bannon was ordered to go over because in one Jap plane that was shot down it was noticed that the two survivors were still in the water. I was ordered to go back and pick them up. I did. I went alongside, and we threw life rings to the pilot and copilot, and they refused to accept them and swam away. Then we started throwing grappling hooks, trying to catch them. We did get the copilot with a grappling hook, lowered some people on a ladder and they grabbed him and hauled him up on deck, but he had been badly wounded and died shortly thereafter. The pilot apparently was not wounded at all. Every time we tried to reach him and grab him, he would fight off the whole thing and swim away. Finally, I lowered a boat and went after him. I unconsciously was in the boat! As we got alongside to grab him, he reached down and pulled a revolver and held it at me. He actually shot, but the bullet didn't go off.

Q: Well, it was wet, I suppose.

Admiral MacDonald: It was so wet. It had been in the water for so long. But my gunners on the bridge always covered such operations with machine guns and they just let him have it and blew his head right off. We did pick up the rest of the body and stripped it down to get whatever we could out of it. His uniform was well made. He had a Luger 38, and the cartridge's firing pin had hit the cartridge but it didn't go off.* We sent all these things in to intelligence to show where these things were coming from. But the thing that I noticed was that their uniforms were handsomely, beautifully made, tailor-made and everything.

That was one of the incidents. We later joined up with the task group on another raid on Munda. Similar things about trying to rescue Japanese survivors occurred later on on numerous other occasions, particularly when we got into more surface actions and sank some Jap ships. In trying to pick some of those survivors up later on, it was the same thing. It was quite noticeable that the Japs had no interest in being picked up as survivors. They'd much rather die, which was completely contrary to the way we

---

*Luger is a trademark for a German semiautomatic pistol.

Americans might have acted.

Q: Did you get any, though?

Admiral MacDonald: No, we didn't. On two other occasions we tried to pick up survivors. They were hanging onto a piece of wood. This was coming back from an operation at night, and we were still within Japanese air cover in daylight. We had noticed these survivors on the way up the night before and marked them on a chart, and the next day on our way back, we thought we'd try to pick them up. They were still there. I went over to them, slowed down, threw life rings, tried to grab them, but they did the same thing as the others. They just up and let go of their wooden plank and swam away.

I queried my boss at the time about what to do. Should I go after them and get them or let them go? And he said, "We've got to get back under our own air cover soon or we're going to be in trouble, so let them go."

There were two others who ended up in a boat that we found. We noticed them on the way back from another operation. We knew where they were, but the Radford was ordered to pick them up, and they did pick them up alive, and they came aboard and were questioned as prisoners.

But, on the whole, the Japs weren't interested in being saved. They had the hara-kari idea.

Q: Why did they make any attempt to cling to boards?

Admiral MacDonald: They did this because in those areas there was a chance--and it did happen in a lot of cases--that in some of these surface night actions a Jap ship was sunk and the survivors in the water drifted down to one of the islands. So it was their hope that they'd drift down to some island and be saved that way, rather than be saved by anyone else. I'm sure of that, because some of the Japs did end up on the islands as survivors, just like some of our people did, too. I think it was just hope, and this is why they didn't want to come aboard us. They were hoping that maybe they could last out until they drifted down to an island.

The destroyers would be ordered up for bombardment operations, then the next night they'd be ordered up on a mining operation or screening the minelaying ships. It seemed that we were constantly on the go, day and night.

Q: Versatility!

Admiral MacDonald: If we weren't bombarding, particularly after we finished bombarding in Guadalcanal and the Japs had evacuated, then the bombardments weren't every night or every day like they used to be. They changed to different tactics or strategy. Knowing that the Japs were coming through certain channels supplying and supporting the airfields at Munda and so forth and getting into Kolombangara and Vella Lavella, we started laying mines up in those areas, and it became a destroyer task to lead the minelayers in and protect them. This also turned out to be some pretty successful operating. We did this under a task force commander and it was just a mining operation by different groups.

Then, all of a sudden, we'd be called in to convoy people. I was ordered out one day with just the Chevalier to head down to Auckland, New Zealand, and report to the commodore of convoys down there. I was told to get down there at a certain time, go through the barrier reef arrangement, down inside the reef, and arrive at a certain hour. I was the senior destroyer man and Captain Wilson was in the Chevalier.* We got down there with good speed and went through the barrier at night. This was a sort of funny experience for all of us but, knowing that we'd got into the barrier, I felt quite safe from submarines, but, lo and behold, the Chevalier, which was riding astern, was contacting submarines all the way down the barrier. So I finally had to tell them, "Please keep quiet and I'll let you know when you have to worry about submarines."

We got into Auckland about 10:00 o'clock in the morning, after going down the coast of New Zealand at night inside the barrier, and I sent a signal over and asked the commodore for information on what to do. He said they were sailing at 12:00

---

*Lieutenant Commander George R. Wilson, USN.

o'clock, so I had to immediately go over to the fuel dock. I wasn't allowed to let anyone ashore, and I ended up being the commodore of the Army division that was going to relieve the Marines at Guadalcanal, all those troops. But I did have the help in my convoy of some destroyers that had just come from the Atlantic. They had never been out in the Pacific before and were convoying this whole Army division from Auckland up to Noumea. Later they were convoyed up to Guadalcanal to relieve the Marines. On the way up, being commodore of the convoy, I was completely responsible for the whole operation.

Here again, you run into inexperienced people not only manning the sonars, but even commanding officers who were sort of nervous and fidgety. After a certain skipper reported a fourth or fifth contact and my boys, who were exceedingly experienced, couldn't get anything, I finally had to shut him up, tell him to keep quiet until I told him when to get worried about submarines in the area. Needless to say, we never did run into a submarine and we got up to Noumea safely, but if I had followed some of these new skippers who had just arrived on the scene and were reporting--I must have had 10 or 15 contacts reported, which required me to shift the whole convoy, radically maneuver it and everything else, for a false alarm. This is one of the tough responsibilities of a commodore of convoys, to weigh exactly whether contacts are actual sounds, whether all this maneuvering had to be done for a purpose or for nought.

Q: Or whether it's a case of jitters?

Admiral MacDonald: In so many cases, for new people to go out there, I used to pray that they could get through their first engagement safely without hurting their own friends, because they get so trigger-happy, and once they start shooting they shoot wildly in all directions and have no control. Even several people who had a lot of experience sometimes reached the point of jumping the gun unnecessarily.

Anyway, this type of operation is what we were being called upon to perform and, of course, the O'Bannon having gone out there as one of the first destroyers and still surviving, we just expected that we would never be relieved to get any relaxation or rest.

This sort of bombarding went on, then the type of operations changed to running up the Slot, the task force running up the Slot, because the Japs were still building up forces on the different islands up the Slot and they were sending down surface forces to protect their movements back and forth. Admiral Ainsworth was still in charge of this task group.

I'd like to bring up another bombardment operation that happened and was rather interesting. This was in the Kula Gulf area, the Kolombangara area, and was to be a bombardment. The usual cruisers were there, the Louisville, the Honolulu, and the Helena, and, as I recall, one of our cruisers had been damaged and we were using the Australian cruiser.

Q: The Australia?

Admiral MacDonald: Well, I went on an operation with the Australia. The Leander was one, but that came into an operation a week later.

Q: That was a New Zealand ship.

Admiral MacDonald: Well, this Kolombangara incident I want to try to recall was somewhere around early July, the fifth or something, and we went in there and the bombardment was carried out exceedingly well, beautifully done. Coordination with the Black Cats was perfect. As we steamed out of the Kula Gulf, we noticed one ship was missing. I questioned Admiral Ainsworth and said that my scope showed one ship missing, and we finally ascertained after a roll call that it was the Strong. The admiral ordered out the Chevalier, which was still under the command of Eph McLean.* The Strong was under the command of Joe Wellings.**

Anyway, the Chevalier and the O'Bannon were ordered back to assist the Strong. We went back into the gulf and we contacted

---

*Commander Ephraim R. McLean, Jr., USN.
**Commander Joseph H. Wellings, USN.

the Strong. She had no communication. We finally found out that she had been torpedoed and she was just lying still in the water. Captain McLean and I decided he'd go alongside on one side and I'd go alongside on the other, and he was going alongside the port side first. He was making a pass at it and I was coming up to go alongside the starboard to take off the survivors. Just as I got close to him, I noticed that he wasn't making a very good landing and he started backing down and he sort of backed into my side. The reason he backed into my side was that he had run into the stern of the Strong and damaged his bow, his sonar, gyro, and a few other things. Anyway, he did get alongside and he took the survivors off, all that he thought were alive. In the meantime we were being shot at by the Japs. Shore batteries had opened up on us. They saw us out there, and they were shooting like mad. Shells were landing all over the place. I was then told to go over there and destroy the shore battery, open up on them, and, of course, stand in between.

So I put myself in between the Strong and the shore battery and started shooting away, while he was loading survivors. We shot quite a bit, and finally he said he'd got them all. Then he said, "My gyro is out and everything; you'll have to lead me out." So I hauled off and led the Chevalier out of the bay. He had rammed his ship enough to do some damage.

Q: But he didn't do any damage to your ship?

Admiral MacDonald: No, he didn't. He just dented the plate a little bit. He didn't back into me because he backed down after colliding.

Anyway, my operation to save them from the starboard side was definitely called off when he made such a lousy approach.

We got out and reported the Strong had been sunk, and then joined the task force back in Purvis Bay.

That particular little accident put the Chevalier out of action for a while and, of course, the Strong was sunk. We thought we had all the survivors, but the ship went down, and after it went down, even while we were fairly close by, there were tremendous explosions, and it turned out that they had set their depth charges for about 50 feet and when they got down there, their own depth charges went off. As a consequence, we thought, well, if anyone was still alive in the water they couldn't possibly have lived through it.

Later on, of course, we found out that there were some survivors and some of them did live, including Joe Wellings, who was the captain, who was in the water. He went through this depth charge explosion. It did do some physical harm to him, but he was alive. Then, weeks later, we discovered that one of his officers also had been in the water and drifted down on the island and was rescued about a month later. He'd been living over there on the island for about--I guess it must have been pretty close to a month.

Q: Who took care of him, the natives?

Admiral MacDonald: No, he was living on his own, and it was Jap-held at that time, that side of it. Later, a Marine raiding battalion landed there. Colonel Liversedge was the commanding officer, and the support group for this Marine battalion were destroyers.* We went in there firing gunfire protecting the Marines landing from some destroyers; they landed over there in that south part of Kula Gulf. This was a raiding party, Marine raiders. The famous Marine raiders went over there.

This was the way life was out there, never a quiet, dull moment, particularly for the destroyers. The cruisers got off a little bit better, because they could stick around until an operation was ready, but we invariably had other missions in the meantime.

Q: Let me ask how the crew of the O'Bannon stood up under this.

Admiral MacDonald: I'm sure they were all quite exhausted but, thank God, by that time they had a great deal of confidence in a lot of things. Too, they thought that maybe the O'Bannon was a special ship that was being well protected.

---

*Colonel Harry B. Liversedge, USMC.

Q: She possessed a guardian angel or something!

Admiral MacDonald: Yes. As a matter of fact, we were called "The Galloping Ghost of the Solomons Coast!" It was felt that we had some sort of a protector there. They felt very strongly that someone was looking out for us. I don't think there were any atheists on board, I'll tell you that.

Several incidents that developed out there were rather interesting.

On that particular bombardment night when we went up there, I had several crew members, I will say they were both black again, who had reached the point of exhaustion. This might help answer your question. I usually told them more or less when we'd get within range of where I thought there might be some activity, so on certain nights when we'd go up and I knew we were going to bombard about midnight, I'd call for calm about 11:00 o'clock and try to rest up in the meantime. We'd usually take off about 6:00 and shoot up there at 34 knots, sometimes. I'd call them about 11:00 o'clock to general quarters.

These two fellows who, there's no doubt about it, just like the rest of them, were getting awfully exhausted and tired, never being able to relax. They failed to go to their lower handling gun stations on this particular occasion, and we got into an action that night. We got through it safely and were on our way back, and the gunnery officer had to tell me that these two men failed to show up in the handling room. I found out that they had been out on deck in life jackets during the engagement.

I called them up. I knew what they wanted. They wanted to be put ashore. They wanted to get a general court-martial or something and live, and I said there was nothing doing. We'd all like to get ashore. So I said, "We're going back up there again tonight and, instead of your being given freedom, when I call for general quarters I'm going to lock you up."

So, that night we went up, and I had the master-at-arms lock them up in the paint locker. We went through an action, firing and all this business. The next day he let them out, and they came up on the bridge practically on their hands and knees. I won't say that they'd turned white, but they were really scared to death and they said, "Captain, we'll never do that again. Please never do <u>that</u> again."

I said, "All right, next time general quarters sounds, you go to your stations."

Well, you know, one of those fellows was a machine-gunner on topside later, and he was one of the best machine-gunners I had. Boy, he could shoot fantastically. It just took this type of treatment to get them over what had happened in the past. It built up confidence in them, the fact that they lived.

The other fellow never failed to do his job, either, but, boy, they did in the first place, and they had to be taught a lesson. This is the way a lot of them felt about feeling that there was no end to this until something radical had to happen, you got lost or wrecked or damaged.

Along that same line, people did get pretty exhausted. My chief pharmacist took a dose of Mercurochrome, and word came up to me that he was throwing up blood. This was just before we were to depart on another night operation. I couldn't let him off because we had to go, but when we finally got in and I found out that it wasn't blood, it was Mercurochrome, this put a different light on it. Anyway, he wasn't too much of a help in those battles, so I let him go ashore because he was really exhausted.

Along the same line, some of my people like George Philip, who was my exec, were just exhausted.* He was such a wonderful guy and so brilliant and able, I just pleaded with them to order him back so he could get a rest, and they finally did. They ordered him back to gunnery school in Honolulu. He was able to get a rest, and he later came out as the commanding officer of another ship. However, he was lost in that ship.

But it was evident. These guys were so loyal they were dying on their feet, they were getting so tired, some of them, really, because it was hot up there. We were pretty close to the equator and we had no awnings, no rugs. It was pretty hard even to rest.

---

*Lieutenant Commander George Philip, Jr., USN, later lost when the USS _Twiggs_ (DD-591) was sunk off Okinawa on 16 June 1945.

People lost weight. They were tired, but, boy, they certainly went to their stations and carried on beautifully when they were called upon.

Following the sort of trend of the action, after we lost the Strong, the following week, as far as task force operations were concerned, we went up the Slot because obviously intelligence had conveyed that there was a Jap task force coming down, and it was to cover some sort of a movement of Japanese troops. So we went back up. As a matter of fact, we went up the day before, the night before, with this information and we didn't encounter anyone, so we came back. But we had had time, and Admiral Ainsworth had worked up a battle plan. We had certain signals for what kind of a deployment we'd go into when we encountered enemy forces. We had all these different plans, and I think it was on the night of the 12th of July or the morning of the 13th we went up there. The word was if we didn't encounter the enemy by midnight, we'd turn around and go back because we'd have to get back under our own air cover.

Well, at five minutes to 12:00, we started picking up contacts. Everyone was all set to turn around and go back. We were all beginning to relax. From 11:00 o'clock until five minutes to 12:00, we were waiting to see what was going to happen and we expected in a few minutes we'd get the signal to haul around and go home.

Interview Number 4 with Rear Admiral Donald J. MacDonald,
U.S. Navy (Retired)

Place: Admiral MacDonald's residence in Washington, D.C.

Date: Tuesday morning, 10 September 1974

Subject: Biography

Interviewer: John T. Mason, Jr.

Q: Chapter 4 is a continuation of the operations down in the South Pacific. Today, I think you want to make some mention of the fact the Americans sprung a surprise on the Japanese and decided to occupy the island of Vella Lavella. It was a small expedition. A landing force under Brigadier General Robert McClure had made a landing on the island on August 15th.* The O'Bannon was a part of the escort for this amphibious force, and I think perhaps you'll take up the story there.

Admiral MacDonald: The Vella Lavella landing is somewhat hazy in my mind, the details of it, because we had been operating as a covering force for so many operations that it would be difficult to single out this particular one. We were constantly covering operations or planning operations and landings all the way up the Slot.

After our landing at Vella Lavella, the Japanese found

*Brigadier General Robert B. McClure, USA.

themselves with a lot of troops not only on Vella Lavella but on Kolombangara, and they had to get them off. This caused a lot of barge activity on the part of the Japanese back and forth to those two islands. That became one of the chief operations during the month of August--the interception of a lot of barge traffic.

Q: How successful were we?

Admiral MacDonald: We were very successful in destroying a lot of the barges. Also, these barge operations were always screened by a covering force of Japanese destroyers. I remember a couple of times--we ran into them--a number of barges with men on board. We didn't do anything to them, because we were being fired at by the Japanese force and the shells were landing on their own barges. We were at full speed and were after the destroyers first. We chased them, but by the time we came back, the barges were hiding and proved very hard to find.

Q: How many men could they carry on a barge?

Admiral MacDonald: They were pretty well filled up with men. There were a number of barges transporting men from Choiseul to Vella Lavella. It must have been in their minds they were going to beef up their forces in Vella Lavella.

Q: And try to push us off?

Admiral MacDonald: Yes, push us off. That type of thing was going on frequently. In the meantime we were changing commodores. Commander Chandler was back in control of a night operation up there, and this night we really did run into a lot of barges and shot up a number.* We really scoured the coast trying to get them all. None of our ships were hit in any of those actions, although we were shot at by the supporting groups. They all steamed away.

Now what happened off Vella Lavella early the morning of October sixth? We had been on a mission the night before in the Slot and were coming back to Purvis Bay when we received word a sizable task force was coming down for an emergency job.

Q: They were coming to dislodge the Americans from Vella Lavella?

Admiral MacDonald: Yes. The task force was in back waiting to run the garrison to Vella Lavella. Early on the morning of October sixth, this force under a Jap admiral was heading south from Rabaul. This progress was reported, and we sent up Commodore Frank Walker in the Selfridge and the Chevalier and the

*Commander Alvin D. Chandler, USN.

O'Bannon to intercept the Jap group.* We were supposed to be joined by four other ships before this action took place. The idea was that six American destroyers could have given the Japs' nine or ten a run for their money.

Q: Were they all destroyers in the Japanese fleet?

Admiral MacDonald: No, one of the ships was the Japanese cruiser Yugumo; the other eight were destroyers. The Yugumo was my target and she was sunk. Our target looked quite large. It looked like a cruiser to me; it turned out to be the Yugumo. The Japs were in two different columns, but we steamed up there at 2231 on October sixth and made contact with the enemy up the Slot.

Before that, we had definitely been picked up by the Japanese night spotting planes. They had been dropping flare buoys right and left.

One thing I must say, we were quite desperate at this time. The Selfridge was just a surface-action ship, and she did not have radar-controlled guns, but she was leading our column. The Chevalier and O'Bannon, of course, were modern ships with radar-controlled gunnery and also dual-purpose mounts. Here was the Selfridge, which could only fire at surface ships, moving up

---

*Captain Frank R. Walker, USN.

there in the lead of the column.

Commodore Walker headed his three destroyers according to the target, and at 2240 the enemy was in binocular range, six destroyers in two groups. There was no surprise at this action, unless the Japs were surprised at three American destroyers with this solid force of six in all. Captain Walker--well, there's a comment about him--but basically we just steamed on towards the Japs at full speed and at 500 yards distance, which is not a very safe distance at high speed, and as soon as we got within range we were all ready to prepare to fire torpedoes, we fired them, and we opened fire. Immediately the bullets were flying. You could see them striking these ships and immediately a couple of the Japs were hit.

Q: Had they not also sent torpedoes?

Admiral MacDonald: They had sent torpedoes and they had started firing. The next thing was that while we were firing, I saw the Chevalier getting hit--I was still shooting--500 yards ahead. It just blew her right off; she was hit on the port side. I gave emergency full speed astern, hard right rudder. I wanted to get out of her way, because she had swung over and we were all making about 30 knots, but I just couldn't avoid her, and my bow ran into the stern of the ship, although the bow had been blown off. She almost stopped dead then and was sort of going down, as a matter of fact.

Maybe in a way, as I wrote my report, my hitting her held her up. She didn't go down right away. The survivors who were later picked up indicated that the water was coming right through.

After that, I saw the Selfridge going up and taking on the other ships, and the next thing was a big explosion and the Selfridge had been hit. All this time, we expected to be hit by Jap torpedoes, too, because we were just dead in the water. Jap airplanes were just buzzing around us like mad. Why they didn't drop bombs right down our stack, I have no idea. They were flying around all the time. We got ready to fire more torpedoes at dead-in-the-water targets, Japanese ships, at quite a distance and we were all set to fire them when, on the TBS, we got word that this group that was supposed to join us in the first place was coming up. They were coming up right in line with the targets, so I didn't fire my torpedoes. I was afraid that maybe they'd hit one of our own.

Anyway, then we decided to pick up the survivors. I made three or four attempts to go alongside, but my bow was so badly damaged I just couldn't steer the thing. She wouldn't go alongside, so then we put our boats out in the water and they went over and picked up all the survivors who were still survivors and brought them on board.

The Chevalier was so badly banged up that there was nothing left forward of her bridge and having hit her stern a little bit, it flooded the engine room. She was a hopeless wreck.

After we'd picked up the survivors . . .

Q: How many survivors did you get?

Admiral MacDonald: I don't think we lost many people. I don't recall the exact number, but probably well over 200 at least.

The Selfridge had gone on ahead, and then she was hit and dead in the water with her whole bow blown off, too. The other group came up after we had all the survivors on board. From my previous experience of ships going down, like the Helena, I left my whaleboats in the water just in case we didn't get all the survivors and maybe they could find a way of getting on board and saving themselves the next day.

After the other group joined up, one of them fired a torpedo into the Chevalier, which was still floating but gone. And the Selfridge apparently had to be towed back. I was getting back under my own steam, although my bow was somewhat damaged.

During all of this action, the thing that struck me so funny was that these planes were all around us all the time dropping these flares and everything but they weren't doing anything. The net result was apparently they were trying to decoy the evacuation of the Japs at that time, and they weren't about to try to get us stirred up. That Japanese evacuation operation apparently turned out successful in the long run.

Q: It was a cover for that?

Admiral MacDonald: I think so.

Q: That they continued this operation. What about the flares? What was the purpose of the flares?

Admiral MacDonald: To mark the spot, a target, just in case they wanted an aircraft, or if there were any Japanese ships around, they'd know where we were. They were always trying to mark the spot or area where we were. This is one of the things that we mentioned in the Chicago incident. They had never seen this type of action, coming from the Atlantic; it was all new to them, and these flares were disturbing.* They didn't know what was coming on. In her case, of course, the Japs sent some torpedo planes down and, of course, this marked the target. But they did this to us all the time up and down the Slot. They knew our track all the way, and we never knew what was going to hit us, whether it was going to be airplanes or whether it was going to be ships.

Q: In this instance, how many destroyers were in the group that

---

*Admiral Giffen was new to the area, but the Chicago and her crew had been involved in the Solomons campaign from the beginning, including the night action of 8-9 August 1942 off Savo Island when Japanese planes dropped flares prior to the surface attack.

came to your rescue?

Admiral MacDonald: Three more destroyers joined up with us, but everything was over and the Japs had all disappeared. Actually, the Jap force totaled, I think, about nine destroyers. The three ships that joined us later were the Ralph Talbot, Taylor, and Lavallette, but the battle was all over by the time they got there. They did see the firing and they saw the Jap ships going down.

Q: How many were lost on the Japanese side?

Admiral MacDonald: Oh, the whole crew of the Yugumo--well, it sank. The strange thing about it, the next day the commander, who was then Ed Wilkinson at Vella Lavella, the beach commander, he sent PT boats up to the area and they towed in my two whaleboats into Vella Lavella. This is not recorded in any of the histories, but it was sent to me in a message by Ed Wilkinson the next day, and my two whaleboats were filled with Japs, Jap prisoners, and those were the only ones who were saved.

Q: They got in of their own accord?

Admiral MacDonald: They got in of their own accord in my whaleboats. They were towed in by the PT boats. This was the first indication we had of what Japanese ships were involved in the battle and how many. That message came through and apparently--I remember it so well--it congratulated me for getting those prisoners in my whaleboats. It never has shown up in any of the historical documents that I know of.

Q: Given their proclivity for self-destruction when about to be captured, why did they permit themselves to be towed in?

Admiral MacDonald: I guess they had no alternative by that time. The PT boat was out there with guns and all that business, and they were towed in.

Q: When you permitted those whaleboats to remain in the water, you were divesting yourself of a safety measure, weren't you?

Admiral MacDonald: Oh, yes, there's no doubt about that. We had life rafts and everything, but we didn't leave that area until daylight and actually we had no air cover up in that area. As cripples, we were very vulnerable to Jap air attacks and we expected them the next morning, there's no doubt about it, and I had the whole crew of the Chevalier on board. Coming back, I hugged the coast and came down through channels that we'd never gone through before in order to stay away from the wide open spaces. No one had ever navigated them, as far as I know, coming down there with a damaged ship.

After we got back, I started writing a report. My battle report was the only one that was available, because the bridges of both the other ships had been blown up, and all their records had been lost. The thing that struck me so funny was that, based on my report, the other two ships wrote their reports and they were completely different! Of course, they imagined a lot of things and they did a lot of things that were not evident. It seemed very strange that the only record was ours. The other two turned in different reports. No criticism involved, but the thing is how did it happen.

We got back to the bay and they surveyed us. They decided to patch up our bow so we could get back to the States. While I was there I went over and saw Count Austin.* He was division commander there and Arleigh Burke was the squadron commander.** We talked about fighting out there, the battles, and so forth. One comment I made that I hoped would be helpful was that in a destroyer action like the one we got into in Vella Lavella, this business of staying in direct column at 500 yards and going at 30-some knots was for the birds when you got into fighting. It didn't give you a chance to avoid anyone. Either they should be sort of staggered a little bit, maybe expanded out to 700 yards.

---

*Commander Bernard L. Austin, USN, Commander Destroyer Division 46 from May to December 1943.

**Captain Arleigh A. Burke, USN, Commander Destroyer Squadron 23 from October 1943 to March 1944.

Q: In other words, that was a textbook arrangement, was it?

Admiral MacDonald: Yes. Oh, yes, 500 yards, full speed ahead, which was fine in just normal steaming, but when you get in an action where you're shooting and firing and everything, you can't watch the guy ahead so much because you're trying to watch what's going on.

Well, that particular action put us out of commission. We had just finished well over a year out there.

Q: It was about time, was it not?

Admiral MacDonald: The first action, but I must say that in my ship no one was hurt, regardless. We weren't hit by any of the Jap torpedoes or shells. I'm not too sure how many torpedoes the <u>Chevalier</u> and <u>Selfridge</u> took, but they were really banged up severely. But there again, we had come through a pretty bad action with no loss of personnel, and yet I think we really were the ones who sank the Japs because our boys just hit the targets the moment they opened up. They were all set.

That concluded our fighting out there in the Pacific.

Q: Do you want to say something about the emotional, mental condition of the crew at that point, as they returned for relief?

Admiral MacDonald: There's no doubt in my mind, after we got back to the harbor safely, there was great relief because then they realized that there was going to be time out for something, whether it was rest and relaxation or something, because we had to be repaired before we could go back. There was great relief from then on, there's no doubt about it. The strain was off, because we had been going up and down that Slot night after night, turned around many times after we were just about ready to go back and told to go back up again. And, of course, one of the big things about this up and down the Slot business was fuel and air cover. We had to go at fairly high speed so we'd get up there at a certain hour and back at a certain hour where we could get air cover. That was one of the things that was always a criterion in these operations, because the Japs were operating from a lot of airports much closer than our people.

Well, that sort of concludes the O'Bannon's first trip out in the Pacific.

Q: Did the entire crew go back to the States?

Admiral MacDonald: Yes, we took the whole crew back to the States by way of Bora Bora. I think I related the incident that happened in Bora Bora, with the change of attitude and conditions. Then we went back to San Francisco, Mare Island. We were definitely back there in December of 1943. We were in the yard there. In the meantime, they had already sent in the dimensions and they had a bow all ready to put on us. We were then repaired and ready to go back. I was there all the time.

The rest of the division, the Nicholas and the rest of them, in a great burst of generosity, were allowed to go up to Mare Island and brought back for Christmas, the Nicholas and whatever other ships were in our division. They were sent back for Christmas, so we were all together.

In the meantime, I flew to New York and got married, went back, took the ship out for refresher training to get her ready to go to Honolulu.

Q: It was an appropriate time to get married, wasn't it!

Admiral MacDonald: Well, we didn't really care years ago.

I was to take her back to Honolulu, where I was to be relieved by Captain Smith.* Captain Smith showed up while we were in Coronado during our training period, but we decided it would be silly to just be riding around as a passenger, so he got permission to relieve then.

I flew back and I was ordered to work with Captain Brown, who was setting up a destroyer commanders' school at Norfolk.**

---

*Commander Richard Wilder Smith, USN.
**Captain Bert F. Brown, USN.

Q: What Brown was that?

Admiral MacDonald: Bert Brown. Not Bill Brown. Bill Brown was commanding officer of the Nicholas.* This was Bert Brown, who had command of another ship out there for a while. He and I were to get this destroyer command school started in Norfolk.

After I got back, my wife and I went down to Norfolk, and we were working on getting this school started.

Q: What was the purpose of this additional school?

Admiral MacDonald: This was to teach the commanders of the new ships, destroyer commanders, how to fight destroyers in war.

Q: And there was no no other such school?

Admiral MacDonald: They had the ASW school down at Key West.** Emphasis was on ASW in the past, and then they had other little schools like radar schools, but this was a school that was designed to combine all the real fighting operations a commander

---

*Lieutenant Commander William D. Brown, USN, was the first commanding officer when the USS Nicholas (DD-449) went into commission on 4 June 1942. Later in this memoir, Admiral MacDonald talks about Captain Brown as skipper of the USS Missouri (BB-63) when she ran aground in 1950.

**ASW--antisubmarine warfare.

was going to be involved in.

Bert Brown had already been there, and I was to go down as a sort of deputy for lectures and so forth.

The new 2,200-tonners were the same hulls virtually as the 2,100-tonners, but instead of five 5-inch mounts they were coming out with three 5-inch twin mounts.* This then was a heavier setup on the same frame as the 2,100-tonners. They were just rolling off the line. They had a different bridge arrangement. They had a bridge arrangement that was taken sort of from the British escort ships, a very tiny bridge, no wings on the sides, and an open-air bridge up above.

Q: This was a British frigate?

Admiral MacDonald: Well, British-frigate style. The British frigate, of course, was just submarine escorting and so forth. It wasn't fighting actions.

I was ordered to take command of one of the 2,200-tonners, but three or four weeks after I'd been down in Norfolk and seen some of these ships, I didn't like them one bit.

Q: Why?

---

*The 2,200-tonners were the Allen M. Sumner (DD-692) class.

Admiral MacDonald: Well, because of the fact that the speed had been reduced; using the same hull, they couldn't make the same speed. They didn't have the same endurance with putting more weight in the same hull. The bridge setup was so bad you couldn't even see what was coming, and they'd had two collisions.

One of my classmates was taking one out, backing out from Norfolk, and he ran into a merchant ship.

So, when BuPers ordered me to take over a 2,200-tonner--and, boy, at that time I felt I could take over a battleship or a cruiser and that's what I wanted--I knew Admiral Denfeld who was up in the bureau, and I wrote a letter to him and said, "Admiral, I don't want to take over command of these ships as they are right now, the 2,200-tonners. They're not, in my opinion, good fighting ships. I'd like to be ordered back to my own ship."*

This resulted in my being ordered to the bureau or, rather CominCh, Admiral King.** This was his approved design, the 2,200-tonner, and he was disturbed at some of the adverse comments. So I was ordered to his staff, although he really didn't want to recognize the fact that the 2,200-tonner was not a good ship the way it was. So I ended up being on his staff for a short period of time, sitting in with some of my friends down in

---

*Rear Admiral Louis E. Denfeld, USN, Assistant Chief of Naval Personnel from May 1942 to March 1945. Admiral Denfeld was later Chief of Naval Operations from 1947 to 1949.

**CominCh--Commander in Chief United States Fleet. Admiral Ernest J. King, USN, served in this position from December 1941 until October 1945.

the Bureau of Engineering and the Bureau of Ships, and we talked about the design of these ships to try to make them better.

At that time, all the people who were in BuShips and so forth who were friends of mine listened to me. So the net result of this thing was that the next group of 2,200-tonners coming out had been cut in half and had additional fuel tanks installed; they extended them ten feet or more.

Q: What about the bridge area?

Admiral MacDonald: They put wings out to the sides. The whole point of the open bridge is not a bridge that you can fight a ship at night in any circumstances, but these ships were going to the Pacific and when they got involved in surface actions they'd never be able to fight them from outside one with the enclosed bridge. They couldn't do it.

They went along with it and finally the net result was that they started changing the design.

Q: How did Admiral King react to this?

Admiral MacDonald: He didn't like it worth a darn, but he accepted it finally.

Q: You mean the evidence was there?

Admiral MacDonald: The evidence was there that his fighting people should be able to tell him how to get these ships ready to really fight.

As a matter of fact, even the twin mounts, having six guns, it should supposedly have made a better fighting ship than the five 5-inch, but the single mounts were still the best producers because if one mount went out, then you've lost two guns. Many of the ships were hit and one mount went out on the 2,100-tonner class, but they still had four. I don't know. The design was cut off a little bit, but they did modify them to that extent. They extended them to where they could build up their cruising radius, but they never did extend them to the point where they could make the speed that we could make because of the weight. And they changed the bridge structure.

While I was sitting there, the Normandy invasion was taking place and Admiral Kirk, who had flown back after the Normandy invasion, was in the office when he was told by Admiral King that he could take his staff because he was going back as Commander U.S. Naval Forces in France.* I was still at that time probably going to go back in command of another ship. King told Kirk he could take anyone back to France that he wanted to, build up his staff there.

Kirk hadn't been in town very long and I knew him. We were

*Rear Admiral Alan G. Kirk, USN.

together at cocktail parties, and he said, "How about going back with me as my chief of staff for operations?"

I was delighted because I thought at that time that the Japanese war would be going on, and it looked like we were going to finish the European war, go back and finish that, and I'd get back to Japan.

Q: Before you launch into that, would you recount any recollections you might have of Admiral King when you were serving there in Washington?

Admiral MacDonald: I can only tell you this. I had known Admiral King way back. I knew exactly what he was like in a lot of ways.

Q: Had you served under him?

Admiral MacDonald: I never served under him. His aide, his perennial aide whom he took everywhere, because of his wife, who was a most attractive person . . .

Q: Who was that?

Admiral MacDonald: Stanton Dunlap.*

I'd met Admiral King out in Coronado when he was ComAirBase.** I used to go to many, many parties with him. I knew how he liked the girls, and what kind of a rough reputation he had as far as naval officers were concerned. So I came back and was ordered to his staff there. I was told that King insisted that we all wear grays and I'd be reprimanded one way or another if I didn't buy any grays and get going with it. Knowing I was probably going back eventually to the Pacific, I wasn't about to buy any grays because Nimitz wasn't about to put on grays out there.***

Q: It was rather unattractive, wasn't it?

Admiral MacDonald: So I was wearing khaki all the time and the only one on CominCh's staff wearing khaki. I know that no one liked it, and I was told two or three times to get out of it, although King himself never said anything to me about it.

He was pretty tough, and one of the things that he was really worried about was the column that Drew Pearson used to write.****

---

*Captain Stanton B. Dunlap, USN.

**As a rear admiral, King was Commander Aircraft Base Force in 1936-1937.

***Admiral Chester W. Nimitz, USN, Commander in Chief Pacific Fleet from 1941 to 1945.

****Drew Pearson was a muckraking syndicated newspaper columnist, the predecessor of Jack Anderson.

Drew Pearson used to attack King quite frequently, and that column was the first thing that he read every day to see how to handle Drew Pearson.

Q: Was Pearson attacking his personal life?

Admiral MacDonald: Yes, he was attacking his personal ways and his naval ways of doing things.

Anyway, as far as Admiral King is concerned, I never really had any real contact with him while I was in his staff and was working there. I was assigned to the training tactical division and working down there with the BuShips people.

Well, when Kirk was told he could build up his staff, he went in and asked King if he could have me go back with him. King said, "All right, that's the end. You get the rest of the staff over there and let's go."

So Kirk and I went back to Europe and into France.

Q: He didn't want him to . . .

Admiral MacDonald: He didn't want him to change his mind to this point of view that he wasn't going to let anyone else go back to Europe. There were enough people over there, and I was the last one he allowed to go back with Kirk.

Q: He didn't permit anyone to raid his staff, anyway, did he?

Admiral MacDonald: Well, I was just on a temporary assignment, anyway. I wasn't on a permanent assignment with King. I was brought up by Denfeld on a temporary assignment, because basically I had been ordered to another ship and I said I didn't want that ship; I wanted my own back.

Incidentally, that particular ship went out to the Pacific and within a month after it got out there it was hit by a kamikaze, the particular ship that I was supposed to take out. I don't know who was sort of protecting me, but someone!

Well, we went back to Europe, first to London, then when the troops started moving into Paris, Admiral Kirk just took his staff. By that time, he had built up a staff with some people he knew were over there, from the commander in chief, Stark's group.*

Q: You went back in August?

Admiral MacDonald: It was right after the Normandy invasion in June. No, I think we must have gone back earlier because we were there in July. As soon as they moved into Paris and took over, we moved in and Eisenhower set up his headquarters in Versailles

---

*Admiral Harold R. Stark, USN, Commander U.S. Naval Forces Europe from April 1942 to August 1945.

and we were at St. Germain.* Our headquarters were right near the Arc de Triomphe, the naval headquarters, and we were living out at St. Germain and had additional headquarters where we set up Nissen huts.

Our task was to work with Eisenhower directly, and the U.S. commander, in order to handle any U.S. naval operations that might be required under him. This resulted in daily meetings with Eisenhower's staff as to what was going on. At that time, of course, the troops had moved on as far as--well, Paris had been completely cleared, but there were still pockets of Germans in the Channel Islands and down around Bordeaux, up in the Gironde. Also, we had to open up the ports, Cherbourg, Le Havre, and then plan to opén up Brussels, the port of Antwerp.

Q: I take it that the ferrying operations that were still necessary for sending troops and supplies to the continent were a bit hazardous?

Admiral MacDonald: Oh, yes. Well, actually, the Germans had been forced back. There's no doubt about that. They had been forced back at that time, and there was terrific fighting going on along the northern part of the European continent. The British were encountering great difficulty in moving, and

*General Dwight D. Eisenhower, USA, Supreme Allied Commander Europe from 1943 to 1945.

Churchill insisted that the Americans not move any faster than the British could keep up so that they would all get up there at the same time.

Q: Keep them in tandem!

Admiral MacDonald: Keep them in tandem the whole way up. There were a lot of operations going on with the Seventh Army in Italy.

We landed right after the Normandy invasion, as soon as they moved into Paris.

Q: Now, Kirk's responsibilities continued to govern the Channel operations, too?

Admiral MacDonald: Yes. Well, the different ports' directors, like Admiral Hall was a subcommander under Kirk in a way, the task force commander, then the admiral who was in charge of both Le Havre and Cherbourg, they all came under Kirk.*

Q: Then there was Sullivan?**

Admiral MacDonald: No, he was the salvage, Sullivan. No, there was a Rear Admiral Wilkes and he had his port commanders under

---

*Rear Admiral John L. Hall, USN.

**Commodore William A. Sullivan, USN.

him, and they were to open up the ports so that supplies could come in this way and do away with the Normandy beaches.* The next thing was to bring ships right into the ports.

Opening up Cherbourg wasn't easy because the Germans . . .

Q: Did Kirk show a personal interest in the opening up of Cherbourg?

Admiral MacDonald: He left it up to his subcommanders; there's no doubt about that, he left that up to his subcommanders. Kirk was supposed to be in an advisory capacity as a vice admiral working with Eisenhower. After things settled down a little bit, I began to work with the French in order to get the French Navy back into the picture to take over some of these ports and to clear them of German pockets. I worked quite a bit in connection with the French then taking over their own ports as far as the west coast was concerned, opening up Bordeaux. We didn't particularly want to use that one, but we did want to use Cherbourg and Le Havre. This was the type of operation I was doing as chief of staff for plans and operations.

Q: Did you have personal relationships with Sullivan yourself?

---

*Rear Admiral John Wilkes, USN.

Admiral MacDonald: No. I knew Sullivan from way back. He was in London several years before, but I never had any relationship. As a matter of fact, I used to go to Cherbourg and to Le Havre just on sort of visits, but I never had anything really to do with it because it was all sort of subordinated down the line.

Q: In retrospect, that was a rather remarkable operation, wasn't it?

Admiral MacDonald: Yes, it certainly was. A couple of friends of mine were ambushed and killed down there when they ran into some German pockets. That all happened at night over there; it wasn't easy, because the troops moved so fast they left these German pockets behind.

Clearing the Channel Islands, because the Germans had some forces over there, they used to raid the harbor of Cherbourg and sink the ships right in the harbor. Then it became an operation of ridding them. They didn't want to go over there and bomb them because of the British subjects, so we were prevented from bombing them out of existence, which we could have done, because of British subjects being there and maybe hurting the British. So that had to be done in a very slow process.

Q: How was it done?

Admiral MacDonald: It was done by raiding and trying to catch their raiding ships, and we did get a few of them at night, in night actions with the small sort of gunboats that they had over there that would come over.

Q: Channel E-boats?

Admiral MacDonald: Channel E-boats or something. They caught some of them at night, and I think a couple of our DEs got banged up and ran aground in a couple of actions, as I recall.*

As far as the Bordeaux thing, we got the French Navy back in the swing. Admiral Rue was in command of the Lorraine and another battleship, and we got minesweepers and so forth and they went in and swept that area and bombarded the pockets of Germans.**

Q: These were the Free French?

Admiral MacDonald: Yes, Free French, but they were navy. Yes, Free French at that time.

I did do a lot of work in the planning of that operation, but the chief of staff of the French Navy by that time was back in

---

*DE--destroyer escort ship.

**Rear Admiral Joseph Rue, French Navy.

the French Navy, Lemonnier.* He was a great friend of Admiral Kirk's and loved to play tennis. On the property that we had taken over, there was a tennis court, and he loved to play tennis, Kirk loved to play tennis, and so did I. One evening he came out with his aide and he was playing in his bare feet.

There were several reasons why we wanted to try to help the French Navy rebuild its morale and spirit, and this operation, I thought--and I had to sell it the whole way through--was to let the French Navy itself remove the Germans from this one pocket.

Q: You had to sell this idea to whom?

Admiral MacDonald: I had to sell it to Admiral Kirk, McGeorge Bundy, and up the way, to try to rebuild their morale and get them back so they could really be helpful again, to tie them in and let them operate this operation rather than for our people who were so busy, particularly the Army Air Corps, and were too interested in the German aspect to the east rather than worrying about what was behind them.**

Q: Why would Kirk have any objections to this effort?

---

*Admiral Andre Lemonnier, French Navy.

**McGeorge Bundy, who served as President John F. Kennedy's national security advisor, was a young (born 1919) intelligence officer during World War II. While serving as military aide to Commander Naval Forces France, he was a captain in the Army Reserve.

Admiral MacDonald: Well, he thought it was sort of a waste of time, as I recall. He sort of felt that this wasn't a big enough operation for him. In a way, you know, Kirk loved publicity. He was a hell of a nice gentleman, he was a real gentleman, but he was egotistical and this way he wouldn't get any credit for it; the French would. But it was a matter of building up their spirit again after it had been deflated for so many years, and it was very successful.

Q: Did this idea of yours spring from your previous experience with the French in Britain?

Admiral MacDonald: I don't think it really sprang up that way. It sprang up when we moved into France and we started talking with the French in various ways, trying to find out where these Germans were and so forth, and then their offering their help. From that point on, as long as they wanted to help and they felt that they could get organized to do it, it was a matter of maybe letting them do it.

In the discussions we had with the French at that time, we also worked hard to rebuild them to a point where they could help. They didn't do that with the Army at that time. That was a different thing, but the Navy still had some ships there that hadn't been destroyed and they were all ready to go.

Q: Did this subject come up for discussion in the staff meetings?

Admiral MacDonald: Oh, yes, I'm sure it did. Actually, there was a Captain English at the time who was sitting on the staff and was advising Kirk a little bit on some of these things, and he was dead against it.* But when I went in, I had to sell it to Kirk. I had to argue what I thought was a worthwhile point to let this thing go through the way we had planned it, and that was to let the French really handle the deal completely, supplying ships, crews, and so forth.

Q: You wanted to revert for a few minutes. You had several recollections of Admiral King.

Admiral MacDonald: The name of Admiral King's perennial aide was Stanton Dunlap and his wife--a beautiful brunette, rather tall--was one of the reasons why King always kept Stanton as an aide. He started out with him as his flag lieutenant and then later, when he was CominCh, he was flag secretary. After the war, Stanton was ordered as commander of the naval air base in Bermuda. Admiral King was very fond of Abbie Dunlap. This I know, and I can remember attending some of the parties we had

---

*Captain Robert A.J. English, USN.

when I used to visit the Dunlaps a lot in Coronado. Mrs. King was never there, but Admiral King was always there. Wherever he went and was entertaining, he would have Abbie as his hostess instead of Mrs. King, which revealed something of the character of the man. He loved women. Several parties that I went to, they had a lot of these sort of glamorous stars from Hollywood present, and he loved this type of colorful life. That was before he became CominCh. It might reveal some of his personal character. He was interested in gals although he had five daughters.

One thing that always seems strange to most people, yet maybe not so strange if you knew him, was that Mrs. King was always way in the background, never out front at all. When the daughters became eligible--I knew most of them--they occasionally used to be seen at some of the parties of the admiral's, but very seldom Mrs. King.

Q: Well, actually, when he was CominCh, he lived in a yacht.

Admiral MacDonald: Yes, he lived on his own yacht, Vixen, although Mrs. King had the quarters at the Naval Observatory.*

*The Vixen (PG-53), King's flagship between 30 December 1941 and 17 June 1942, was replaced by the Dauntless (PG-61) for the duration of the war.

Q: Now to get back to the staff in Paris. Do you have any more to say about your close working relationship with the French? What was their general attitude when you first came upon them in Paris?

Admiral MacDonald: Well, of course, they were most friendly and most anxious to do anything that we wanted them to do. I'm sure the basic attitude of the people on Eisenhower's staff was not to pay much attention to them, because they didn't want to be bothered with that; they had bigger things to do.

Q: They had a job to do.

Admiral MacDonald: They had a job to do, and they didn't want to worry about all of that.

It soon developed as far as we were concerned what the Navy's participation was going to be. About this time, in the fall, they were getting plans ready to move into Germany across the Rhine and so forth, and this is where we had to play quite a part in making sure that if they got up to the Rhine River, at least we could get our troops across, assuming that all bridges would be destroyed and there would be no way to get across. So this is what part of my main planning was, and I had to make frequent trips up to General Bradley's 12th Tactical Headquarters in Luxembourg and work with him in connection with the requirements for the three different armies that he controlled, find out how we could get the troops across.*

Q: Bring them in from the Channel?

Admiral MacDonald: Yes. This was after we got the port of Antwerp opened up, and it was not an easy thing opening up the port of Antwerp because it was pretty badly mined, and, actually, the Germans were still firing V-2 missiles into the port area. They apparently weren't destroying the city as much, but they were very accurate with the V-2s which were heading right in the harbor area for a long period.

Q: Whose task was it to clean out that harbor?

Admiral MacDonald: Well, this is a little confused. It was under our jurisdiction, as far as the Navy was concerned, but we must have been working with the British on this. But the British had nothing to work with. I just don't recall exactly how. I made a number of trips up to Antwerp. We had a port authority there, a U.S. Navy port authority, but I've forgotten now how the arrangements were made. We had minesweepers sweeping in there.

---

*Lieutenant General Omar N. Bradley, USA, Commanding General, U.S. 12th Army Group.

Q: But always under bombardment from the V-2s?

Admiral MacDonald: The V-2s, and they were a terrible nuisance for a long time.

Anyway, working with the Army to get them there, first, we had to get these LCMs and LCVPs up to Antwerp and unload them, 50 of these big 50-foot--I've forgotten now, but they were about 12 feet wide and 50 feet long--LCMs. We had to get them into the port and then it was a matter of getting them transported down to the different armies, all set up and with Navy crews. This was another thing that had to be done, Navy crews had to man all of these boats. So we had a Navy organization setup of coxswains, crewmen, and engineers. We had to then find out how to transport the boat down there and it worked out that we could use the big 25-ton tank trailers, put these boats on tank trailers and haul them down. The organization had been set up under Navy crews as far as the arrangements were concerned.

We decided in order to camouflage the whole operation, the boats basically were moved at night and the crews all wore Army uniforms. All the time they were up there in the different areas, they were messing with the Army, wore Army uniforms, yet they were all Navy under Navy command.

Q: Just as a footnote, what would have happened to these men if they'd been captured?

Admiral MacDonald: Prisoners of war just like any other soldiers.

Q: They wouldn't have been penalized for wearing the wrong uniform?

Admiral MacDonald: I don't think so. I don't think that point ever came up.

Along with this, we started getting the troops across and everything, and we had to figure ways when the engineers finally built some temporary bridges, how we could protect them from floating mines and all that business coming down the river. They never envisaged that our troops would move so fast that we would have trouble trying to protect the crossing of the river for the different armies.

Q: Let me interrupt and ask a question about German intelligence. Was it still active and accurate enough to know about the existence of these landing craft and guess your purpose in getting them there?

Admiral MacDonald: I don't know exactly what intelligence they had on it, but it seemed as though they weren't informed, they didn't know what was going on. We had these pools of boats with each army, the First, Third, and Fifth Armies, in order to get them across. Then we also had to plan protective booms. We had netting, we had all kinds of devices, just so that once we got the temporary bridges--the engineers put in temporary pontoon bridges--so we could protect them and they wouldn't be blown up all the time. We had to swing booms across above the current.

Our own boom people went over there, Navy boom people, to help on this operation.

Q: What were the problems involved in the pontoon bridges? How wide was the river at that point and how swift was the current, and that sort of thing?

Admiral MacDonald: Well, it's the Rhine River. I'd say at these places it was pretty close to a quarter of a mile, anyway. They weren't too sure exactly where they were going to go across at this stage, but the thing was to get all the equipment up there that could handle the number of troops and tanks and trucks, and get them across just in time to hold the other side; then the engineers could go ahead and build the bridges.

I worked with the people and they did have, originally, a date in November when they were going to launch their drive, so we had to have everything all ready. The thing about getting the boats up there was a real difficult problem, because these were big, 50-foot boats, and the roads went through a lot of narrow towns. We had to get them around certain square corners and so forth. They almost knocked down the sides of buildings. We had a terrible time getting all these 50-footers, 12 feet wide, through a lot of these narrow streets.

Q: Were you given the task of building roads to do this?

Admiral MacDonald: No. We used the old roads, but it did take a lot of Army tank trailers to move these boats down into position, and we set up training headquarters on some of the smaller rivers before we ever got to the Rhine, you know, launching the boats from the tank trailers to get them into the water. Those LCMs are heavy equipment.

Q: Were these fresh crews from America?

Admiral MacDonald: They were regular LCM crews that the Navy had. They were all experienced coxswains. Apparently, they had been used definitely in the Normandy invasion.

Q: How large a crew did this require?

Admiral MacDonald: An engineer, a coxswain, and a couple of crew hands for each big boat.

Q: And there were how many boats as a total?

Admiral MacDonald: As a matter of fact, each army had about 50.

Q: So you had quite a contingent of men.

Admiral MacDonald: Quite a contingent of men up there, and they were all still in the Navy but living with the Army and looking like the Army. We had to get them up there and trained because the original push was planned for November '44 when they were really going to push across the Rhine. That's when the British had moved up to a point where maybe they could move, too. One of the reasons we never moved faster was that the British were so slow up to the north.

Q: You mean there were so many obstacles in their way?

Admiral MacDonald: Yes, too many obstacles in their way.

All this planning of movements was being done in the Versailles headquarters.

One person Kirk used to take along to all the what they called the "chief of staff meetings" while we were in France was McGeorge Bundy. We all lived in the same chateau, about eight of us, and McGeorge Bundy was one of the most brilliant men I think I've ever run into. He had no real position with us. He was just sort of an assistant. Gordon Grayson was the flag lieutenant and Commander Cragg was the flag secretary, but neither of those attended any of these meetings; it was always McGeorge Bundy.* I worked with McGeorge Bundy to a certain extent. He had no fitting into the organization except he was always there.

Q: He was kind of an alter ego to Kirk?

Admiral MacDonald: That's right. He spoke fluent French. As a matter of fact, I even got him to instruct all our officers in French so they could make out a little bit better. He taught us French, but, on the other hand, he was the guy who sort of kept Kirk on the right track all the time. He was just a brilliant guy, unbelievable.

Q: How many stripes did he wear?

Admiral MacDonald: He was an Army captain, I think, and he went with Kirk to all these big meetings, in the beginning. Then when things had boiled down to a lower level, I would meet with the operations people.

Q: Let me ask one more question about the crossing of the Rhine and dealing with Admiral Kirk, General Bradley, and others of

---

*Lieutenant J.G. Grayson, USNR; Lieutenant Commander R.T. Cragg, USNR.

that sort. In retrospect, did you anticipate all the problems that developed, or were there some that you overlooked?

Admiral MacDonald: We anticipated all the problems, I think, including the fact that we figured that a lot of Germans would try to escape into Switzerland, Lake Constance. We anticipated their getting some fast Chris Craft, armed Chris Craft type, for patrolling. This was all done in advance, before they ever made their move, so that we could seal them up and not let them escape.

Q: Very astute to have thought of that angle!

Admiral MacDonald: I will say this, now that I remembered it when we were discussing the French. We were talking to the French about that and the availability of boats and craft in order to accomplish that aspect of the mission. The French were very interested in trying to help us seal off Lake Constance, too.

Q: And did they actually?

Admiral MacDonald: Yes, they did. They actually did help in that respect with the manning of the boats that were going to patrol down there. Our people didn't man them and worked it out with the French trying to prevent it. This looked like quite an escape route for a lot of them, to cross over into Switzerland via Lake Constance, and they could have done it with their own private boats. We had to get boats, and they had to be equipped with searchlights and all kind of stuff in order to stop them.

Q: As it developed, were there many who did attempt this route?

Admiral MacDonald: Yes, there were some. I don't recall exactly the results on that.

What happened was that just about a week before they were ready to go, everything was all set. By that time we had Antwerp opened up to the point where it was pretty safe to bring these ships in there.

Q: Had the V-2s been quelled?

Admiral MacDonald: Not exactly. They were still firing them periodically, but it hadn't been stopped yet because they were flying from Peenemunde, the V-2s. No one had stopped that.

Q: But Peenemunde was under heavy bombing.

Admiral MacDonald: Yes, but they never really knocked any of them out. As a matter of fact, when I used to go up to

Luxembourg the V-1s--they were still firing V-1s--were just crossing over the housetops. Boy, it was still scary. They were still firing V-1s and V-2s.

Our main operation had been bogged down by the Battle of the Bulge. The Germans obviously knew that we were getting ready for a push, so what happened, as I recall at this late date, the Germans had launched an attack, the Battle of the Bulge, to seal us up, slow the whole thing down, so we didn't get going on the operation until the next spring.

In the meantime, we had cleared out the pockets all right, opened up the harbors.

Q: You mean this was on the Atlantic?

Admiral MacDonald: Yes. Then Kirk's staff, of course, started working in conjunction with Admiral Ghormley, who was then prospective Commander U.S. Naval Forces in Germany.* He was sitting over in London, building up a staff.

Q: London?

Admiral MacDonald: Yes, he was back in London, and he was Commander Naval Forces Germany, if and when they moved in. So

---

*Vice Admiral Robert L. Ghormley, USN.

then we had to start working with them, assuming that we were going to join up when we got in there. This was when we got all involved in a lot of future plans that were coming up. They sent us draft plans of what to do in Germany, de-Nazification, demilitarization, de-industrialization, plans to look over and how we had to draw up plans--we didn't have to do them because this was the German side, how to handle the demilitarization of the German Navy. But the basic plans were coming over to us to look at and comment on.

Q: Was that Ghormley's principal objective? I mean, he was going to take over there?

Admiral MacDonald: And sit down and talk, as I will tell you later as we go on here, talk with the Russians.

There were two plans that came over and I had to look at them in my official capacity, and they were very disturbing to me.

Q: But you were still in Paris?

Admiral MacDonald: Oh, yes. We were in Paris until late in the spring of 1945. This was the fall of '44 and we were bogged down by the Battle of the Bulge. That took a lot of attention on the Army's part.

Also, we were involved with the fact that our boys were still up there, our Navy troops, with the boats.

Two plans came over. One was what to do when we moved in and the unconditional surrender of Germany and the demilitarization, de-Nazification, and de-industrialization. I looked these things over and I just thought how can we do these things. This was when I used to talk with Lindbergh about it.* We can't destroy this nation. We can't do these things. And I was told, "Yes, we can."

Q: You obviously didn't agree with Morgenthau, then, did you?

Admiral MacDonald: I didn't agree with Morgenthau or his plan, and when it came up to the unconditional surrender part, that might have been all right. The fact was that they had in mind not treating these people like they had been good opponents and we had won and so forth. They were going to make prisoners of war out of them.

Q: The whole nation?

Admiral MacDonald: Yes, they were going to accuse the whole outfit of being murderers and everything. Well, that's what the Nuremberg trails and everything was. This was the type of action

---

*Charles A. Lindbergh.

that was being talked of at this time how to handle, and, boy, I tell you it made me sick.

Q: How did others react to this? How did Kirk react to it?

Admiral MacDonald: Well, Kirk, you know, wasn't paying much attention to it. I had to write up the comments. I don't know, he was sort of dashing around Paris, being seen with attractive girls and all this business. It was a lot of fun.

This is the type of discussion I had when Lindbergh came over there and both of us were really quite upset.

Q: How did he happen to come over? Tell me about that.

Admiral MacDonald: You know he had been out in the Pacific. He had been with my brother; he lived with my brother out in New Guinea for about three months. My brother was a fighter-bomber commander out there.*

Q: In the air force?

---

*See Colonel Charles MacDonald, USA, "Lindbergh in Battle," Collier's, 16 February 1946, pages 11-12, 75-76; Collier's, 23 February 1946, pages 26, 28, 30. For more on the exploits of MacDonald's brother, see Edward H. Sims, American Aces in Great Fighter Battles of World War II (New York: Harper and Brothers, 1958), pages 189-209.

Admiral MacDonald: In the air force, the Army Air Forces, at the time. Lindbergh was out there to teach the boys how to fly more economically and reach out further distances, which at that time they had to do because the islands were pretty large steps.

Q: And he was there as a civilian, was he?

Admiral MacDonald: He was there as a civilian. He wasn't allowed to fight.

Q: But he did, didn't he?

Admiral MacDonald: Well, my brother took him on a fighter mission, and he almost lost him, too. My brother shot down a plane that was going to attack him, and he finally set up a plane for Lindbergh and he did shoot one down. That resulted in my brother being recalled, but nothing ever came of it.*

Through him, when I was here in 1944, before I went with Kirk, I saw Lindbergh. He was back here working with the Army as a sort of consultant. We had dinner with him several times, my wife and I, and we discussed a lot of things, at that time mainly

---

*During the war Lindbergh used his aviation expertise to benefit American pilots. While flying an Army P-38 from the Fifth Air Force on a mission to observe fighter coverage of a bombing raid on Guam, he shot down a Japanese plane. Since he was not supposed to be engaged in combat--being a civilian--the kill was not made publicly known.

about the Pacific. Then, all of a sudden, he shows up in Paris.

We had, in addition to our St. Germain headquarters where we were mostly staying, additional places if we got stuck in Paris, the Royal Monceau Hotel. The Navy took that over, and we used to put up Navy people there on a transient basis and the rest of the big organization was housed there and operated in the Paris headquarters. Lindbergh showed up there, and he was talking about different things in connection with what was going to happen in Germany.

Q: Was he on any kind of an official assignment?

Admiral MacDonald: Yes, he was over there as some sort of advisory capacity with the Army. As a matter of fact, the Army really appreciated his help on a lot of things. Probably he was over there to try to tell them about the German Air Force as far as he knew about it.

One of the things that bothered him so much was that he couldn't go to London. They wouldn't allow him back in England, and he used to talk about this quite a few times at our sessions at dinner. Ever since the beginning of World War II when he indicated that the Germans were pretty strong and everything and he didn't feel that the British probably were capable of handling it, they forbade him to go back to London. He couldn't get a visa to go back, even though he was in Paris, and he was hoping that maybe someone could help him so he could go back to London, but no one was able to. The British wouldn't accept him.

That was one of the policies that was very disturbing. But the other thing that came up at this time was that someone, it was General Marshall, had sent over a document to Eisenhower and wanted his staff comments on it in connection with setting up a separate air force in the United States.* I was ticked off to be the Navy representative, to sit with an Army officer from G-3--later a retired general--and an Army Air Corps officer. We sat down and we took this paper in connection with the establishment of a separate air force and discussed it to write up Eisenhower's comments on it.

Right off the bat, it was a 2:1 proposition. The Navy itself, from our point of view, my point of view, couldn't afford, after seeing what had happened in my dealing with the British in the beginning, to see the Navy losing its air arm, its own air arm.

Q: As the Royal Navy did.

Admiral MacDonald: But, boy, I'll tell you, the discussion got hot, to where the Army said, "We'll go along with a separate air force provided we can get the Marines put under us."

---

*General of the Army George C. Marshall, USA, Chief of Staff, U.S. Army from 1939 to 1945.

And the Air Corps said, "We'll back the Marines going under the Army and we'll all vote against the Navy having a separate air arm."

And this is the kind of comment that was written up by Eisenhower's staff, two against one. Now, as far as I know, this came directly in to Eisenhower. It never filtered down to any of the Navy people like Stark, sitting over in Europe, or anyone else.

Q: Did Kirk see this?

Admiral MacDonald: He didn't know about it. I was the one. I sat in on these meetings for a few days while we were reviewing these papers, and I came back and said, "Admiral Kirk, we've got to do something about this thing right away. I don't think that Stark, if he does know about it, is doing anything to stop it. These people are working to take away the Navy's air arm and the Marines away from the Navy, and set up a separate air force."

Well, Kirk was very interested.

Q: I would think he would be!

Admiral MacDonald: He was very interested.

So I drafted a dispatch and we kicked it around. Shall we send it to Stark? Maybe Stark would just drop it. But we have to get this back to King, that this is what they're thinking of. The war was still going on, but we've got to get this back to King. These people, right after this war is over, are going to opt for a separate air force, and this is wrong.

Mind you, my time, in relating this, is a little off, because it came a little bit later than I thought. Anyway, Kirk went along with this. He drafted it and we discussed how to send it, whether to send it through channels, and then decided that if we sent it through channels it was liable to get bogged down and no one would pay attention, and King should know about it. We sent it to King.

Q: With information to Stark or what?

Admiral MacDonald: Unfortunately, we didn't, and that created a bombshell.

Q: This went over Kirk's signature, did it?

Admiral MacDonald: Oh, yes. It created quite a disturbance. In the first place, King immediately went to Stark and found out he didn't know anything about it. He felt badly he wasn't informed, and King said, "We're not going to worry about that; we've got a war to fight."

The next thing was eventually Kirk was recalled. He was sent back and given another job.* I guess my timing on this is a little off, because Kirk didn't leave until we'd just about moved into Germany.

But this is the type of thing that was going on. We tried to alert the Navy about this difficulty early, but King said, "I'm fighting the Japanese war. I can't be bothered."

Q: Well, what was the wisdom of General Marshall in raising this particular issue at this time, when the German angle was not completed and the Japanese was far from completed?

Admiral MacDonald: The Army operates a lot differently than we do. They have so many people on their general staff, just sitting around doing nothing, except writing papers, and they were getting all ready for the future, getting things all buttoned up so that the minute everyone was off balance and knocked out, they could push through their program. There's no doubt about it, they saw a great opportunity to get the Marines. This is why Marshall's staff was working on it. They wanted the whole Marine operation, from the air aspect of it to the amphibious aspect of it. This is one of the things that came up

---

*Rear Admiral Kirk was reassigned from his dual position as Commander U.S. Naval Forces France and Naval Commander to General Eisenhower in July 1945, was promoted to vice admiral, and then served on the General Board until his retirement the following March.

in these meetings. I was the only one sitting there. Everything on the ground was to be Army, everything in the air would be Air Force, and everything on the water would be Navy. This is the concept that they were working on. Everything in the water would be Navy, ground--Army, air--Air Force. They saw a great opportunity, a lot of these empire builders, particularly in the Army Air Corps, of selling this because the German war looked like it was coming to an end when this thing broke. We had moved in in the early spring of 1945, got across the Rhine, and although we did use the boats a lot and even later on they kept the boats up there on the Rhine and even formed the U.S. Naval Rhine River Patrol, and that patrol stayed up there for years.

Q: How useful did the boats actually prove to be in the crossing?

Admiral MacDonald: Very useful in the very beginning. They carried lots of troops, but there was no opposition on the other side.

Q: They were little ferryboats?

Admiral MacDonald: They were little ferryboats, and they were transporting people very fast. Also, the fact that there was no opposition, when the Battle of the Bulge was stopped and they finally were able to move the next spring offensive, they found that instead of all the bridges being destroyed, the Remagen bridge was only badly damaged, which helped a great deal in establishing a bridgehead on the other side. That bridge, they didn't have a chance to blow up the whole thing, but that was the only bridge that was left and it was a way down. But, having that, they were able to spread up the river, and we had no opposition on the other side when the Army began to move.

So the Navy did transport as a ferryboat arrangement, and when Patton made his move, they moved at night in the boats under fire, under gunfire.* There was opposition there.

Q: At the original crossing?

Admiral MacDonald: Yes, the original first crossing. They moved at night and were under gunfire, but there was no opposition afterwards and they moved pretty quickly. The only thing was trying to slow up General Patton. He wanted to move up into Berlin but couldn't get permission. Montgomery was finding it very slow moving and Churchill put the heat on and the pressure and said, "Look, everyone's got to slow up. We all have to move together."**

---

*General George S. Patton, Jr., USA, Commanding General, U.S. Third Army.

**Field Marshal Bernard L. Montgomery.

We'd have been in Berlin, and boy, it would have been very helpful to have taken Berlin right off the bat, because later the Russians moved in.

Eisenhower had great difficulty working with the Russians and trying to get a line of demarcation, of where they were going to stop. The Russians never stopped at the river that they said they were going to stop at. They just moved on! It was pretty difficult.

When the forces moved into Germany, I then was shifted over as deputy chief of staff to Admiral Ghormley from Kirk's staff because Kirk had been recalled. This dire message we sent to King infuriated him, and they recalled Kirk.

Q: Why did it infuriate King? Was it because it was not through the chain?

Admiral MacDonald: It wasn't through the chain, number one. I think that was our original mistake, but if we'd sent it through the chain, I think it would have been bogged down, because those boys in London were just footsie-footsie with the Army. But they had no forces to control over there in London and they just played footsie-footsie with the Army. We were the only operating people.

Q: That leads me to ask you a question that has always occurred to me about the validity and the worth of the Stark mission in London. You were an operational man and saw it from the operational point of view. How valid was this mission of Stark's?

Admiral MacDonald: Well, after the Normandy invasion, of course, there wasn't too much, except working with the British. They were still escorting ships, and this is what they worked with the British on, getting convoys through and so forth. It was still an operational setup, but also it was supposed to have been sort of a policy-planning setup. The British Navy controlled the whole Normandy invasion operation, as far as the Navy was concerned. That was under the Royal Navy, and Kirk was just a subordinate.

Q: Admiral Ramsay was the big man?*

Admiral MacDonald: Admiral Ramsay was the boss. Admiral Ramsay then moved to Paris as the Royal Navy representative. He should have been more or less on an equal basis with Kirk, but having worked with Eisenhower in London, they always considered that Ramsay represented the Navy. We were just purely U.S. Navy and only U.S. Navy forces in France. This was one of the things.

*Admiral Sir Bertram H. Ramsay, Royal Navy.

Stark had a group of people over there who were interested in things, like Pat Flanigan--he became a commodore and his interest was petroleum, getting oil there--and he had an operation going on.* And Monty Pryce, who stayed over there indefinitely.** And one of the reasons Monty never went anyplace--he just stayed in London instead of moving around--and later married a British girl. Those people loved the living. It was an enjoyable life, and when they used to come to Paris they'd live it up like mad.

I will say that Army life in Paris and on the continent was certainly nothing like life as a naval officer.

Q: You told me off-tape that Admiral Kirk had a technical division to his staff in Paris concerned about gathering information on German ordnance and what have you.

Admiral MacDonald: Yes. Once the forces had moved into France, it became very evident that, as far as a lot of the technical requirements of the Navy were concerned, they could be best fulfilled by having people shifted over to France. On Kirk's staff we did have a technical group whose job, of course, was going up with the armies and going in with the armies to areas where they could get a hand on the latest things as far as the

*Commodore Howard A. Flanigan, USN (Ret.), deputy chief of staff.

**Commodore Roland F. Pryce, USN, head of the operations division, Commander Naval Forces Europe staff.

German services were concerned. This played a big part in our organization of trying to get the latest German technical data.

I will say that there were a lot of hangers-on who were sent over to Europe.

Anything that developed in the way of opening up an area, our technical people were in there to try to find out, and they had certain objectives. Of course, that technical staff had been built up in Europe fantastically. In the beginning, at one time, of course, they were working with the British, but now it was a matter of getting the German technical knowledge, finding out what it was all about. Particularly there were great stresses on about three or four different points. One was the missile area. This was one area, the guided missile area, where the Germans were far superior.

Q: As was evidenced by the V-2?

Admiral MacDonald: That's right. And the other area that really the Navy was so interested in was in connection with the submarine area, their high-speed submarines, their use of hydrogen peroxide as fuel, and also the snorkel. This area was very important to the Navy, and this is why our people were right there and ready to move in when they could, not only to get the information but to try to get their hands on the German technical people who knew about all these things.

Q: Peenemunde was one of the main objectives?

Admiral MacDonald: Oh, yes. Our Navy people were to try to enlist right away some of these technical people into our hands. Of course, as far as the overall thing was concerned, there was the fact that the Germans had developed the Messerschmitt, which was the first jet plane that was ever seen or used in action. This is another area where they were so anxious to get the knowledge, and in the mine area because the Germans were so superior, and radar, and communications. These were all areas where we definitely wanted to get our hands on the latest things as soon as we could.

So that, actually, when the forces moved in, our technical group also moved right behind them. They took over a house not far from Wiesbaden. They operated their headquarters there, and they had technical people coming and going and operating after we moved into Germany, before the war was over. I went up and visited the headquarters several times. It was a delightful place. It really belonged to Mr. Busch from St. Louis.* We took it over and staged as headquarters a transient hotel for our technical people.

---

*August A. Busch, Jr., was then an officer on active duty with the Army. Before World War II, he was vice president of the brewery Anheuser-Busch, Inc. In 1946, he became president. In 1956, he became chairman of the board as well, holding that position until 1977.

I remember that this is one place I went up to with Forrestal, who came over on a trip, and some of his experts.* This is where we stayed. It was very delightful, a beautiful place. The Germans had been using it as a home for women who had gotten pregnant. What do you call it, a maternity home for unwed mothers.

Q: Until the babies came?

Admiral MacDonald: That's right. They were using it. When we moved in, they got out and we took it over.

The technical thing was very important, because in certain areas we knew that they were well ahead of us, and we were trying to grab the people who knew these things and could get them. Wernher von Braun was grabbed right away.** I don't know who grabbed him. I guess it was the Army and not the Navy.

Q: Our boys did their bit of grabbing?

Admiral MacDonald: That's right, we were in there to grab, too.

Now, along this grabbing way, all of these staffs, including Eisenhower's staff, had groups of people who had objectives and

---

*James V. Forrestal, Secretary of the Navy from 1944 to 1947.

**Dr. Wernher von Braun, technical director of the Peenemunde rocket and development center from 1937 to 1945, where he is credited with developing the V-2 rocket.

not military objectives, sitting over there, trying to grab up what they could get their hands on, particularly in a big way.

Eisenhower assigned us a brigadier general. He was supposed to have been our civil defense operator, and we were supposed to talk about civil things. But without a doubt, his idea was to grab the stock certificates of any company he could get, grab them up. He was over there with ulterior motives, and I, being the deputy chief of staff, had to conduct the staff meetings every morning at 9:30. He used to sit in there as the representative of that particular section, and he really contributed nothing to our Navy staff or any of our operations or anything.

This is why I went up with Ghormley, who had a headquarters in Frankfurt, not far from Eisenhower's staff, which had taken over the I.G. Farben headquarters building. They took that over as SHAEF, as the commander in chief's main headquarters.* The Navy then took over some other quarters, and we all requisitioned some houses, so we had houses in town and outside.

At the same time I had to set up a setup in Berlin for Ghormley, because all of these meetings with the Russians were taking place in Berlin. The discussions with them were all taking place up there, rather than in Frankfurt. That's where the Russians were. So we took a very nice house for the admiral

*SHAEF--Supreme Headquarters Allied Expeditionary Force.

on Bodensee for his headquarters. Actually, Admiral Ghormley, while he was there, although he was responsible for the carrying out of the whole objective--(well, of course, this was after the war) of demilitarization of the Navy and getting along with the Russians--the biggest deal with the Russians was how to split up the German Navy, and this is why Ghormley's talks with the Russians were so important.

Q: Ghormley, in turn, was under Stark?

Admiral MacDonald: He was under Stark; he worked with Stark. They were the closest of friends, but, as I recall, we reported directly back here to Washington because those discussions were something like the ABC papers, discussions with the British originally.* The whole thing was what shall the Russians take and what shall we take, and try to split it up, dividing up the spoils from what was left of the German service. Who could get submarines and so forth, and who would get this and get that.

This was part of what Ghormley did, but this was after the war. It was well after June of 1945; this was going on into the next year. I can remember in June when the unconditional surrender was finally accepted of the German Army, the fact that Eisenhower's headquarters was still in Reims, France. He had

*ABC--American, British, Canadian plans.

moved from Versailles up to Reims. His tactical headquarters was then in Reims and this is where they flew in the two commanders in chief of the different services to accept the surrender. These fellows came in full-dress uniform, the head of the German Navy and the head of the German Army.

Eisenhower didn't receive them. Bedell Smith received them.* They came in and signed the agreement of unconditional surrender. They had their swords and everything and they turned over their swords to Bedell Smith. There were all these officers, and no smiling, no comments from either side. These guys were beautifully dressed, and the Americans were just in sort of battle fatigue stuff.

Q: Why didn't Eisenhower receive them?

Admiral MacDonald: He wasn't going to lower himself, because he already considered that we had put into effect the de-Nazification and de-industrialization plan. The minute the war was over, that went into effect, and I'll tell you more about that.

The thing is that these fellows turned over their swords and this was another stabbing blow to me. These guys signed, turned over their swords as acceptance of the surrender, and, instead of

---

*Lieutenant General Walter Bedell Smith, USA, who was Eisenhower's chief of staff.

being congratulated for the good job of fighting that they had done, the poor guys turned around and were marched off to jail, hauled off to jail. It was unbelievable.

Q: This was a continuation of that policy that came over?

Admiral MacDonald: That was the policy, yes. They hauled them off to jail. There they were in full-dress uniform, whereas the Japanese, with General MacArthur, came in full dress and all this business, signed, and went back to their places.* These guys went off to jail.

That de-Nazification thing was that no U.S. person could even talk to a German. He couldn't even talk, he couldn't be seen, he could have nothing to do with the Germans, nothing to do with them. The de-industrialization part was to destroy all of their industry, and they did start on destroying them, tearing out everything.

Q: This had its roots in what, the Nazi attitude towards the Jews?

Admiral MacDonald: Yes. Oh, yes, they were going to make them an agrarian nation, and they weren't going to give them one bit

---

*General of the Army Douglas MacArthur, USA, who accepted the Japanese surrender in Tokyo Bay on 2 September 1945.

of consideration for existence. The demilitarization was to divide the spoils completely and all that business. It was the most terrible thing I've ever seen.

Q: To revert for a moment to Lindbergh, when he arrived in Paris, he expressed himself in this area.

Admiral MacDonald: He and I were in agreement. I talked to the people who were working on that plan in the Navy in London, and I said, "How in heck can we go along with something like this? This isn't American. This isn't the way we've been brought up. If someone has fought a good battle and so forth, you congratulate him, if you win, because you don't say you're no good to start with and therefore I haven't won anything. Nor did it pick up your own morale. You lick someone who was worthwhile."

The thing was unbelievable. I couldn't understand it. Then they told me, "Forget it. Look what we did to the Indians. We took the whole country away from them. Don't worry about it. Look what's going on all over the continent. Look what they're capable of."

I had little voice to try to protest that, but we did have a little.

Q: Did Lindbergh speak out in any way?

Admiral MacDonald: No. He wasn't in a position to. He wasn't in the chain of command over there.

Q: He was suspect, anyway, because of his attitude at the beginning of the war?

Admiral MacDonald: Yes. No, he wasn't involved in that except to comment to someone like myself.

Q: Was there any reflection of General Eisenhower's attitude toward this whole policy?

Admiral MacDonald: No, but, you know, I haven't touched on certain aspects of things that developed here, and maybe I'm not getting it exactly in the right time frame.

Eisenhower was up at Reims and, at that time, in the House of Representatives we had a Naval Affairs Committee. This was in the fall of 1944. The Naval Affairs Committee with a liaison officer, who was Don Ramsey, was coming over to Europe, and we got the word to make arrangements for them.* We didn't know exactly what they'd want to do, because there wasn't any real naval action that they could look at, except go and see some of the Navy troops up in the front line.

---

*Rear Admiral Donald J. Ramsey, USN.

They came in to Paris, and we had set up some sort of meetings with them and made travel arrangements.

Q: Did Vinson come over with them?*

Admiral MacDonald: Yes, Vinson was there, Hebert, Lyndon Johnson, Cole, the whole damned Naval Affairs Committee practically, at that time came over there.** Lyndon Johnson . . .

Q: He was in the House at that time?

Admiral MacDonald: Yes, he was a member of the Naval Affairs Committee in the House of Representatives. This was in '44.

They came over there, so we had set up these trips and so forth. I did because that was my job, to handle that type of an operation, too. I had in my office three or four telephones, red, white, orange, and so forth, and the red line was a direct line in to Eisenhower. We had arranged for the Naval Affairs Committee to go up to see Eisenhower in his headquarters. I was sitting in the office and the telephone rang. I picked it up. I've forgotten what he called me, but I said, "This is Commander

---

*Representative Carl Vinson (Democrat-Georgia).

**Representative F. Edward Hebert (Democrat-Louisiana); Representative Lyndon B. Johnson (Democrat-Texas); Representative W. Sterling Cole (Republican-New York).

MacDonald."

And he said, "This is General Eisenhower. I have with me here [and this was on the red line, a direct line] a number of the Naval Affairs Committee members. I want to make sure while they're over here that they see everything they want to see and they get to go every place that they want to go."

I said, "Well, I think we've already sort of arranged this, General," and so forth.

"Well, I want to make sure," and this was all in front of these people. "I want to make sure that no stone will be unturned so that they get everything they want." Knowing damned well that it was nothing but a boondoggle for them, anyway.

I said, "Well, General, that's fine. I think we have done about everything we could possibly do, but, just in case, who should I contact up at your staff if I need more help?"

He gave me another general's name, I didn't know him, but he said, "You contact him and he'll make sure that everything they want will be done."

This was a good show for Eisenhower. He was selling himself in a big way. I'm only pointing this out because this was one of the first indications that this guy had other ambitions.

Q: He had some savvy as a politician?

Admiral MacDonald: Well, he was playing politics. The only

thing, as I will tell you later, after we moved into Germany, I used to, as deputy chief of staff--Commodore Robertson was chief of staff, an old commodore, a wonderful guy--I did all the work. I had to go down every day and be at the chief of staff conferences at Eisenhower's headquarters.* Bedell Smith was the number two man and he ran the show, and all these other division operators were generals. I mean G-1, G-2, G-3, G-4, and G-5, all this business, were all generals, and they had these briefings every morning at 9:30, a decision-making arrangement. And I sat there representing the Navy every day. If it hadn't been for Bedell Smith, Eisenhower wouldn't have gotten anywhere. Bedell Smith ran that show and he ran it well.

Q: He was a very bright man, too, wasn't he?

Admiral MacDonald: Yes. He was not a West Pointer, but he was bright and he was able, and there was no fooling around with Bedell Smith. I used to sit there--here I was still a commander. I took over the job and I should have been pushed up to at least a captain, because I was holding meetings and some of the officers under me were captains, so I used to have to tell captains what to do.

But, by that time, my reputation was so good that rank didn't

---

*Commodore Marion C. Robertson, USN.

mean an awful lot. People listened. I had established a pretty good reputation and so forth regardless of rank. The British officers assigned to our staff all had to sit in subordinate to me--they were all captains. But I would sit in with the generals as a commander. No one seemed to worry too much about me. Maybe I should have pressed a little bit harder to get the proper standing like the British always do, but they treated me fine at those Army meetings. When it would come around and Bedell Smith would ask, "What do you think the Navy will do about this?" and I'd tell him what we had in mind, what we were going to do, and so forth, and it was a very interesting thing.

So far as I know, the only thing Eisenhower read every day was Stars and Stripes and the gripes from the troops, and he'd try to nail those down.* He was building up his popularity; there's no doubt about that.

---

*Stars and Stripes was (and is) a newspaper published by the armed services overseas for reading by U.S. servicemen.

Interview Number 5 with Rear Admiral Donald J. MacDonald, U.S. Navy (Retired)

Place: Admiral MacDonald's residence in Washington, D.C.

Date: Thursday morning, 5 December 1974

Subject: Biography

Interviewer: John T. Mason, Jr.

Q: Well, sir, this is Chapter 5, and you have more to say about your tour of duty in Europe as the war was coming to an end. You have more to say about your duty which was approximately a year with Admiral Ghormley in Frankfurt and Berlin.* So would you take up the story there, please. Tell me, for instance, about going up to Berlin, which is where the conversations with the Russians took place. Were you present at some of these conversations when the fate of the German Navy was discussed?

Admiral MacDonald: No, I was not present in Berlin at any of those conferences, but we did work on some of the papers down in Frankfurt. I made several visits to Germany in order to see that everything was going well, to Berlin, at the time and to see that Admiral Ghormley was well taken care of. But his meetings with the Russians involving the splitting up of the German Navy, what forces were left, and the splitting of the spoils involving their

*Vice Admiral Robert L. Ghormley, USN, Commander U.S. Naval Forces in Germany from December 1944 to December 1945.

merchant marine and any other marine craft that were still in existence, including such things as the destruction of their building capabilities. These things were handled in Berlin.

Q: From your conversations with Admiral Ghormley, did you learn how these discussions went? Were they conducted in a smooth fashion, or were the Russians obstinate, as they have been on other occasions?

Admiral MacDonald: The Russians were no different than they have been on other occasions. Their demands were always greater than we wanted to accept, and this was one of the difficult things that Ghormley had to deal with. They wanted more and more and were not easy to satisfy.

Q: Was he a patient man?

Admiral MacDonald: Ghormley was a very patient man and a very practical man. He had to be patient in dealing with the Russians on the problems that he was working on.

Q: Did they discuss such things as the scientific advancements of the Germans? I mean the Peenemunde outfit, was there any division of spoils there?

Admiral MacDonald: No. As a matter of fact, we didn't even have a chance to get involved in that because the Russians took over that area right off the bat. That's why, after the war, they made such fantastic strides in the space area, because they got some of the real top people. The only person we were lucky enough to get was Wernher von Braun, who was working up at Peenemunde. Apparently, the Army Air Corps people were able to get him nailed to the mast.

Q: We knew in a general way what we would like to have from Peenemunde. Why were we not more alert to the possibility of getting it before the Russians?

Admiral MacDonald: Well, I won't say that we weren't from the sort of complete military service side, but the Navy's concentration was basically in the Navy area and this really involved submarines and mines and so forth. The missile thing was a little beyond us in the Navy, and this is why Ghormley's involvement just sort of pinned down to that area, as far as dealing with the Russians was concerned.

Q: Was the Army also dealing with the Russians in Berlin? Did they have a staff there?

Admiral MacDonald: I'm sure they did, but I was unaware of it.

I know that in Frankfurt there were a number of Russian officers sort of working with the Eisenhower headquarters, and Anthony Biddle was the liaison individual between the Russians and the Americans.* Also, Bob Murphy, Jake Beam, and Fred Reinhardt were advisors and translators.** What they were talking about along that line, I'm not too sure now, but basically I think it was trying to divide up Germany, their lines of demarcation. Another thing that I do remember, and Ghormley was involved in this, was the splitting up of Berlin and Vienna and the sectors.

Q: You mean the divisions?

Admiral MacDonald: The divisions and movements, where the troop lines would be, who would move back to where and so forth. And the Russians were very tough on that point, as you know. Later that became one of the agreements at Potsdam, where Truman and Churchill had to go and come up with an agreement on the actual division.*** But the planning part and working out of some of these details in advance was being gone into by the Army people.

---

*Anthony J.D. Biddle, Jr., ambassador to the Netherlands, Norway, Yugoslavia, and Czechoslovakia.

**Robert D. Murphy, Jacob D. Beam.

***At the Potsdam Conference, 17 July-2 August 1945, preliminary details of the intended administration of Germany were discussed by the Allied leaders, and part of eastern Germany was assigned to Poland.

Q: What was the overriding issue there? Was it status?

Admiral MacDonald: Not only status, but the Russians wanted to grab as much as they could, and they were in a pretty strong position. Because instead of stopping at the Oder, as they should have done originally, they kept on going and they had Berlin. And, once they had it, they weren't about to give it back. The same thing was true in Vienna; the Russians had moved in and taken over all of Vienna. Then it was a matter of our trying to recover enough so that the Russians didn't have the whole thing.

Q: To maintain a toehold!

Admiral MacDonald: A toehold, at least. This is how they split up Berlin into definitely three parts, Russia, England, and the United States, but France was holding out for a part, too, and this was also a problem that had to be faced up to--how far would they be able to accept France as a partner in this coexistence. These were the sort of problems that had to be worked out, and Ghormley was working on that type of thing.

Q: And the Russians weren't helpful at all?

Admiral MacDonald: They certainly were not helpful. As a matter of fact, it was a long time before we were able to get even a zone, sector, in Berlin that we could call the U.S. sector, because the Russians had taken the whole city. They'd taken it all. As a matter of fact, they were well beyond. That's why even today we have to operate through a corridor.

When I first went up there, I went up to a place called Lubeck, because that's where some of the minesweepers and so forth were. We were getting minesweepers ready to operate and sweep the mines at Lubeck, and we moved through there freely. All of a sudden, the Russians came in and took it over, and it was closed to us. We could never get it back. That's exactly what happened. We couldn't hold the Russians back. Even today we have to operate through a corridor to get into Berlin.

On many of my trips going up there when the trains reached the border of the corridor, even though the Russians and we were allies, they would inspect our papers, check us out, check everything, stop the trains, and Russian troops would go through there. We had a terrible time trying to get into Berlin via any way, except flying.

Q: What was the reaction of the American military there, on the ground, to this sort of thing?

Admiral MacDonald: Well, I think we had been had. That was our indication.

Another very deplorable thing. When I went up there to Berlin the first time, when we were setting up headquarters for Ghormley, here were the Russians all over the city. They looked bedraggled, their uniforms were poorly fitting, they all looked like Asiatics. They were young kids, probably 16 or 17, and their overcoats were dragging on the ground. And they were moving in with all their belongings with horse-drawn wagons. It was the most deplorable sight I've ever seen. Here we have such a mechanized modern setup, and here they moved in to take over Berlin with nothing but--I described it at the time as rabble--and no coordination.

I think in a previous comment I made mention of Harry Hopkins, when he came back from Russia and, just to give you some idea, when he asked Stalin what the United States could do to help, he said, "We don't need any help, except rifles."

And Harry asked, "What do you mean, just rifles? Don't you need some other equipment?"

"Oh, no, I have 17 million troops under arms but we don't have enough rifles. What we have to do is make sure there are enough rifles for the front line and when they get shot down the next wave moves up and takes over."

But my point is that they had so many people under arms, and I don't know what kind of control they had over these people--I've heard so many stories even from friends who were in Hungary and so forth, about how when the Russians moved in they just slaughtered everything, horses and everything. There was no control. It was like wild hordes moving into some of these areas.

Q: From the steppes?

Admiral MacDonald: Yes, from the steppes. The thing that impressed me at that time was that the front-line troops were sort of Mongolians and Asiatics. They weren't white Russians like you see so much on television in connection with Moscow. They were other people. This is a thing you have to always keep in mind if you get involved with Russia, that Russia isn't just all one particular ethnic group.

Q: Now, you associated, by virtue of your connections and your job, with the brass. How did the top men feel about this whole thing?

Admiral MacDonald: You know, very few of them even indicated their feelings. I was one of the few people who really spoke out a little bit in connection with some of these things. I think that is because none of those people had been under fire themselves. They had never gone through being exposed to death day after day, and they had a different attitude. Mine was a very fatalistic attitude, in a way, so I felt there were a lot of things we were supposed to do and, getting back to Ghormley's job, he was charged with the top assignments in carrying out the demilitarization, de-Nazification, and non-fraternization, as far as the Navy's personnel was concerned. He was charged with that, there's no doubt about it, and, basically, that was what we in Frankfurt had to do besides just trying to get along with the Russians.

Q: Didn't he have personal reactions to the frustrations?

Admiral MacDonald: Yes, he did, but, you know, he never really spoke too severely about it. He was carrying out his duty. He was a most obedient servant of his commander, and if he was told to do something, this was what he was going to do. He may have had the feelings, but he certainly kept an awful lot of them to himself in connection with this.

I think probably several times when he'd come down to Frankfurt, we had a nice house out in the country where he'd spend a weekend or something, he would talk about his feelings a little bit, but I just don't recall well such things.

Q: What were your specific duties?

Admiral MacDonald: I was deputy chief of staff. As a matter of fact, I ran the show because the chief of staff was Commodore

Robertson, who really was just a grand person and an elderly person and he was just sort of a figurehead there. So I had to conduct our staff meetings every morning. There were several Army colonels who were liaisons with us, a Captain Seymour of the Royal Navy, who was liaison. I had a lot of liaison people, and we had staff meetings, and we worked over specific papers that were sent up from the headquarters, or when I'd go down every day to the chief of staff meetings at the headquarters--where, as I mentioned before, I represented the Navy as a commander and everyone else was a general or something--they would bring up the problems that existed that had to be solved. They would want the Navy's reaction and we would have to draft whatever we were going to do along those lines.

Also, we were charged with taking care of all the naval matters throughout. These things were going on all over the place, at different ports in Germany where shipbuilding was still going on, construction was still going on, how to destroy it. And, of course, at the same time we had set up what they called the Rhine River Patrol, which still is in existence, as far as I know.

Q: Tell me about that.

Admiral MacDonald: That stems from the operation when we moved all these LCMs and LCVPs up the Rhine River to get the Army across. As I mentioned before, we had to use a lot of them in the very beginning, in the first several months, I guess, until they got some pretty good bridges built across, and they would have been more useful if Remagen hadn't remained somewhat usable. That was one reason why it wasn't the big operation that we had planned. Those boats were up there and rather than send them back, they set up a patrol arrangement where these boats would be operating on patrol, just to patrol the river and make sure that things were going all right.

That Rhine River Patrol became a command that is still in existence, as far as I know.

Q: Were you at Remagen when Churchill made his famous visit there?

Admiral MacDonald: No. No, I was not at Remagen when Churchill made his famous visit. Incidentally, I was called upon to make a broadcast on television in connection with the Rhine River crossing on one of the anniversaries of the landing in Normandy at Schenectady, New York.

Q: This was in recent years?

Admiral MacDonald: Yes, in the middle Fifties, I think. They asked me to come up and talk about the Rhine River crossing on television, which I did. I don't know exactly the date; I'd have to refer back, but I'm not sure even then I could pinpoint it. I was asked questions about that, why we did it and how we did it and so forth at the time.

But, along with the planning of that whole operation, as I think I've also mentioned, I used to go up to the 12th Army Group's tactical headquarters, General Bradley's headquarters, and, of course, he was delightful every time I went up there. He had me for lunch, a wonderful person, very cool and collected. I worked with his planners in connection with getting all the necessary equipment up there.

I think I've also covered the fact that we had a regular organization, Navy organization, charged with the actual operation of the boats.

But that thing didn't break. The Rhine River Patrol setup slowly eroded down to just the Rhine River Patrol, and what happened to all the boats, I have no idea at the moment, but they were pretty well worn after a while.

Q: Incidentally, we were talking about the reaction of staff members to the Russian attitude. Since you associated with the British, do you have any idea how they reacted to this?

Admiral MacDonald: The British, I don't think, ever wanted to have anything to do with the Russians, in the first place. We were the only ones, and this goes back to my first trip over there when we did deal with the Russians in connection with a directive from Roosevelt to see how we could help the Russians, Harry Hopkins's mission, to see how we could help. One of the results of that was conversations with the Russian admirals who were in London. The British didn't show any interest in any of this at all. We were the only ones who showed any interest in connection with trying to find out how to help the Russians. I think Roosevelt was the only one who was putting pressure even on the British to get the Allies to attack Germany from the east. This was one of Roosevelt's plans, to get the Russians hitting the Germans from the east so we could hit them from the west.

I remember in all those conversations, and this also was Ghormley in connection with his first trip over there, talking with the Russians, and I being his flag lieutenant, I used to have to set up the meetings and deal with the aides of the Russian admirals in London. The Russians couldn't do a thing. Ghormley talked with them, and then he would find out that they would listen, then say they would give us a reply after they heard from Moscow.

Q: They were just errand boys, weren't they?

Admiral MacDonald: They were just errand boys; they had no say at all. They couldn't tell you anything. They never did tell us anything. They never told us a thing. This was one of the things, but later on, there's no doubt about it, we did get some better communication because, otherwise, Hopkins and Harriman and the rest of them wouldn't have been able to fly into Russia without a little bit of coordination from the Russian side.* The British were flying the planes from Scotland over Norway into Archangel and so forth. The people were then picked up by Russian planes and taken to Moscow.

There was a Russian embassy in London. It was still open, but as far as I know the British weren't dealing with them one bit. Well, they had their hands full, anyway, just fighting the Germans, and we were the ones who were really sincere about getting the Russians in on this thing.

It paid off a little bit later, because even in Ghormley's conversations I think they were more friendly to the American point of view than they were the British. The British sat in on the same meetings that Ghormley was sitting in on in connection with splitting up the spoils. The funny part about it, as I remember, is that the only thing they got was one of the training cruisers, the Horst Wessell, which we have now at the Coast Guard Academy.** They got the other one, the only two sailing vessels

---

*W. Averell Harriman, U.S. ambassador to the Soviet Union, 1943-1946. Back in 1941 he had gone to Russia to set up a working relationship after that nation was attacked by Germany.

**The Horst Wessell, built in 1936 by Blohm & Voss, was renamed Eagle when she was annexed by the United States.

that are still in existence. The Germans had two of them and they used them for training ships. That's about all the British wanted. I think later they sold theirs. They got it and then sold it. We still have the one we took, and it's still in use.

As far as I know, the British involvement on our staff in Germany--I had a British captain, who used to keep the British side pretty well informed as to what we were doing, but he never seemed to interfere much, except pass information along. I don't recall right now trying to get an answer out of him. Oh, yes, several times I did put some questions to him, and this was one of the amazing things. I asked him how they would do a certain thing. It became a well-known fact with me that any time you asked an English officer how to do something, he almost came up with the same answer that any other English officer would come up with, what is good for the King or the monarchy is the way that they're going to handle it. But if you asked all the American officers around the line, you'd get ten different answers. We had no continuity of policy or thinking, or no sort of fundamental training that would encourage us to do things in one way. You'd get ten answers from ten Americans, but one answer from ten British.

Q: Simpler to deal with!

Admiral MacDonald: Yes. However, they were pretty stubborn,

too, the kind of give and take. They wanted a lot of things, too.

They were watching us and that was the main thing they were doing, because they also had British headquarters set up in northern Germany, a comparable setup to what we had, and they took over a certain area.

Q: Up to the Baltic, you mean?

Admiral MacDonald: Yes, because that was the area assigned to them, and they had the same British organization. They worked at getting the ports open and the North Sea mines swept and things like that. In the sweeping of the minefields up there, we used the Germans, their equipment, and German people, and lost quite a few of them. They lost some of the boats and they lost a lot of people.

Q: Did they resist?

Admiral MacDonald: No, they didn't exactly resist. As a matter of fact, the Germans were very humble about a lot of this. The way we put this non-fraternization thing in there, we treated them like criminals, every one, so they were pretty humble because they were starving to death. There was no connection for getting any money; there was no connection for where they were going to get their food. They were most appreciative of even getting a job where maybe they could get something to eat. This was a deplorable setup. People were just starving. They were rationed down to about 1,100 calories supposedly a day, but they couldn't even find that. It was a pretty bad period for them.

Q: Would you talk at this point a little more about the de-Nazification program that we insisted upon?

Admiral MacDonald: Well, the de-Nazification program was to get all of the leaders and all the top officials and lock them up. Anything that smacked of the Nazi Party, they just grabbed them and put them in jail, and tried to break the whole thing up.

Q: These were military prisons presided over by our Army?

Admiral MacDonald: They were military prisons presided over by either the British--definitely, there were three big sectors. The Russian sector, which included Berlin and well on past that; the British were way up to the north; and we had down in the area through Bavaria. The French had only the little area around Lake Constance, bordering on their own boundary there.

The de-Nazification thing was just to try to grab everyone who'd even been associated with the Nazi Party.

Q: Was there any cooperation on the part of the German populace in this area?

Admiral MacDonald: No. Everyone was scared to death. As it collapsed, a lot of people who even thought that they would be nailed to the Nazi Party went into hiding. It was complete elimination of the Nazi Party from top to bottom. These lists apparently got circulated around and then, of course, these guys all ended up in jail.

Then later the Nuremberg trials were another concept. The top leaders were then supposedly tried under a new law which the Americans dreamed up.

Q: A new international law?

Admiral MacDonald: Yes, which we dreamed up. Anyone who had anything to do with the prosecution of the war, if you're the loser, you can be blamed for anything. This is exactly the concept that they tried to--well, they supposedly proved in the Nuremberg trials by conducting the trials and putting a lot of these people to death.

Q: Who actually authored this idea?

Admiral MacDonald: It was authored right here in Washington by

Justice Robert Jackson.* He was the one who drew up what you might call charges and so forth, and the objective was to set a precedent so that no nation would ever want to fight anyone else because the top leaders would be held responsible, particularly if they lost.

Q: Were our military people not concerned that this could be a boomerang on other occasions?

Admiral MacDonald: Yes. This is the most disturbing factor to me, too, sitting there seeing these papers and what was supposed to be in their minds. That was another one of the areas that I personally was very disturbed about what we were doing in Germany, and the Nuremberg trials were just another. As I said to everyone I ever talked to over there, "You'd better not lose the next war or everyone from the top to the bottom in our government and in our military is going to be hung as criminals." What we were trying to do was build up this particular precedent where it would frighten anyone else from ever starting a war, and this is what they had in mind.

Q: It's somewhat idealistic!

---

*Robert H. Jackson, Supreme Court Justice from 1941-1954.

Admiral MacDonald: Very idealistic but, boy, the consequences if you lost would be unbelievable. Every man, even the people who were involved in industry, the top industrialists because they made chemicals or made munitions or something like that, they were treated as war criminals, too. An awful lot of them were put to death. They were hanged, and that was the result of the Nuremberg trials.

At the Nuremberg trials, the British and the Russians also had judges sitting there, but there was no defense. It was all a prosecution type of deal. I went up to those trials and got sick to my stomach, seeing what they were doing. I couldn't stand it. It was terrible. It was building up something that we could never live with. The times were such and the hatred of the Jews for the Germans was such that this was going on.

I spoke out, but, boy, my voice was like a whisper in a wilderness or something in connection with these things, because this was all dreamed up right here. Morgenthau without a doubt had a fantastic influence on getting this thing set up.* I realized in other words with what was going to happen in Germany that Morgenthau's hatred and bitterness was unbelievable. His family originally came from Germany and, apparently, they were mistreated there or something. But this wasn't true because there were an awful lot of Jews who were top people in industry

*Henry Morgenthau, Jr., Secretary of the Treasury from 1934 until 1945.

in Germany even when we took over, a lot of them, all of the big chemical companies, a lot of the top scientists were Jews and they were still there, running them. So why this thing built up this way, I have no idea, but it was one of the things that was terrible. The fact that most all of those people who were tried in the first Nuremberg trial were convicted and sentenced to hang, and they were hanged.

Q: You were there for how long a period?

Admiral MacDonald: I was there until July 1946.

Q: I mean at the trials.

Admiral MacDonald: Oh, I went up there twice just to see what was going on, but I knew this thing was coming through because I'd seen the papers coming into Eisenhower's staff. I was with the Army's planning group there.

Q: Did you find some people who shared your point of view on the planning staff?

Admiral MacDonald: Damned few.

Q: They were all vindictive?

Admiral MacDonald: No, I won't say they were vindictive, but they were the type of people who are obedient to their commanders without voicing--do what the commander said, never expressing their views. If they were told to do something, they went ahead and did it and would try to get approval on that.

What I think was wrong with their setup is that none of these guys who were working--and some of them I know very well around here and are holding big jobs even today--they had never been in actual battle themselves. They'd never had to carry the responsibility of doing something and making sure that you won. Their job was sitting down dreaming up what to do and plans, and never carrying responsibility. This is what I told, I think, in an earlier interview in connection with McGeorge Bundy. McGeorge never in his life, particularly in his naval career with us, carried responsibility, but he was a smart, intelligent guy, there's no doubt about it, and he did do a lot for us. But you get a different view if you have to carry the responsibility yourself.

As far as their attitude was concerned, it wasn't expressed too clearly to me at any time, and then I don't think I even asked them. I expressed my views and maybe some of them agreed, but I'm not sure.

Q: Was there any likelihood that some of the men being tried in those days were also similar people in that they followed orders?

Admiral MacDonald: I'm sure they were. I think that is exactly what they were doing. They were following orders, carrying them out, but also in that involvement of the Nuremberg trials there were a lot of top industrialists, manufacturers comparable to the president of Du Pont or the president of General Motors or something like that.

Q: Krupp himself was tried, wasn't he?

Admiral MacDonald: Oh, yes, but he later was given a life sentence or something and he got out.* A lot of them who were given life sentences are still in jail because no court has ever been convened that I know of to get a lot of them out. I'm not sure whether they're still alive, but a lot of them were convicted and sentenced to hang right then.

Q: The most highly publicized one of the German criminals, so to speak, was Hess, of course, and he's still in jail.**

---

*Alfried Krupp von Bohlen und Halbach, president and chief owner of Krupp Works, Germany's principal armament factory. He was arrested in 1945, tried in 1948, and sentenced to 12 years imprisonment and confiscation of his fortune. The verdict was overthrown by a U.S. high commissioner, and in 1951 the factory was restored to the family.

**W.R. Rudolph Hess, Hitler's deputy and second in line to succeed him. On 10 May 1941, he flew solo to Britain--without the knowledge or approval of Hitler--with a plan for the alliance of Germany and England against Russia. Upon his arrival he was incarcerated in the Tower of London as a prisoner of war and remained there until October 1945 when he was moved to Nuremberg to stand trial before the International Military Tribunal. Hess was sentenced to life imprisonment, which he is currently serving as the sole prisoner at Spandau.

Admiral MacDonald: Yes. He wasn't involved in the Nuremberg trials. He was still a prisoner in England. He was brought back much later, and in a different court altogether he was sentenced to life. Hess escaped from Germany. As a matter of fact, Hess landed before we even got into a war and was held prisoner in England. He didn't like what was going on, apparently, and he wanted to try to negotiate some sort of peace arrangement at the time.

I hope we never lose a war like World War II, or our people will be sorry we ever established the precedent of the Nuremberg trials.

Q: It wasn't such a major factor at the termination of hostilities with Japan, was it?

Admiral MacDonald: No. Japan was treated entirely differently. You might give MacArthur a great deal of credit for how the situation went, because I think he was planning entirely differently. He wanted to go back as a great savior and so forth to a lot of places like the Philippines, go back and be recognized as a great person in even Japan. So they did the whole thing differently in connection with the Japanese, but I will say this. One of the reasons maybe why a lot of this planning that went into what they did in Germany that didn't affect Japan is that all the origination of this was right here in Washington, and the hatred was really against the Germans in our government at that time, rather than against the Japs, and we didn't pay too much attention. It was a Navy-fought war in the Pacific, anyway, just as the other thing. The Navy really fought the Pacific war and the Navy's attitude was entirely different from the Army's attitude. As a matter of fact, the Navy carried the whole war, really, in the Pacific and our whole upbringing and everything else was entirely different.

Q: Also, was it possible that we'd had time to reflect a bit on what had been accomplished at Nuremberg and its possible consequences in the future?

Admiral MacDonald: No, because the Japanese war ended in August 1945 and these Nuremberg trials and everything came on much later.

Q: Yes, I know.

Admiral MacDonald: I think probably even in the spring of 1946. As a matter of fact, even when I left there in 1946 we had not relaxed our three different categories of what to do with Germany. The non-fraternization thing had just barely been relaxed to the point we needed help, laborers, sort of slave-type labor, and we were hiring the Germans to work in our messhalls and our laundries and so forth, and to carry out all the menial tasks. That type of fraternization had started, but you still couldn't go down and talk to any German in an office or anything like that. Along that line, the Army had a special what they called intelligence group that was watching our own men all the time to see whether they were carrying out this non-fraternization.

Q: Like the OGPU![*]

Admiral MacDonald: Like the OGPU, and if they weren't, they nailed them to the mast and sent them home. They were called on the mat immediately if they got too friendly with the Germans. I had several dealings with this intelligence group in connection with some of our troops who had gone into my wife's cousin's house and stolen some very valuable property. I went to them in connection with this. But that's another thing in connection with the way the troops moved in and just took over everything, silver, china, and particularly general officers moving into the houses that they requisitioned. When they saw something, they just packed it up and shipped it home.

A lot of these things were very disturbing to me. I don't know how I even continued in the capacity over there, but I was

---

*OGPU was the internal state security organization in the Soviet Union, a predecessor of the KGB.

always hoping, in the beginning, to get back and fight the Japanese.

Q: Were some of our people concerned about getting hold of the collections of General Goering?*

Admiral MacDonald: We had so many people who were over there with ulterior motives, it was unbelievable, like people trying to grab shares of stock in I.G. Farben, trying to get control. We had brokers from New York, investment people, who were over there for only one purpose, to grab as much as they could in the way of investments and so forth.

Q: How did they get there?

Admiral MacDonald: I don't know how they got there. That's one of the points I want to make. There were so many people coming over they'd obviously sold a bill of goods here to the headquarters, and it was true of the Navy, too, except the Navy was a little different. They sent people over with no job in mind and no way we could fit them into our organization, and we treated them as sort of visitors, but they roamed around and wanted services and they looked around and so forth.

---

*Field Marshal Hermann W. Goering, head of the German Luftwaffe, owned the largest private art collection in the world.

In General Clay's civil relations department, he had people over there who were brokers.* I remember one guy whose only interest was--he knew all about I.G. Farben, and his only interest was to grab as much of the stock as he could, because at that time the banks were closed and people were so poor and starving that if they had 100 shares of I.G. Farben, they wanted to give it to you for a package of cigarettes or something. Of course, most of their certificates are bearer notes, so whoever had them owned them.

My wife's family, having relatives over there, I made several trips to their different places to check things out a little bit and see how things were.

Q: How could you do that, though, with the policy of non-fraternization?

Admiral MacDonald: I just went ahead and did it.

Q: Were you trailed?

Admiral MacDonald: They were all kicked out. The Army had already requisitioned their home.

I went into one place, the Mumm house on the Main River.

---

*Lieutenant General Lucius DuB. Clay, USA, deputy military governor.

Q: What house?

Admiral MacDonald: Alfred Mumm, the champagne people. I knew one of the sons in New York, and he asked me to see what was left of the place. Well, it had been taken over by the Army, but the first time I went there, all the pictures were still there; the Army had requisitioned it. They had beautiful paneling that they had sent down years and years ago depicting Bible scenes, wood carving, in this particular room, a great big library-type room, beautiful wood carving, all the silver-framed pictures. Everything was there. They'd just moved in, the Army was in, threw out the Germans, took over the house. They did this all through. These things always upset me.

I went down there and the carvings and everything were there. I admired them and later I got a little information. These carvings had come out of London a long, long time ago and had been put into this whole wall, paneled all of the wall.

After three or four months, I had an occasion to go back there again, and the paneling had all been removed, shipped out. No one knew where it went. Fantastic! Except I know that the people were sending carloads of parcel post packages back to the United States. I ran into that in connection with their taking all kinds of silver and china and all these things. There was no way to stop it. We allowed it. They just grabbed everything, valuable pictures of art and tapestry. This is one thing where I did get involved with one of the troops living in one of the villas that belonged to the family. They had taken the tapestry off the wall, so I went to the intelligence people and said, "Look, someone's been in this house, taken the very valuable tapestry, and I'd like to get it put back."

They did cooperate on this thing. They finally checked it down to a guy who'd been in there and he had already wrapped it up and sent it down parcel post, this great big package, to send home. As I say, it was a very valuable tapestry, Gobelin tapestry. You know, they cooperated on this particular item where we got this tapestry back in the boxcar; after unloading the whole boxcar, they found this package and we got it back.

Q: It was returned to the owners, was it?

Admiral MacDonald: Returned to the owners, yes. Achim von Meister was the owner of this particular villa. As a matter of fact, my wife's family used to rent it during the summer. But they took their silver, they took everything. This just happened to be one item that I worked on and got it back, but here it was on its way to the United States. That's the type of thing that went on.

Q: It sounds like a rereading of history, Attila the Hun and so forth.

Admiral MacDonald: No different, I can assure you, the way they moved in, no different. This is why the Navy is such a clean operation in comparison with the way the troops usually handle things. I was very disturbed about that.

In Frankfurt, on Eisenhower's staff, he had a political advisor called Mr. Robert Murphy, and his two top assistants were Jake Beam, who later became our ambassador to Moscow, and Fred Reinhardt, who was our ambassador in Rome. Both of these people I had known very well. I had worked with Jake Beam in London in 1941. We got together a lot on all kinds of functions, but their jobs really were to advise Eisenhower in connection with how to deal with the Russians and also, supposedly, other political matters. But knowing these two people, not that I personally had to deal with them directly, but just being with them so much, I certainly knew how they thought in connection with all these things. There's no doubt about it, they were the go-betweens between the other governmental officials, particularly the Russian liaison people, and Eisenhower. Frankly, I don't know what all they accomplished. Both of them were not only German linguists, but also Russian linguists, and they were very able men.

Q: Did you know Robert Murphy, too?

Admiral MacDonald: Oh, yes, I knew Robert Murphy, but he was an older man on a higher-level capacity. My association was with his two assistants, who were friends.

At the same time I was over there in Frankfurt, I obtained through the Army a house close to the headquarters and the one out in the country and it was next door to Tony Biddle. He had the house next door, and we got together quite frequently in the evening for dinners and so forth because of our association.

Q: How did the policy work when you had a house and you had to have help, I mean this policy of non-fraternization? How did it work with the Germans?

Admiral MacDonald: The Army requisitioned and took over the houses. Then they were responsible for getting help, and they eventually hired German servants to come in and keep them clean and make the beds, keep the house clean. But, frankly, the people were working for virtually nothing, but it gave them something to do, and I think definitely the ones who were working in the main officers' mess and so forth in the headquarters at least got their meals.

Q: How did you staff your own house?

Admiral MacDonald: Well, through the Army. We had to apply and get help through the Army. They assigned us help, particularly in Frankfurt. In Berlin, I've forgotten what branch of the Army it was, but I think it came under the military police. They hired Germans to take care of the houses. In Ghormley's house in Berlin they hired a couple of German women to take care of it. Supposedly, they were screened before they were allowed to do it. The thing about it is that I never saw them, really, because they would come in during the day, when you weren't there. But you did see them at the officers' mess in the headquarters. They had a couple of big officers' mess.

Q: How did you arrange it if you had a dinner party in your own home? How did you do this?

Admiral MacDonald: Well, there's no doubt about it, we could get commissary food, and I'm sure, as I recall now, we had some stewards. We had a couple of stewards at that time. The generals all had stewards assigned to them, just like they do here, but we had to use German personnel as soon as they cleared them just to take care of the necessities of life.

There's one thing that I haven't covered here. We did set up a little group in Vienna and they were based at the Bristol Hotel.

Q: And what was their purpose?

Admiral MacDonald: Their purpose was the same purpose, actually the Austrians were to find out about demilitarization, non-fraternization, and so forth, as far as officers were concerned.

Q: Did you go down to Vienna?

Admiral MacDonald: Yes, I flew down there several times.

Q: That was under the American sector that was under Mark Clark, wasn't it?*

Admiral MacDonald: I don't remember who was there when I was there. All I can remember is that right plump outside was the Russian sector, and the Russians seemed to have about three-fourths of the city. The Americans and the British were confined to just one street, or strasse, and the Russians even had the hotels all along that. And we couldn't go into the Russian zone. They wouldn't allow us anywhere near the Russian zone.

Of course, from a family point of view at the time, Baroness de Rothschild, who had plenty of property over there, and I had known her in the past, came over. How she got into Germany, I

---

*General Mark W. Clark, USA, commander of U.S. occupation forces in Austria.

don't know, but she did via some high government official's okay, and came to see me and asked me if I could check on her property, which was in the Russian zone. Well, I couldn't even get through. They had a barrier set up.

Q: This was in Germany?

Admiral MacDonald: In Vienna, a place called Lindau in Austria. I couldn't get anywhere near it.

Also a first cousin of my wife, Willie von Meister, had married an Austrian girl, and her family was still alive, and they asked me to check on them and also they sent me a whole carload of CARE packages which I tried to deliver in my airplane. I think I made a couple of trips with CARE packages. Those people were still alive but living under terrible conditions, elderly people cornered in a little room. As a matter of fact, the Russians were somewhat ruthless in the way they moved into Austria. They just took it over, and actually the first thing they did was set up their own monuments. Instead of the beautiful monuments around like Schonbrunn Castle and so forth, they had a great big concrete-block arrangement and a tank sitting up on top of it or Russian guns or something.* They had monuments all over the place indicating the Russian victory, in

---

*Schonbrunn Palace in Vienna had been a summer home for Austrian royalty.

the place of all these beautiful artistic things!

You couldn't even deal with the Russians in Austria. It was impossible. There was no way of communicating with them.

Q: Doesn't evidence show that they intended Austria to be theirs, as they did Hungary?

Admiral MacDonald: They wanted to take over Austria, too. Fortunately, we were able to stall them in connection with the tripartite division of Vienna, and we never were able to really take over any section of Austria except in Vienna. The Russians controlled it.

Q: Our mutual friend, Eleanor Dulles, had something to do with that.*

Admiral MacDonald: However, I will say that Vienna was not badly destroyed like the cities in Germany. There was no real bombing of any great consequence. The only damage that was done was done by the Russians by artillery fire and so forth. It was pretty well intact when we got up there. If they'd allowed Patton to do what he wanted to do, we'd not only have had Berlin but we'd have had Vienna, too, and he could have done it. But this is all

---

*Eleanor Lansing Dulles, financial attache to Vienna from 1945 to 1949.

hindsight, and it probably would have been still preserved quite a bit.

When we were in France under Kirk, there was a man called Lieutenant Peter Hoguet, who was sent over to us.* We had no assignment for him, so we told him to think over what he could do to be helpful, and he dreamed up the proposition of surveying all of the ports along the coastline. Well, we got an airplane for him.

Q: On the North Sea?

Admiral MacDonald: Yes, along the North Sea, along the Bay of Biscay, down along the Mediterranean, all the port coastlines. He photographed all of this and later blew up these pictures of all these ports, so that if we ever have to use them again, it's a fantastic portfolio of all these ports as they were then.

Q: Where did he come from?

Admiral MacDonald: He came from New York. Later, as a matter of fact, Peter Hoguet was running for Congress from New York City, Manhattan District, about two years ago, but he unfortunately wasn't elected. He's still living in New York. But this was

*Lieutenant Peter W. Hoguet, USNR.

just another case of someone who came over there with nothing to do. I don't know how helpful all of this surveying will ever be in the future. At the time, it looked like maybe we might never have a chance to do just what we were doing, so he surveyed all of these areas, and these are on file somewhere.

The other thing I wanted to mention was that in Germany I was talking about some of the people, particularly after Glassford relieved Ghormley, one of Glassford's aides . . .

Q: This was William Glassford?*

Admiral MacDonald: Yes. One of his aides was Seymour St. John, who was quite an intelligent man who later became dean or headmaster of, I think, Choate School.** I think I mentioned something about him before, but I just did not recall his name, so I'm trying to fill it in.

Q: Tell me about the termination of your tour of duty with Admiral Ghormley.

Admiral MacDonald: Well, of course, Ghormley was sent back and Admiral Glassford relieved him. I think Ghormley retired then.

---

*Vice Admiral William A. Glassford, Jr., USN, Commander U.S. Naval Forces in Germany from 1946 to 1947.

**Lieutenant (junior grade) Seymour St. John, USNR. Between 1947 and 1973 he was headmaster of The Choate School.

Q: Glassford was quite a diplomatic type, was he not?

Admiral MacDonald: Yes, and he was a very grand person, very meticulous in appearance, very personable, and very sociable. He loved that aspect of life. He just filled in where Ghormley left off in the same type of duties, although Admiral Glassford spent a lot more time in Frankfurt than Admiral Ghormley ever did. I used to see him all the time.

Q: Why would he do that? Were negotiations with the Russians less onerous at that point?

Admiral MacDonald: Yes, I would imagine so. I think things had quieted down, and he stayed more or less around Eisenhower's headquarters, although I won't say that Eisenhower had any more communication with him than he did with Ghormley. As a matter of fact, I don't recall that Eisenhower ever dealt with Ghormley or Glassford. The only contact that I know was the chief of staff meetings. Otherwise, both Ghormley and Glassford were working with the Navy. They weren't working with the Army at all. But we had to carry out the Army's plans and we were left more or less on our own to do it.

Q: Does this imply that Eisenhower's attitude was almost exclusively an Army attitude and it wasn't a joint command?

Admiral MacDonald: No, I didn't mean to imply that, but when we moved into Frankfurt when he was up there, his main job was U.S. Army, because the British had their own setup, the Russians had their own setup, and he no longer was the Supreme Allied Commander over the British after we moved into Germany and the unconditional surrender, and they changed the name of his command to U.S. Army, Europe. Eisenhower then became really the top U.S. commander there, no longer the top Allied commander.

Q: I see. There's quite a distinction there.

Admiral MacDonald: Quite a distinction.

Q: And this was when hostilities ceased?

Admiral MacDonald: After that. When we first moved into Frankfurt, of course, he was still the Supreme Allied Commander, Expeditionary Forces, and so forth, but as soon as Germany surrendered, as soon as they'd built up their headquarters, the British moved in up north, the Russians, and all this business, his main job then became the job of the U.S. Army. He was still dealing with these people, and I will say, along this line, that the British didn't go along with all of our concepts about what to do with the Germans. They never carried out this de-Nazification, non-fraternization thing at all. They immediately went out and hired the Germans to work in their messes and to work in their homes and everything else. They didn't go and destroy everything in the British sector. They didn't do that at all. Their treatment of the Germans was entirely different from ours.

Q: This was one European to another?

Admiral MacDonald: That's right. Their treatment of everything in their area was just the way they wanted to do it. It had no bearing on the Morgenthau plan or anything, although this was agreed on at a high level, but they didn't carry it out, not in the same way. While we were sort of ruthless in a lot of the things, they just didn't do anything. They started fraternization right off the bat, as far as getting the people they needed to do the work and to do the jobs like in the ports business. They were responsible for clearing the different channels of mines and so forth, and they went right ahead and took the German boats as they were and German crews, and off they went. This is the type of thing they were doing.

Their attitude in this was different. I can't speak too well for the Russians, because I don't know exactly how they dealt with the thing, except we did know that they took over the whole area and it's now East Germany.

Eisenhower's status definitely changed. As a matter of fact,

I left before he came back and he had been consulted by Lodge and so forth, I think he then had definite political ambitions to be President.* As a matter of fact, when Eisenhower returned to this country, they gave him a tremendous ovation down there. At that time, I was allowed to fly back, and my wife and I watched this parade in Washington. I was still on duty in Germany, but I came back just for this thing.

Q: How long did you serve with Admiral Glassford?

Admiral MacDonald: I don't recall exactly when he relieved Ghormley, that's the point. Right now, I'm not too sure, but I served with Glassford, I think, even longer than with Ghormley, and I returned in 1946.**

Q: Do you want to talk about the results of the Ghormley-Glassford mission in terms of what we actually got, what the Navy got, as a result of these negotiations?

Admiral MacDonald: Well, years ago I saw the papers, saw an awful lot of the material in connection with the discussions of how to split things up, who would get this and that, and how was

---

*Senator Henry Cabot Lodge (Republican-Massachusetts).

**Vice Admiral Ghormley was relieved in December 1945; MacDonald left Germany in July 1946.

it going to be divided. I remember seeing the lists of the ultimate agreement where the Russians would take so many ships, which type, and so forth, but I don't specifically remember too many specific names except the Prinz Eugen. We were allowed to get the Prinz Eugen and, of course, this was another job of what we had to do, equip her and get her ready to sail back to the United States.

Q: Did we know then what we were going to do with the Eugen?

Admiral MacDonald: We didn't know that we were going to use it as a target out in Bikini, in the atomic tests out there. We didn't know at that time, but what we wanted to do was get it back here so our engineers could study all the engineering aspects of it and the construction and so forth.*

Q: It was one of the most modern . . .

Admiral MacDonald: It was the most modern ship that was still in existence. We got that. The Russians were more interested in getting the submarines, I know that, the German submarines that

*The Prinz Eugen surrendered to the British at Copenhagen on 7 May 1945 and was transferred to the Americans. In January 1946, she sailed from Wilhelmshaven for Boston with both American and German crews. She survived atomic tests at Bikini Atoll on 25 July 1946 but sank on 22 December 1946 after being towed to Kwajelein.

were still available, and the minesweepers, and the merchant ships. I think we probably had to concede a hell of a lot to the Russians on the merchant ships and the submarine aspects of it. As a matter of fact, I don't think we were too interested in getting too many. I think the British wanted only one or two submarines so they could look them over and that was it.

I've seen the list, Jack, but just don't recall the divisions that were agreed upon in the ultimate papers.

Q: But in an overall sense, did we achieve what we wanted?

Admiral MacDonald: Yes, they achieved an agreement. Then we went along to try to carry it out, to try to turn over these ships to the Russians and so forth and trying to hang onto the ones that we were supposed to be getting, because the Russians would have taken the whole damned thing if we hadn't fought them a little bit. They would have taken everything they could have.

Q: When you left the staff in Frankfurt, you returned to the States and you took up a very interesting job in the Navy Department. It had to do with operational intelligence. Do you want to talk about the background for this job?

Admiral MacDonald: Operational intelligence was a new concept that evolved during the war in connection with operational matters and intelligence in order to carry them out properly, and this was a new division in the Chief of Naval Operations' department. Actually, we were not under what was called the Office of Naval Intelligence, which was a separate division. We worked directly with OP-03, who was the Deputy Chief of Naval Operations for Operations, and our job was to plan all kinds of operations that might happen in the future. At the same time, one section that we had was involved only in connection with the Russians, and the heading up of that particular section I didn't have too much to do with because he was on the same level, that was Kemp Tolley, a Russian-language specialist.* He kept abreast of all the facts and everything about the Russian fleet and Russian personnel, whereas in my setup we were involved in planning operations and keeping the CNO briefed on any operations that were going on, tactical operations.

Q: Your area was Western Europe?

Admiral MacDonald: No, I had the waterfront.

Q: But not Russia?

Admiral MacDonald: No. Russia was an exclusive section of

*Captain Kemp Tolley, USN, whose reminiscences are included in the Naval Institute's collection.

operational intelligence.

This was a little difficult because it was such a new division and just exactly how to operate. Admiral Carl Espe was the top man in operational intelligence when I was working there and I had one of his branches.*

Q: Was it not in some sense a duplication of what ONI was doing?**

Admiral MacDonald: Yes, it was, but this was to put things down for future use and also to prepare training manuals and so forth for future use in connection with dealings in certain areas. One of the manuals that we had to turn out was how to deal with prisoners of war in connection with getting information from them. That was one of the manuals. We had an operational organizational arrangement. We put operational intelligence officers into the fleet commands and then had to assign people to fill those billets. Peter Belin was one of the operational officers sent to the Sixth Fleet. Later we had to find a billet for Admiral Forrest Sherman's son-in-law. Peter Belin was the first one I sent over to the Mediterranean, and these people then had to obtain operational type intelligence. We drew up a fantastic manual of what the requirements were, the intelligence

---

*Captain Carl F. Espe, USN.
**ONI--Office of Naval Intelligence.

requirements for operations. This wasn't being done in ONI. They were keeping different files.

Q: But they had their naval attaches, I mean, and kept their prewar responsibilities.

Admiral MacDonald: Well, this was tied in with reconnaissance and exactly the type of material that you would need, say, for a beach landing or something like that. How to plan for reconnaissance photographs, what was required, and all that. This was just putting it into manuals for training purposes, and I would say that it wasn't much of an assignment as far as I'm concerned. I was a little disappointed.

Q: Did you meet with cooperation or some antagonism on the part of ONI?

Admiral MacDonald: No. No, we didn't work with them except in connection with getting a lot of our material. I talked with a lot of the experts in ONI to help us along with filling in these manuals we were writing. In order to write these manuals--particularly the one on who held prisoners of war and trying to get information--the drawing of manuals on how to do it and what to do, I was allowed to bring in some reserve officers who'd had some experience, who sat down and wrote paragraphs or chapters on how they handled certain things. We put that together for future use. These were secret documents and they may be still secret documents.

Q: OSS was still in existence, was it not?*

Admiral MacDonald: Well, that's another thing. OSS was going out of existence and they were starting this CIA thing. That was another thing that I had to do. In this particular job I was handling the personnel side of it as well for operational intelligence. We were ticked off to go to the CIA when they were first setting it up, and when CIA was first set up under Vandenberg, was it?**

Q: Yes, General Vandenberg.

Admiral MacDonald: The requirement for personnel was only military and particularly in all the spots, so we ran into difficulty there. I did send over some captains--who had quite a lot of experience even in intelligence--to CIA and find out that

---

*OSS--Office of Strategic Services, formerly known as COI (Cooperative for Information); later known as SSU (Strategic Services Unit); currently the CIA (Central Intelligence Agency).

**Lieutenant General Hoyt S. Vandenberg, USAF, Director of the Central Intelligence Group from 1946 to 1947. The first director of the Central Intelligence Agency was Rear Admiral Roscoe Hillenkoetter, USN.

they were working for a recently appointed brigadier general who was much younger than they were and had less experience. So, after we'd assigned certain people, we found out that we were having a terrible time getting people to even want to go anywhere near the CIA because of the way Vandenberg's group had set it up and elevated to the ranks their people in order to control the situation, and then asked us to fill in in the lower echelons.

Q: And also ONI, because they took ONI personnel, too?

Admiral MacDonald: Yes. Well, the initial setup just was very sad for the Navy because in the four or five divisions that they set up, my gosh, there weren't any of our experienced personnel in the area of intelligence that they were dealing in who had the rank to fit in with this seniority. The Army had promoted them up into temporary ranks and they were sitting on top of them.

We ran into this in connection with the British, too. They do the same thing. The Navy never was able to learn this thing until later on, that in order to maintain control, you promote a guy in rank even though he's the youngest one. We never did this because of our whole setup and principle in the Navy.

Q: The selection system?

Admiral MacDonald: Not only that but the rank structure in

ships. In other words, no one but a captain can command a big ship, and unless you command a big ship you can't go any higher. So we were hamstrung by the fact of this emphasis on commanding a big ship and pinning it down to the commanding officer's rank sort of kept everything blocked below.

Q: How important did this particular division prove to be, as a new division, for the CNO?

Admiral MacDonald: I wish I could answer that question, but I can't, because in my mind I couldn't see the importance of it at all! At the time. I was not involved with the briefings, which were done by Admiral Espe, and were tied up definitely with the Russians at the time. I wasn't in on that. I know that the hush-hush section that was the all-Russian setup did come up with briefings that probably were helpful.

Q: They maintained a sort of semi-war room type . . .

Admiral MacDonald: Yes, definitely, a locked-door arrangement and no one could get in, all that sort of thing. Oh, yes, they were watching what the Russians were doing all the time.

Q: Was there any cooperation or any contact between your outfit and the British mission?

Admiral MacDonald: In operational intelligence, no. This was solely the U.S. Navy, purely a U.S. Navy arrangement.

I will say that on this level it was not, but the British had a tremendous mission group here at the time and they had been evolved down to working with their opposite numbers in the areas in which they were involved, except, of course, the chief of the British mission who would deal with the top people, I suppose. I've forgotten now who was CNO, but I think it was Nimitz.*

Q: Yes, immediately after the war, it was.

Admiral MacDonald: If there was anything to do with them, why, they probably dealt with the top level, but we never had anything to do with them.

Q: Did your outfit have anything to do with the plans that were being activated to decrease the scope of naval activities and cut down on ships and personnel?

Admiral MacDonald: No, we had nothing to do with that in what we called OP-03Y. OP-03 is, as I said before, the Deputy Chief of Naval Operations for Operations. He was responsible for that but our division was not, not our section, you might call it. We

*Fleet Admiral Chester W. Nimitz, USN, Chief of Naval Operations from 1945 to 1947.

were not responsible for that. That was all on a different level.

I, of course, got involved in a lot of other things when I was back in the Pentagon later, but not at that time. As a matter of fact, that particular tour of duty was nice in a way, being here, but it really wasn't--with the war not going on, it was what you might call a very dull assignment for me, anyway.

Q: Well, it brought you home to your family.

Admiral MacDonald: That's the whole thing. At first, I thought maybe it might be helpful, when they first told me where I was going, but it didn't turn out that way because what happens is you fall right back into line with your rank and everything fits in.

Q: Were there any indications of what came to be the Defense intelligence setup? Were there any moves in this direction towards a unified . . .

Admiral MacDonald: No, not at this time, because CIA was just getting under way, the Central Intelligence Agency, and I don't think they were as far-reaching at that time, although the Army and the Navy had to supply officers to them, but they hadn't grabbed out to get full control of the whole defense setup at that stage. I frankly don't know exactly, maybe they had it in mind then, even in the two years I was there, it was awfully hard for us to get people to go there at all. It wasn't very big and it wasn't very attractive.

Later, when we finally had Admiral Hillenkoetter, who took over CIA--I wasn't around then exactly, but I remember going to several briefings over in the headquarters when he was head of CIA.* I'm not too sure whether he relieved Vandenberg, but I think he did, and I think there may have been a change then in the organization where the Navy was able to get a few people up into the jobs that were more sort of controlling positions.

I do remember that Vandenberg set it up, and we had to try to find some intelligence officers who were good to send over there. I think people like Hank Jarrell, who was a great Chinese expert, was still a captain and just as a comparable arrangement was probably ten years senior to the guy who was his boss!** He was just recently promoted. This type of thing didn't work to help any of our people wanting to go over there.

Q: Naturally it didn't!

Admiral MacDonald: And even after they got over there, the morale was so low you couldn't keep them over there. They wanted

*Rear Admiral Roscoe H. Hillenkoetter, USN, was the first director of the Central Intelligence Agency.

**Captain Henry T. Jarrell, USN.

to get out of there. It was just not a setup for the Navy at the time.

Q: Did you have any close relationship with the State Department, working in the area that you were working in?

Admiral MacDonald: Not in operational intelligence. We didn't work with the State Department at all. At least I had nothing to do with it and Espe, who was the head of the operational intelligence division, didn't have anything to do with that. He did work with ONI a lot. As a matter of fact, I did, too, to get a lot of information, but my chore really was to produce a lot of training manuals, the organization for future use, and things like that.

Q: I would think that some of the monographs and so forth maintained by ONI would have been of real value to you in preparing your manuals.

Admiral MacDonald: Well, we wanted to get a separate identity from ONI, so one of the things I did was draw up our own little seal. We published a monthly magazine called *Operational Intelligence*, giving all the dope of our buildup and organization and so forth. Basically, the thing at the time was to get billets assigned in the various fleet staffs that they didn't have before, just for this type of operation, which was mainly the publications we put together in connection with reconnaissance, getting pictures and so forth, getting a terrain type and the altitudes and the depths and the waterlines. This is the type of thing. It was very involved.

Q: That's precisely what we did in ONI, too!

Admiral MacDonald: It probably was, but apparently it wasn't reaching the operational forces in time. This way you'd get it right off the bat, the operational forces would. This is one of the reasons why, I guess, the necessity for operational intelligence came up, the fact that, sure, they had all this information in ONI, but it wasn't getting to the people who needed it at the time they needed it. Probably this is basically why it started this way.

Just like, you know, in Overlord and so forth they had to have coverage of beaches and depths of water and tides and everything right at the moment.* I think this is one of the reasons why. ONI probably had all this material, but it wasn't there the minute you had to have it.

Q: It was classified!

---

*"Overlord" was the code name for the June 1944 invasion of Normandy.

Interview Number 6 with Rear Admiral Donald J. MacDonald,
U.S. Navy (Retired)

Place: Admiral MacDonald's residence in Washington, D.C.

Date: Thursday morning, 30 January 1975

Subject: Biography

Interviewer: John T. Mason, Jr.

Q: Admiral, we begin a new and interesting chapter today. In 1948 I think you had an interview with President Truman and the results of that were soon apparent. Do you want to tell me about that?

Admiral MacDonald: I was in the Navy Department, in operational intelligence, and received a call from the naval aide, Admiral Dennison, saying that he'd like me to come over and talk to President Truman.*

Q: Had you known Dennison before that?

Admiral MacDonald: No, I didn't know Dennison at all before this.

I went over to the White House.

*Rear Admiral Robert L. Dennison, USN, naval aide to President Truman from 1948 to 1953. Dennison's memoirs are included in the Naval Institute's oral history collection.

Q: Did you have any idea what was coming up?

Admiral MacDonald: Dennison didn't particularly tell me what it was all about. Anyway, we had this appointment with President Truman. When I went in, I was wearing my decorations and so forth and Truman remarked about that.

Q: That they were fairly extensive!*

Admiral MacDonald: He made a very favorable comment about how many decorations I had at the time and said, "How would you like to be the commanding officer of the Williamsburg?"

I said, "Well, Mr. President, I'd be very flattered and honored to have the job."

And he said, "Well, Larry Freeman [who was the commanding officer] is leaving," and he'd like very much if I'd take over."**

Q: How did he get a latch on you?

Admiral MacDonald: Admiral Leahy was one of his top military advisors, and Admiral Leahy still had his office in the executive

---

*MacDonald's decorations included two Navy Crosses, three Legions of Merit, three Silver Stars, two Bronze Stars, and a Presidential Unit Citation.

**Captain Charles L. Freeman, USN.

offices at the time, and his top aide was a man called Commander Kelly.* Kelly had known me and suggested my name. I think also the Bureau of Naval Personnel may have--at the time I was a senior commander and I think the commander desk probably mentioned it to them over there at the same time that maybe I was the best one for the job. So it was just a matter of being called up and asked to come over, but I will say that Dennison didn't give me any clues until I walked in to see Mr. Truman.

Q: That's being a typical aide, isn't it?

Admiral MacDonald: Mr. Truman was a delightful person.

After I committed myself, it was just a matter of getting the dates straightened out to take over. From that moment on, it was certainly a different life. My association as the commanding officer there lasted about three and a half years, until the fall, I think, of 1951.

Q: Were you under the naval aide or under whom?

Admiral MacDonald: Basically, I worked for the naval aide in this particular job. However, I received an awful lot of my instructions directly from the President. I would say yes, I

---

*Fleet Admiral William D. Leahy, USN, chief of staff to the Commander in Chief. Commander William D. Kelly, USN.

sort of worked under the naval aide, but for all my administrative details, budget and everything, I had to work with the different bureaus. I didn't come under the Chief of Naval Operations. We were just an entity there that existed at the pleasure of the President.

Q: Give me some idea of the scope of your job as skipper of the Williamsburg and the other duties.

Admiral MacDonald: At that time, the Williamsburg had been converted into the presidential yacht. It was Hugh Chisholm's transatlantic yacht that he had built back in 1930. Its name was Aras, "Sara" spelt backwards. As I understand it, it cost him about $750,000 to have it built at Bath Iron Works during the Depression, and he had a very large crew on that ship.* When the war came along, instead of giving it to the Navy or selling it to them on a temporary basis for a dollar, like so many people who owned big yachts did, Chisholm held out and sold the ship outright.

Q: For a stated price?

---

*Hugh J. Chisholm was a wood-pulp magnate who had taken delivery of the Aras on 15 January 1931. The Navy acquired the vessel on 24 April 1941.

Admiral MacDonald: For a stated price, with no stipulation that the ships would ever be returned to Hugh Chisholm. The Navy just bought it, and I think they paid nine hundred and some thousand dollars for it at that time. They were then going to make a flagship out of it for the Icelandic patrol; the commanding officer who was stationed in Iceland was supposed to use it as his flagship. It wasn't a good seagoing ship, particularly when they started putting guns and a few other heavy weights on it. It wasn't that stable and had no watertight compartments.

Q: It was designed for speed?

Admiral MacDonald: It was designed just as a comfortable yacht, transatlantic yacht.

Q: What kind of specifications? What size?

Admiral MacDonald: It was 244 feet long and the tonnage was about 1,800 displacement, and it had a draft originally of about 14-1/2 feet.

Q: What sort of speed did she achieve?

Admiral MacDonald: She had twin diesel engines, and even when I had her, we could get up to 14 knots full speed, but I imagine when she was originally designed she could go a little faster than that, because after the Navy took her over they sent her to Iceland, but she was so unstable and frightening that they sent her back and she was tied up to the dock in Norfolk as the Commander Training Command Atlantic flagship, and just stayed tied up at the dock.

Q: What sort of a crew complement did it require?

Admiral MacDonald: Hugh Chisholm, I understand, originally had about 75 people on it. It was a pretty big operating ship. He took it to Europe, I think, several times, the Mediterranean and so forth. When it was the flagship, Commander Training Command, I don't know how many people, but I would say it probably had close to 175 people on board.

So, when Truman became President, he wanted a yacht. They had the old Potomac that Roosevelt had, which was sort of a converted minesweeper type, and Harry Vaughan, who was Truman's aide, was a lot more ambitious about getting a more suitable ship, so they sold that one to the Governor of Maryland and looked around for another.* This USS Williamsburg, having been bought by the Navy and made a commissioned vessel, they selected that and sent it over to have it converted into a yacht. Well,

*Major General Harry H. Vaughan, USA.

in the conversion process, they put a complete new deck on it, they air-conditioned it, they redecorated a lot of it, and put a lot of special communications equipment on board and so forth, so that actually the draft--well, when they ran it through the stability test, they found out that they would have to do something about stability, so they put a couple of hundred tons of pig iron down in the bilges to try to make it stable. That drove the draft down to about 18-1/2 feet.

Q: It cut down on the speed, too, didn't it?

Admiral MacDonald: It definitely cut down on the speed, but, as I say, we could make about 14 knots in fairly calm weather, but it did have two beautiful diesel engines.

One thing that wasn't done very satisfactorily by the yard was that there were really no watertight compartments in that ship. It had wooden doors and no way of sealing it up. If it got hit, it would just go down like a rock. That's why we always had to be very careful.

Q: Wasn't the Secret Service concerned about that aspect of it?

Admiral MacDonald: No. Actually, the minute the President got on board, the Secret Service just relaxed, because it was my responsibility. We never had more than three Secret Service at any time, and they didn't even hang around. The minute they got on board, they just sort of moved around and so forth.

Q: Sat in deck chairs!

Admiral MacDonald: The President had a whole suite of rooms on one level, which was put on, and that's one of the reasons they had to weight it down on the bottom. Then in this little sitting room up there, they had a piano. There was a lovely little lounge room and two very elaborate bedrooms, one for him with a bath and one for Mrs. Truman and Margaret with a bath. Then on the lower level they had a lot of compartments for passengers and guests and had a big lounge in the back. That opened out onto the deck and we had awnings out there with quite a deck space in the back. We had a specially designed poker table there and a piano. The dining room was really a very elaborate dining room, which could seat, when we put up two different tables, quite long tables, probably 30 people very easily at a seated dinner in a very nice way.

Of course, in order to serve the President properly, we had a lot of messboys assigned to us, stewards and cooks and so forth. There must have been a couple of dozen altogether, stewards and cooks and messboys.

Q: So the kitchen facilities must have been very extensive.

Admiral MacDonald: They had charcoal-broiling arrangements and everything else. We had a fabulous setup just for the presidential mess, and that was separate from the crew's mess.

We had on board at all times a crew of possibly 175 men, engineers, radiomen, and all this business, and at the same time--I didn't realize it at the time--but Shangri-La, which was the camp that was built for Roosevelt--Ben Moreell built this camp up in the Catoctin Mountains and, of course, as long as he was Chief of the Bureau of Yards and Docks, the money was coming to handle the camp. But when he left, the camp was never put under anyone, so they just put it under the Williamsburg, and there was no crew or anything to man the camp, so this was another assignment that was tied in to the Williamsburg, handling the camp.

Q: Did you have to take your crew up there?

Admiral MacDonald: Well, I had about 30 people permanently assigned up there, carpenters, electricians, and so forth, and whenever the President would go up there, we'd send up stewards and additional people.

Q: How large was Shangri-La, Camp David now?

Admiral MacDonald: Well, it's one tremendous big lodge, and then when Truman became President, a special little house called the Truman House was built, which had two bedrooms, a sitting room, its own kitchen arrangements, and so forth, well-insulated and off to the right. They called it the Truman Cottage.

Q: What sort of acreage?

Admiral MacDonald: The acreage involved, what we really used, couldn't have been more than about 13 to 15 acres there, but it was tied into a lot of land that the government owned, because they had OSS camps, training camps, and CCC training camps up there, and they were off at a little distance.* We had a swimming pool, and then we had little bunk houses scattered around the different paths, and this was where the Secret Service and any additional people bunked. Then they built a great big what they called sort of community building, and this was the bunkhouse for the crew, messhall, and this is where they showed the movies. It was a great big bunk building. The messhall was used for recreational purposes, movies, and so forth. That's where the crew lived.

We did all of our work ourselves because no one had any money. I can remember when we wanted to try to renovate and build a patio on the back, scrape it down and cut down so that

*OSS--Office of Strategic Services; CCC--Civilian Conservation Corps.

the view would be clearer from there. I went to the Chief of the Bureau of Naval Personnel to see if I could get the money from this contingency fund, because we had no money assigned and the camp was on no one's budget.

Q: Why didn't it rightfully come under the White House itself?

Admiral MacDonald: The White House had no budget to amount to anything at the time. Actually, my budget--and later on I'll tell you exactly--was only less than $100,000 to run the Williamsburg, two other boats we had, which at that time were called the Margery and the Lenore--the Lenore was the boat they used to call the Secret Service boat; it was a 105-foot yacht. Later they changed it to Barbara Ann, the Fitzgerald, and all these other different names. Anyway, that always followed us when we were going down the river as a sort of a pickup boat if something should happen. Its mission was to come alongside and get the President off right away if something happened.

Now, when I talk about the crew members, we had crews for both of those boats, too. The Lenore, being a 105-footer, it would depend on what we were using it for, how many people we'd put on board, but basically it was a crew of five or six, ordinarily, assigned to it all the time, and about the same number to the Margery, which was another little boat, a 75-foot boat, which they bought from Fisher Brothers at one time. That was used for sort of daytime cruising up and down in small parties.

The Williamsburg, being a commissioned vessel, supposedly we were not allowed to serve liquor, but the Margery was a noncommissioned vessel just like the Sequoia, so that if they were just going to give a little evening party where they wanted to serve cocktails and there weren't too many of them, we'd use the Margery. She, being noncommissioned and they didn't have to keep a log, didn't come under the Navy Regs in the same way, so we could serve cocktails on board. So sometimes they would use the Margery to go down the river in the early evening, have cocktails and everything, and then come back for dinner on board the Williamsburg.

Q: The President, as Commander in Chief of the Navy and the Army and Air Force, could, when he was aboard, assert that he was the commander of the Army and have liquor, could he not?

Admiral MacDonald: I made no issue out of that. I always had on board all kinds of whiskey in the back, in the President's area. What he did was what he wanted to do. There were no questions. No one ever checked it or anything like that. I used to go back many times; he'd invite me back, to play poker. President Truman loved to play poker.

But to get along on this allocating of money and budget, that

$100,000 had to keep all three of those boats in working order. We were responsible for the camp, and we were responsible for the train. If we had two cars, they were presidential train cars, special train. Wherever the President went, we sent the stewards and the cooks and so forth on the train and saw that our supply officer would get all the food and everything to take care of that and to keep the train clean.

You talk about why didn't the White House give us money. When they wanted to paint the White House one time, there was no money available to do it, so they came down to me and asked me if I could give them, I've forgotten how many thousands of dollars from my budget, to paint the White House!

Q: Things have changed because there is a fund for the White House now.

Admiral MacDonald: Yes, a maintenance fund. The setting up of the White House mess was something that was done by Admiral Dennison and myself. Admiral Dennison felt that it would be great to have a Navy-run White House mess in the White House, down below.

Q: What did they do before then?

Admiral MacDonald: They all had to go outside.

Q: On a rainy day they had to go to the snack bar!

Admiral MacDonald: Yes. So, our of my poor old Navy budget, we had to get the furnishings, and Dennison had a great flair for taste and liked nice, good things, the chairs and the furniture and the rugs and all that stuff. And who ran the White House mess? My stewards, on a daily basis. We worked out menus and so forth, and the stewards from the Williamsburg would go up there every day and run the White House mess arrangement.

Q: The customers at the mess would pay, would they not?

Admiral MacDonald: Yes, they would sign a chit and they were billed at the end of the month. There were flat fees for certain things, like there would be, for one price, the hot-dish arrangement that would be hot soup or something, and then one or two sandwiches, and that's about all, but it was in very nice surroundings. We had nice furniture, tablecloths, and all that sort of thing, and nice china.

And that's another thing in connection with money. It was hard to get, but the President in the middle of all this changed the White House seal--Truman changed the seal because the eagle was looking in the wrong direction. Someone called it to his attention, and they had to change all of the china, change the whole seal around! Well, then we worked with the Lenox china people to have all new china and all this business.

Those were just some of the things. Later on, after Eisenhower took over, he made one trip in the *Williamsburg*. He went down to Annapolis and when the *Williamsburg* came in--Turner Joy was Superintendent, he asked me to come over and meet with the President.* I did and I said to President Eisenhower, "I understand you're going to put the *Williamsburg* out of commission. Mr. President, you have no idea of the advantages of having the *Williamsburg*. In the first place, it's what the people wanted to provide for the President and it's not that expensive to operate. In ten minutes you can get away from the White House and everything and you can just do as you please."

He said he realized he had made a terrible mistake. It was his brother who convinced him that, economically, to sell himself and to get votes he should go on an economy program, and one of the things he was going to do away with was the luxury of a private yacht.

I just thought here was $100,000 that the people were providing to run that yacht for the President. He didn't know what the advantages were, and then, when he became President, the Air Force absolutely was delighted because all of a sudden they spent $5 million building Lowry Air Force Base and their headquarters and everything out in Denver for him. The Air Force

---

*Vice Admiral C. Turner Joy, USN, Superintendent of the Naval Academy from August 1952 to August 1954.

and the Army were always very disturbed in connection with Truman and the yacht.

Q: So it became an interservice rivalry!

Admiral MacDonald: Oh, it was awful. They never could get their hands on the President because the President [Truman] loved to come down to the yacht. He'd call up many times. As a matter of fact, he was on board two or three times a week. Many times he'd call up on the telephone--I had a direct line to the President--and he'd say, "Captain, I'm coming down for lunch today."

And I'd say, "Are you bringing anyone else down, Mr. President?"

And he would say, "No, so if you'd like to have lunch with me, I'd love to have you."

He'd come down and we'd have lunch. I'd sit there and listen to him. I learned a lot from talking with him at some of these luncheons. After lunch, he'd go up and have a nap, and this he did every day regularly, he would nap, and I had a pharmacist's mate who was a masseur and he would then give him a rubdown. Then he'd go back to the White House about 4:30.

He had a group that he liked to play poker with. He had three different groups. At that time Clark Clifford was one of the secretaries and Clark organized one group and he had a couple of people organize different groups.* The President really loved to get away, and sometimes he'd come down on a Thursday. He'd have poker parties that night and about 12:00 o'clock at night some of the people would leave, the rest of them would go down the river with him. Many times, when we left at night like that, I'd only go down to Quantico, maybe, and anchor, or, if we left early enough, we'd go way down to Blackstone Island, and he'd stay on board for the weekend and we'd be back up in Washington Monday morning about 7:30.

Q: To complete the thought on Eisenhower, when did he do away with the _Williamsburg_? Did he retain the smaller boats?

Admiral MacDonald: He retained the two smaller boats.

Q: But he changed the names?

Admiral MacDonald: Yes, he changed the names and named them after his granddaughters, the _Barbara Ann_ or something. They used them and even the Kennedys used them a little bit and changed the names. But those were noncommissioned; they were not the yacht. People called them yachts, but they were not suitable

---

*Captain Clark M. Clifford, USNR, naval aide to the President, 1946. Clifford was a close advisor to Truman. He later served as Secretary of Defense, 1968-1969.

for the type of thing you needed for a presidential yacht. They had bunks, all right, but I mean the quarters--well, the Margery could sleep six people just in ordinary type quarters arrangement, nice little rooms, but we never used them that way.

Q: But we've never had a presidential yacht since then?

Admiral MacDonald: No.

Q: Nixon used something.

Admiral MacDonald: He used the Sequoia. At one time, years ago, I think in the Thirties, the Sequoia was for a brief period called the presidential yacht for Roosevelt, before he got the Potomac. Since then, it was always considered the Secretary of the Navy's little yacht. The Secretary of the Navy ran it all of the time. It was a noncommissioned vessel, and they had a commander assigned as the officer in charge.*

Q: How big a ship is she?

Admiral MacDonald: The Sequoia is about 100 feet, I guess, but very narrow--maybe it wasn't quite that long, maybe 90-some feet--a very narrow arrangement, and they had some bunks there. The Secretary of the Navy could take parties down the river a

*The Dictionary of American Naval Fighting Ships indicates that the USS Sequoia (AG-23) went into commission in 1933 and was in that status intermittently to 1935. After that, she was "in service."

little way, but it wasn't good enough for anything more than just river work. It's still being used for little private parties, trips down to Mount Vernon and so forth, and they have a crew of an officer in charge and, by having an officer in charge, they didn't have to keep a log. This was the whole thing and they didn't have to then comply with Navy Regs. That's the advantage of having a ship that's noncommissioned versus a commissioned ship.

It was nice and still is--Trumpy overhauled the Sequoia, half a dozen times. They call it the presidential yacht, but really it hasn't been a presidential yacht. The President uses it, but it's always been the Navy's, the Secretary of the Navy's.

I used to take President Truman down the river so often, sometimes there would be a period when we'd be going down every weekend. Sometimes we'd go out in the bay and stay out a week or so, anchor over around Patuxent, go up through the Chesapeake Canal and so forth.

Q: What about communications on board?

Admiral MacDonald: Oh, we had very elaborate communications. I think I even mentioned in a previous conversation about the scrambler.

Q: Yes, you did.

Admiral MacDonald: There wasn't a scrambler in the United States. I knew all about them, but we couldn't get any scrambling equipment. It didn't exist in the United States, but I got them working on it at the time, because the President used to be called occasionally, sometimes on political matters, and if he sounded off and was pretty frank and blunt sometimes in his comments, and if he said, "What the Sam Hill are you doing this for?" or something going over the air clear, this wouldn't have been good!

But we did, we had good communications equipment, the best the Navy had at the time, and we even got a radar, a small one, because it wouldn't take anything else, a small radar to try to help us. But in the river channel work, radars weren't any good because the channel's too narrow, the Potomac River channel. The channel is supposed to be dredged to 25 feet, from Washington on down, but in some places it's less than 75 yards wide. You have to stay in it all the time or you run aground. I know the _Potomac_ people, Dayton Clark and even Count Austin, when they were in the _Potomac_, I think they ran aground in that little _Potomac_ several times going up and down the river with Roosevelt.* I had a little better luck.

Q: That would be embarrassing!

---

*Lieutenant Commander Augustus D. Clark, USN; Lieutenant Bernard L. Austin, USN.

Admiral MacDonald: What I'm saying is that Truman loved to go down that river. To get back to the tie-in with the Sequoia, I took President Truman, his wife, and Margaret down one weekend, as we got under way in the afternoon--I guess it was either Thursday afternoon or Friday afternoon--about 4:00 or 5:00 o'clock. I was up on the bridge and we went by the Sequoia. The President was standing up there with me, and Margaret was standing up there. As we went by the Sequoia, Margaret said, "Whose boat is that?"

And I said, "That's the Secretary of the Navy's boat." Then in front of the President I said, "You know Mr. Johnson borrowed the Chief of Naval Operations' little converted PT boat to go down the river last weekend on a little party, supposing he was going to stay down there overnight.* They went down Saturday afternoon, the stewards prepared a meal for them, and they anchored off Mount Vernon. They wanted to turn in rather early and they turned in and then discovered that, in order to keep the lights on, the generators had to be kept going, and the generators were right under the bunks. So the Secretary of Defense, Johnson, told a chief to get under way; they were going back. So about 10:00 o'clock, they returned, instead of staying down the river."

So, as we got in the week before with the President, I was

*Louis A. Johnson, Secretary of Defense from 1949 to 1950.

off the ship, on a Monday, because the crew always was off on a Monday if you were down the river at the weekend, and Johnson sent his captain naval aide down to look over these yachts that the President had. When I returned on Tuesday, Commander Gay, who was my executive officer, came up to me and said, "Secretary of Defense Johnson had his aide down here looking around. They want one of the President's boats for the Secretary of Defense's yacht."*

When I told the President that Secretary Johnson was very upset and wanted a boat like the Sequoia, the President said to me, "What the hell does he want a boat for? He's not going to be around that long."

Boy, did I have to keep that under my hat! And within one month Secretary of Defense Johnson had his walking papers. That was just one of these many incidents that used to happen.

The President was a great person to have. You know, he never caused me any trouble. I would ask him, "What would you like to do, Mr. President?" or something like that.

And he'd say, "Oh, you work out something and go ahead." It was so easy and so delightful.

We did have three and a half years of different groups coming on board. The President loved to play poker in addition to napping and walking in the morning. Sometimes a lot of these

---

*Commander Jesse B. Gay, USN.

poker players wouldn't be able to stay on, as I mentioned before, so they'd play poker until about midnight, and then I'd have to get under way after they went ashore, and then we'd have a seaplane--at that time our mail and everything was delivered by seaplane--and we'd see different passengers arrive and the poker session would start up again in the afternoon at 4:00 o'clock.

Q: What sort of staff did he have with him when he went on these trips?

Admiral MacDonald: He never had any staff except what we provided him with. I had yeomen who would take things down for him.

Q: But no permanent secretaries?

Admiral MacDonald: He had no permanent secretaries. He would have some of his staff--people like Secretary Clark Clifford would go with him sometimes.* Vaughan, he loved to go, too, and would be with us, and General Landry, who was the Air Force aide, used to go.** His naval aide went most of the time but not all the time. But as far as outside staff, personnel who worked in

---

*Clark M. Clifford, Special Counsel to President Truman from 1946 to 1950.

**Brigadier General Robert B. Landry, USAF.

executive offices on a lower level, he never took any of those with him; he just used our own facilities. And we had them.

Q: How different from now!

Admiral MacDonald: Oh, yes. As I said, there were only three Secret Service people. The thing is that we used to go down that river and back on weekends, the President would be up on the bridge, and all these boats coming over and waving, the President would wave to them. There was no thought of something taking a potshot at him or anything like that. It was a different time. These little boats would come alongside and wave, and no one ever made an attempt to do anything rash or anything like that. It was a very nice tribute.

Q: It's hard to realize that it was a relatively short period in time.

Admiral MacDonald: Yes, and there was a lot of dipping of colors and all this nonsense. Of course, we had certain ceremonies when we went by Mount Vernon. We had to get the crew up and they'd all stand at attention and salute, quite historic. Well, I mean, we'd render honors as we went by.

McCormick-Goodhart had a big place down there and he had a big flagpole, and every time we'd go by, he'd dip his colors and we'd have to dip our colors.

I had to take Truman off on certain specific missions. We used to go down to Key West. That's the other thing that I didn't mention.

Q: The Little White House. That was under you?

Admiral MacDonald: That was under us, too. We had two houses down there and whenever the President was going down there, I'd send by air a supply officer and steward and so forth to get it ready. Then we'd bring all of his stuff down, and Truman went down with us a couple of times on the ship from Washington.

Q: The Inland Waterway?

Admiral MacDonald: Oh, no, we could never go by the Inland Waterway. We'd go out in the ocean, and it got damned rough! But every time we went to Key West and the President was with me, we had a destroyer escort, which I'd pick up down the Chesapeake Bay, and the destroyer escort would carry the press and so forth and would follow us down, outside in the ocean. The other boats never went. They just stayed up in the navy yard. As a matter of fact, sometimes the Chesapeake Bay got a little too rough for the Lenore, which was our usual river escort, so that we had to have a destroyer escort when we were operating in the Chesapeake

Bay.

Q: Tell me about that Little White House. It required extensive renovation, didn't it? Was that in your time?

Admiral MacDonald: Yes. Well, it was where the commanding officer of the station lived, originally, but he moved out into another place and they fixed that up for the President. They completely redecorated it. It was fully equipped with everything essential and, of course, it had a custom-built poker table.

Q: And whose budget was this?

Admiral MacDonald: Fortunately, that was under Key West's budget! But the personnel to man it were all from the Williamsburg. When the President was there, it was my personnel who managed that house and another house that we maintained for all the guests, which was really another house with a living room and bedroom and everything fully equipped, but we didn't operate any dining room service or anything like that over there. We only did that in the main house, and the overflow guests stayed on board the Williamsburg. Some of them, like Vaughan and Dennison, they lived on board the Williamsburg, and I always tied up at the dock there. We made several trips over to Havana. We took Margaret and the Truman family and a lot of the aides over to Havana on a couple of trips from Key West. Basically, we went to Key West twice a year. Usually we'd go down there in November up until almost Christmas, and then maybe we'd go back in March, for all of March. In the meantime, people would be flying back and forth all the time and there'd be a changing of personnel in connection with whatever message he was working on. We had a regular communications setup down there, a shack, and the communications people at the White House were Army people. Now, they would go down and they would operate the shore communications at Key West, Army communicators. But, as far as Shangri-La was concerned, that also was an Army communications setup--Fort Ritchie provided a lot of the equipment.

Basically, Truman had a certain routine and way of life. For instance, we'd go down and anchor, and several times I even went alongside the dock at Quantico. But we'd anchor off Quantico if we got under way late, and in the morning, about 6:00 o'clock, the President would like to get up and walk.

Q: Before breakfast?

Admiral MacDonald: Before breakfast. I would go ashore with him and we'd walk around Quantico in the morning, at 6:00 o'clock, when people were all still asleep. If I went, the Secret Service didn't give it a thought, they didn't follow us at all, and that was true the many, many times during the summertime when we'd go down the river and we'd anchor at Blackstone Island, and the President used to go in for a swim. And who would be standing by to save him and so forth but myself and my executive officer, who were swimmers. We'd get our clothes and so forth, and the President would go in and have a swim off the gangway. The Secret Service would be standing up on the dock, but they wouldn't be ready to go in and save him.

I just know that it was an easy time for the Secret Service, that period in time, when the President went aboard a ship. The responsibility, in a way, was ours because the Secret Service has no control over the commanding officer of a ship. So it was a funny thing. The ones who used to go on a lot of these trips with him, of course, were the top ones assigned in the field, and Jim Rowley, the head of the Secret Service, went on most of the trips with us, and another one of the senior men.*

Truman liked to take his walk and he'd actually nap after lunch, and at 4:00 o'clock in the afternoon, if he was on board or at the Little White House, he'd start a poker session, which lasted until dinner. He'd have dinner, cocktails--they liked cocktails. Then after dinner, he might have another poker session that would run up to 11:30 or 12:00 o'clock. He loved to play poker, and, as I mentioned earlier, they had different

*James J. Rowley, who at this time was special agent in charge of the White House detail. Between 1961 and 1973 he was director of the Secret Service.

groups that they'd organize. How much they played for depended on which group he had. Certain groups like Fred Vinson, Clint Anderson, George Allen, and some of those people--the sky was the limit.* I mean they just played with no real limit. Then he had a group . . .

Q: That were poorer!

Admiral MacDonald: A sort of $700-limit group. If they went down and played poker over a weekend, the most they could lose would be $700, because every hand they'd always put something in the kitty, and once you were down to a $700 loss, you borrowed from the table and you couldn't lose any more. Then, if he just had the staff when he couldn't get one of the other gangs, he'd have people like Dennison, Vaughan, and other members of the White House staff, Clark Clifford and some of the rest of them, they had, say, a $100 limit. But he just liked to play poker and he loved Old Grand-Dad whiskey. I always had to have plenty of that for him.

Q: What was his winning ability?

---

*Fred M. Vinson, Chief Justice of the Supreme Court from 1946 to 1953; Clinton P. Anderson, Secretary of Agriculture from 1945 to 1948; George E. Allen, former head of the Works Progress Administration.

Admiral MacDonald: Oh, he used to win. He had a great time. It relaxed him. And there were those pianos on board, little pianos.

Q: Upright pianos?

Admiral MacDonald: Yes, little upright pianos. He had one up in his own little lounge, one down in the main lounge, and he had one in the dining room. On several parties, we'd have a special musician come in there and play.

The thing that I haven't mentioned is that we had special meetings on board the Williamsburg because of our staff-dinner capability and all this business.

Q: What kind of meetings?

Admiral MacDonald: Well, Churchill--high-level government meetings. They'd come down there and the dining room, which could accommodate--a very elaborate dining room arrangement, very beautifully decorated and maintained--they'd have their business sessions and have their meals. The wonderful thing about it from the security point of view was that we were in the navy yard, and at that time, you know, Marines guarded the gates and very few people could get in unless they were cleared. So that did help, too, the fact that at that time the navy yard was a sort of secure area. This probably helped the Secret Service a great deal, too.

Truman often told me, "It's just wonderful, I can get away. In ten minutes I'm away from everything, no telephone calls." Everything had to be checked out before we ever bothered him on telephone calls or anything like that.

Q: What were his working habits?

Admiral MacDonald: He was an early riser, walked, and did most of his work in the morning. When he was going back to the White House, he would start working again about 4:30 and go on until the evening. Of course, when he was on a weekend trip or something, it was a different story. Basically, his working habits were in the morning, up until noon, and most of the people who had to get papers cleared with him or something worked with him around 10:00, 11:00, or 12:00 o'clock, up to that hour.

I know that in the drafting of the State of the Union and budget messages, all the different legislation, drafts were constantly being flown in, checked over, and worked with him at that time. People would come in for special conferences. We had about everyone on board who meant anything at the time, various times.

Q: With such an uncertain schedule, you had to maintain almost a constant state of readiness, didn't you?

Admiral MacDonald: Oh, yes, we were ready to go at any time. The only situation was that if we were out over the weekend, I usually gave Monday off to my crew, except for the watchstanders.

Q: He understood that so he didn't make plans on Monday?

Admiral MacDonald: Yes, because usually in a case like that, we'd never come back until Monday morning. He'd want us to come back and we'd be tying up at 7:30 Monday morning at the gun factory. I had to plan my trip back to be alongside the dock at 7:30 on Monday morning.

We ran like a railroad schedule. I knew how long it would take me to go to different places. Several times he had to go down to Norfolk for various reasons, speeches or something, and we'd take him down. We'd have to arrive at a certain hour because of the honors rendered to him and so forth.

Usually things had to be well-organized by clockwork. Even the arrival going from Washington to Key West, we'd notify them in advance exactly when we were going to arrive so they weren't standing around waiting unnecessarily. I'd have to give my speed and time and all this business to hit it on the button.

Q: Did you go with him on the train when he . . .

Admiral MacDonald: No, I never went on the train with him, but Dennison did several times.

I'll take that back. There was a period when I was in Key West and Dave McDonald was Dan Kimball's aide, and Dave had a very serious operation, so they sent him down to recuperate at Key West.* That's when I really got to know Dave fairly well because he used to come over to see us when he was based at the hospital there.

Dennison became very ill at one time as a naval aide and was laid up in the hospital for three or four months, at which time I was sort of acting naval aide. One of those trips was the Army-Navy game trip when the President went up and I went up with him to the Army-Navy game.

Q: You traveled by train?

Admiral MacDonald: By train. So I did go that particular time that I remember well, and the funny part about it, they were all Army people--Vaughan went, Landry went, Truman went, and myself. I was the only Navy guy. That particular year, the Navy was not the favored person so I got points from all of them, and it was

---

*Captain David L. McDonald, USN; Dan A. Kimball, Under Secretary of the Navy at the time of this incident in 1950. The memoirs of Admiral McDonald, who served as Chief of Naval Operations from 1963 to 1967, are included in the Naval Institute collection.

the first time that Navy had won in a long time. I won $10 or $15 from Vaughan and Landry, so I cleaned up on Navy on that particular trip!

On that train trip, my supply officer, who ran the stewards and so forth, had to make sure that everything was there; we had our stewards go up with us. The stewards, you know, serve coffee and sandwiches and things and take care of the situation at the game as you sit there.

Q: You returned the same night, did you?

Admiral MacDonald: Yes, we returned the same day on the train.

So I did really go on the train once with him. This was a special train. It was equipped just like any other private car, and the car was maintained down at the Naval Gun Factory, which was called the Naval Gun Factory at the time, just for Presidential use.* He used it, of course, on one of his trips around when he was campaigning, a whistle-stop type of arrangement, he used that train and my stewards went with him.

As a matter of fact, I had this wonderful pharmacist's mate who really could give you a wonderful rubdown, and that guy

---

*The Naval Gun Factory is currently known as the Washington Navy Yard.

always went with him, because the President, you know, after a nap loved to get a rubdown.

Q: To wake up fast.

Admiral MacDonald: I had two doctors. As a matter of fact, instead of using a White House physician, he used my doctors. These fellows would take care of all the people attached to the White House staff, also the President. That was something else again that Eisenhower didn't realize. Instead of having a White House physician stationed there, he was stationed on the *Williamsburg*. He was a Navy doctor and he used to take care of the people, and under him was this particular fellow. He had two corpsmen in there, one a chief, and the President just loved to relax and get a rubdown, shower, and go back up to the office. He liked that type of thing. That's why he used to come down for these special luncheons.

Sometimes, as I mentioned before, when he'd call and say he was coming down for lunch, he'd bring a guest or two, but, I would say on at least a half-dozen occasions, he said, "Well, if you'd like to have lunch with me, if you're not doing something else, why, I'd love to have you." I'd have lunch with him and he'd tell me things to sort of get my reaction. Several times he would ask, "What would your reaction be?"

The one incident that really was sort of outstanding in my mind was in connection with MacArthur. He was so upset in connection with how MacArthur was acting out in Korea--this was after we'd gone to war out there--and he said, "You know, I'm the Commander in Chief, and here's one of my subordinate commanders who will not carry out orders. I just have no alternative--there's no alternative open to me except to fire him." This was before he fired MacArthur. He said, "This fellow just won't obey orders."

Q: Did you have to give a reaction to that?

Admiral MacDonald: Yes, he wanted to know what I thought of MacArthur. I remember at the time I said, "Well, Mr. President, you can't be the boss in a military organization and have people not carry out the orders, really, or you lose control."

I won't say that what I said had any bearing. His mind was made up, but he discussed that item. He discussed in connection with Eisenhower on another occasion. I will say in connection with Mr. Truman, when I went on board, Mr. Truman didn't know anything about the Navy, he really didn't. He was all Army. He thought the world of any Army commander. Marshall was his great hero; Eisenhower had been a commander, so he thought he must be great, too.* He really loved the Army, and one of the things that Dennison and I had to do was sell the Navy to Truman, because his whole life had been Army, and we did. We were successful in convincing him that the Navy was something, too.

In connection with Eisenhower, he wanted Eisenhower to be a Democrat and definitely he wanted to groom him to follow Truman.

Q: Did he have any reason for thinking he was a Democrat and that he would . . .

Admiral MacDonald: He was a Democrat originally.

Q: Eisenhower was?

Admiral MacDonald: Oh, yes, and Truman appointed him to head up the new organization that later became NATO, the Supreme Allied Commander, after the war, he tried to build him up and keep his image high, and it virtually broke his heart when, all of a sudden, Eisenhower shifted over to the Republican Party. Truman knew definitely that Eisenhower was going to run for the Presidency.

---

*General of the Army George C. Marshall, USA, whom Truman appointed as Secretary of State (1947-1949) and Secretary of Defense (1950-1951).

Q: Had he had conversations with him on this?

Admiral MacDonald: Very little. You know, they didn't talk too much. He talked with Marshall all the time. They were close, although Marshall never came down to the Williamsburg. But he did talk with Marshall a great deal and had great respect and admiration for him. It was through Marshall that the President wanted to have Eisenhower groomed to follow him, but not until they were ready for it. Then, of course, Lodge went over there and the Republicans talked him into changing over to the Republican Party, then they started grooming him in a different way like getting him the appointment as president of Columbia, changing his image.*

Q: That was a Republican . . .

Admiral MacDonald: This was a blow to President Truman. This was a real blow to him because he was such an enthusiastic Army man and he would have done anything for these top Army people.

Q: Do you remember particularly what he said when he talked about Eisenhower changing?

---

*Dwight D. Eisenhower took over as president of Columbia University 7 June 1948. He remained in that post until taking leave on 16 December 1950 to become Supreme Allied Command Europe as the NATO military command was being established.

Admiral MacDonald: Well, he liked to swear a little bit.

Q: Use colorful language?

Admiral MacDonald: Yes, colorful language is it, "stubborn Missouri mule" and all that stuff. He was very upset. I don't remember his exact words, but he just was so upset that he didn't know what to do when he found out that Eisenhower was not going to be a Democrat and follow him, and could possibly run against him. I just remember his discussing it one time.

This was just one of the incidents. The other one that I remember that really made quite an impression on me--I never knew anything about the atomic weapon--and at one luncheon arrangement he said, "You know, I've had to make some terrible decisions." He was talking first about Potsdam, and he did remark about his going over there to Potsdam and he was so badly prepared to take over the situation, he just didn't know what the score was at the time, whether he had lost ground for the United States by his actions at that time.

Q: Didn't he realize, however, that he was going to be catapulted into this job?

Admiral MacDonald: I think it came so fast he wasn't prepared. Roosevelt never talked with Truman to brief him and keep him up to date on things.

Q: But wasn't he aware of the President's state of health?

Admiral MacDonald: I don't know that he was aware that he was going to die that soon. As you know, the war was coming to an end, anyway. He was catapulted into this, and he wasn't really prepared to do this, but he said he had to make these momentous decisions.

Now, what I'm leading up to is he was talking about another great decision following the Potsdam deal that he had to make which he said bothered him a great deal. He was the only person who could make the decision and that was to tell them to go ahead and drop that atomic weapon. So he reviewed the situation to me, and for the first time I even asked him a couple of questions about the size and everything. I had no idea what these weapons looked like. He told me the exact weight and length and all this business, also the fact that the whole point behind dropping the weapons, of course, was to possibly end the war earlier and save a lot of lives, the same old thing you hear all the time, trying to save lives and shorten the war. This was a decision he had to make. If they dropped and were successful, this probably would hasten the end of the war. It absolutely did, but look at the destruction and look what happened on this thing. This was just another one of those great decisions he had to make.

Later on, with that knowledge and so forth, politically when he started trying to hold this atomic weapon as a big club over everyone's head, we had the know-how and we could do this, this then became a political arrangement which was all wrong.

As I mentioned in one of our earlier conversations, I was always very close to Admiral Nimitz, used to play tennis with him. He and I were talking one day just on a walk and we were talking about this atomic weapon, and Nimitz said, "It's just another weapon. It has to be dropped at the right place at the right time. Why all this hullaballoo of thinking it's going to be the end of everything? It's all wrong."

That was just one of the things. We held this weapon over their head for a long time, but no longer because even the Chinese now probably have developed a weapon. It's no longer the great club to keep everyone in line with.

Q: It's a matter of two clubs now, or three clubs!

We haven't talked about Mrs. Truman and daughter Margaret and how frequently they came with the President to the Williamsburg, how frequently they went to the Little White House and to Shangri-La.

Admiral MacDonald: Well, actually, I have to keep this sort of separated in different areas. As far as the Williamsburg is concerned, the President did take Mrs. Truman and Margaret, I would say, on an average of about once a month and it would be just a family trip down the river for a couple of days.

Q: Were they good sailors?

Admiral MacDonald: They were excellent sailors because of the fact that the ship was large enough that in the river and even in the bay it wasn't uncomfortable for them. We even had a couple of birthday parties with Mrs. Truman and Margaret on board, at which time, I remember, we used to go and anchor over near Patuxent, then they could fly some guests in and have them picked up from Patuxent.

Now, as far as down at the White House in Key West, yes, Margaret and Mrs. Truman used to go down all the time, but they always sort of operated independently. I don't think the President ever went up to Shangri-La--at that time it was called Shangri-La. It wasn't changed to Camp David until after Eisenhower took over--every time the President went up there, Mrs. Truman always went with him.

The President was very much of a family man. It was a close-knit family. Mrs. Truman was a wonderful person. She was always in the background but always nice and pleasant. Margaret, of course, was trying to be a singer, and the President was always very sensitive and touchy on any comments that might border on her talent or ability.

Q: His famous letter to Paul Hume![*]

Admiral MacDonald: That's right. In that letter he blew his stack. He really loved his family. The President and Mrs. Truman had relatives--as a matter of fact, the President brought his mother on board one time, on the _Williamsburg_, and his brothers and her brothers and sisters came and went on a little trip. As a matter of fact, I will tell you this. A number of times Mrs. Truman organized luncheon parties for women alone, at which times we took the _Williamsburg_ down almost to Quantico and they'd have lunch and so forth, just a ladies' luncheon party, and then come back the same day. We had quite a few of those when there were only Mrs. Truman's guests, women.

She never said, that I can recall, that she loved the _Williamsburg_, but, on the other hand, she never said she didn't, either. As far as I can recall, any time the President asked them to go, they went; they nearly always went with him.

Q: Did Margaret have dates on some of these occasions?

Admiral MacDonald: No, Margaret never had dates on the occasions

*On 6 December 1950, _Washington Post_ music critic Paul Hume wrote an unfavorable review of Margaret Truman's singing performance at Constitution Hall the prior evening. Upon reading Hume's remarks, the President immediately dashed off a scathing handwritten note that was later widely publicized.

of being around the Williamsburg or Key West, because there were always so many staff members who were around there. There were people like George Elsey, Clark Clifford, and a lot of those people never had their wives there, most of them never had their wives, so there were always what were called spare men around.* That's one of the things about the trips to Key West. Mrs. Truman and Margaret used to go, but none of the other wives ever went.

Q: It must have been lonesome for them, then?

Admiral MacDonald: Well, they went back and forth quite a bit. They did not stay all of the time. We always used to stay at least three weeks, sometimes a little bit longer. Dennison would be there and Vaughan and Landry. They lived on board always because they liked to live on board. None of the people had their wives except the President.

Q: How frequently did the President resort to the use of a plane?

Admiral MacDonald: He had a plane called the Independence and it was operated by a Colonel Williams, who was a delightful person,

---

*George M. Elsey, Truman's administrative assistant; Clark M. Clifford, special counsel to the President.

and Williams's plane was always available at Key West over at the air station.* The President, after a couple of bad sessions at sea, didn't particularly like to go down in the ship, so he would fly down there. That plane was always available, but he only had the one. It would bring passengers up to Washington and bring them back and things like that. That plane was there, and the President only used it when he was coming or going to Key West. As far as going to Shangri-La is concerned, they always drove. At that time they always drove.

It became very evident to me up there, and I tried to get in and talk with the President about it one time, that we should have a helicopter pad up there so that instead of the two-hour-and-a-half trip up to Shangri-La--the roads were narrow then, they weren't like they are today--he could go up there by helicopter. Well, it was just right after that that they put the pad in, but I'd tried to get it in a year or so before.

Q: The helicopter wasn't in such general use then?

Admiral MacDonald: It wasn't in use at all. We weren't using it at all. For instance, the helicopter was not in use and we used to get our mail by seaplane. We had little seaplanes stationed over at Andrews Air Force Base. They would take the mail down

*Colonel Francis W. Williams, USAF.

and land not too far from us, wherever we were, and we'd send a boat out to pick up the mail and even deliver people for them to take back.

No, the helicopter hadn't come in, but it was obvious to me at the time that the helicopter was coming along and that the only thing we could do would be to put a helicopter pad up there, and it was done. It's done and that's the way they go there now. As a matter of fact, after Eisenhower took over and the Army moved into Camp David, although the guard situation--that's another thing I didn't mention. Whenever the President went up there, there was a Marine detachment from the Naval Gun Factory that always went up there as security people when he was there, a whole Marine detachment. We kept so many Marines up there all of the time that when the President was there we really had a whole detachment of Marines sent up, but we had the facilities for them up there.

Then, when Eisenhower took over and changed the name, the Army took over and put up a great big fence and built new barracks. They built a lot of other new things and moved practically a whole brigade of soldiers into the area, put in fabulous communications systems, of course, underground and all this business. They changed the whole setup.

I think it was probably a year or so afterwards I was up in that area and I wanted to stop by and see what Shangri-La looked like. I was no longer in command of the *Williamsburg*. I couldn't even get near the establishment. The Army wouldn't let you in. They had these great big high wires with electric arrangements. The security had changed completely.

Q: When you were on the Williamsburg, did you have anything to do with the contingency plans in case of attack or what have you, the safety of the President? Were those underground areas constructed by that time?

Admiral MacDonald: No, they weren't constructed. They were just being talked about. They were just in the phase of getting them all under way. That's a good question. That was the phase when they were just beginning to work on it. One of the reasons why the President probably used us more than you might imagine was that there was a period here, during this time, when the White House was being rebuilt, renovated. The President was living over at the Blair House, and the Blair House was not a very happy setup for them, and that's probably why he got out of there as fast as he could all the time. That was a year's arrangement or more when they kind of rebuilt the White House.

Q: Well, they discovered to their horror that it was ready to fall down!

Admiral MacDonald: Oh, yes, a lot of what they called the beams and everything were pretty well rotted out. I've got a lot of things from the beams in the White House.

Q: That was at the time they built the Truman balcony?

Admiral MacDonald: Yes, that's right. There was a lot of discussion at that time whether they were going to renovate or rebuild it, exactly what they would do. A decision had to be made whether they would confine everything to the dimensions that existed or enlarge the whole thing and really change it completely. They finally came up with the idea that they'd renovate it, using the old dimensions, and this really was very restricting.

I'd like to tell you a rather interesting story about changes. It was later on when President Johnson was President. We had a birthday party here in Washington for President Truman, and the President was staying at the Mayflower. He came east just for this particular party, which we had set up at Bolling Field, and we had the wives and the old staff that he had present at Bolling Field. It was a delightful luncheon arrangement, a delightful period, and when Truman got up to recognize the party and thank us and so forth, he said, "When I looked around this room and I see these 40 or 50 people who used to work with me and run the government, we all seemed to work together. We knew what we were trying to do. No one was working at cross purposes.

Once we'd decided on something, we'd all work together on it. Here are the 40 or 50 people who used to run the whole government. Now they have 2,500 people doing the work that you 40 were doing, and no one knows what the other guy's doing. There's no chief of staff coordinating it, there's no way of coordinating what the Sam Hill's going on in the White House."

I thought that was a wonderful remark and it came from President Truman--that they had blown up to such an extent that it was no longer an effective, efficient organization in that executive office. I do know that Truman had meetings with his closest members of the staff. They'd make decisions, and then they all worked together to push them through. It was a good sort of happy arrangement.

Q: Do you think it would be a correct surmise to say that when he was living at Blair House and it was so limited in its size, that this may have been one reason why he was so anxious to get down on the yacht so frequently?

Admiral MacDonald: Oh, I'm sure of it, Jack, I'm absolutely sure of it. I think he hated living in the Blair House. It just was all wrong. Cramped quarters, nothing personal about it, just a cold sort of VIP house arrangement. Without a doubt in my mind, this was one reason why he got out just as much as he could, and it was very easy for him because in ten minutes from the White

House he was down there and could take off his coat and do whatever he wanted to do.

Q: Did he ever remark on that attempt on his life as he came out of Blair House?

Admiral MacDonald: He did, but, you know, it's very vague in my mind now, but the attempt wasn't really on him because he was inside. It was the fact that these people were trying to break in and the policemen outside--I think it was Puerto Ricans at the time that were shooting and everything. He had just gone in the house. They were trying to break in. He was very disturbed. I remember he did remark about it and was very disturbed that such a thing could happen.* He never really thought this type of thing--just like, morning after morning, when he was in town he'd be out walking in the street, along Pennsylvania Avenue at 6:00 o'clock in the morning, and only one Secret Service man with him. He never had the fear that someone was going to do something to him, and he never had the fear on the ship, with all these boats constantly coming up. Sometimes a lot of them were very poor

*On 1 November 1950, two Puerto Ricans stormed the entrance to Blair House while President Truman was on the second floor taking an afternoon nap. Thirty-one shots were fired in three minutes; one of the assailants and one White House policeman were slain. Though Truman had a very conciliatory policy towards Puerto Rico, his would-be attackers hoped the turmoil surrounding his assassination would provide the climate for their country to declare independency.

navigators and it was a little dangerous, but they would be waving and he would wave back. I will say this, that usually when I was going up and down the river, definitely in the daytime, he was always up there on the bridge with me, just standing and talking and looking around or waving, and, boy, the people were thrilled to death to see him up there.

Q: That was a lovely, peaceful time.

Admiral MacDonald: It was. It was a wonderful time.

Q: You might tell me something about some of the outstanding personalities in the White House in that era, the men with whom you were in contact daily.

Admiral MacDonald: At that particular time, Admiral Leahy was there and still helping the President in a military advisory capacity.*

Q: When you first went there?

Admiral MacDonald: That's right. He was still there and, as a matter of fact, he made several trips with us on the

---

*Fleet Admiral William D. Leahy, USN.

Williamsburg, and he remarked one time when we were out in the ocean and it was a little rough, "This old ship has a movement all of her own. She just swings her tail and bounces in all directions."

He didn't enjoy exactly cruising in the Williamsburg very much, but then he never really went with us very much, Admiral Leahy. When he was there, he used to come up in my cabin and the naval aide's cabin because we had our own little mess up there.

Q: He was succeeded by General Bradley, was he not, in that capacity?*

Admiral MacDonald: I don't know that anyone really took over that job exactly. I think the job just died out after Leahy left. Then there was Clark Clifford who was an up-and-coming bright lawyer who used to do a lot of the speechwriting and drafting of legislation for the President. He was very smart and able. Every time we went to Key West, Clark was with us. He was one of the secretaries and he handled all the legislation and budget writing type of thing, and Clark was a good tennis player. He and I used to play tennis quite a bit down in Key West at the

*General of the Army Omar N. Bradley, USA. In early 1949 when Leahy resigned as Truman's military advisor, Bradley was Chief of Staff of the Army. In August of that year he became Chairman of the Joint Chiefs of Staff, a position he held until 1953.

Casa Marina. I guess he was an outstanding tennis player when he was younger.

Connelly was the appointments secretary to Truman.

Q: Matt Connelly?*

Admiral MacDonald: Matt Connelly. He used to go down to Key West but never stayed there. He was always invited by people up around Seaview, up on Miami Beach, so he just disappeared. Once we arrived in Key West, he just took off and went with friends to the Bahamas and every other place. Although he was always in Washington and when I used to have to go to the White House occasionally for certain arrangements or ceremonies that they were having or something like that, Matt was always there when the President was at the White House. He never went with us on the Williamsburg. Matt Connelly never went out there.

Clark Clifford was in one of the groups and he organized one of the poker party groups, and that particular gang was sort of Stanley Woodward and . . .**

Q: He was rather suave, wasn't he?

---

*Matthew J. Connelly, secretary to the President.

**Stanley Woodward, chief protocol officer, Department of State.

Admiral MacDonald: Oh, yes.

Stuart Symington--they had this group, Smathers, all sort of attractive young people at the time, were one group that the President played with--Smathers, Symington, Stanley Woodward, Clark Clifford.* Clark used to be told to organize that group. I don't know who the Sam Hill was organizing the others, except Fred Vinson used to organize the expensive group. I know that. The President and Fred Vinson were very close. They were really close together, and Vinson used to set up these expensive deals, the George Allen gang.

John R. Steelman, who was the sort of secretary for labor matters, unions, and so forth, never went on the Williamsburg on any of our parties, but when we went to Key West--I have to always add this because he sometimes spent two months out of the year down there--Steelman would go down there for a while.** He liked to go down there, but what he was doing, I don't know. A lot of his helpers were down there all of the time. As a matter of fact, several of them moved up into high jobs since then. They would always be down there because they loved to be down there, to be close to the scene, but what they were doing, I don't know.

Bill Hassett was another one of the corresponding secretaries

---

*W. Stuart Symington, Secretary of the Air Force from 1947 to 1950; Representative George A. Smathers (Democrat-Florida).

**John R. Steelman, chairman of the National Security Resource Board from 1948 to 1950.

for the President.* I don't know whether you recall who he was or not, but this man had a fabulous memory for quotations from the Bible, unbelievable knowledge, and he could recall things from the testaments and all that business. He used to write letters for Roosevelt in the beginning.

Q: Yes, he was with Roosevelt.

Admiral MacDonald: He drifted over with Truman, so he wrote the letters that Truman had to sign that would go to, say, the Cardinal or the Pope. One comment I heard made was that Hassett could write a letter turning something down in such a way that it almost seemed like it was yes! He had such fluency of expression.

Now, Hassett was sort of a sickly man at one time. He'd had his problems. I think he had been an alcoholic at one time, but he'd straightened out of that, and he used to love to come down on the *Williamsburg*, but he never participated in a poker party or anything. He just liked to be there. Every evening, particularly if we were anchored or something, he'd come up to my cabin. The guy was wonderful. He would talk about Pope John and he said, "The fellow's done more in two years than all the popes in the last 1,000 years." Pope John's ecumenical council and all

---

*William D. Hassett, corresponding secretary to Presidents Roosevelt and Truman.

these things, he said. But he could quote everything. He got his experience as a newspaper columnist in World War I. He never married, was very able as far as diction and writing the English language was concerned. He was another one of the secretaries who used to do a lot of writing.

One of Clark Clifford's assistants was Charlie Murphy, who just recently left his job, I think, with CAB, Civil Aeronautics Board.* Then there were people like George Elsey, who had worked for Morison in the history.** George was working also in connection with speechwriting and the drafting of messages. He was another one who loved to go down there. I'm not sure that George was married at the time, but I think he was, but he was always there as a spare man because they liked it down there. The weather was usually good during the periods that we were down there.

While I'm talking about this, I might as well tell you that one of the things the President did like to do down there was swim. We had a little place at Key West that they called Truman Beach. He used to walk from the White House down to Truman Beach and go for a swim.

Q: In the ocean?

---

*Charles S. Murphy, administrative assistant to President Truman between 1947 and 1950.

**Samuel Eliot Morison, author of the 15-volume History of United States Naval Operations in World War II.

Admiral MacDonald: Yes, in the ocean. The only thing we had to do when he went down there was watch out for sharks.

Q: Was he a good swimmer?

Admiral MacDonald: He could swim around. He wore his glasses all the time that he was swimming. He'd keep his head up. He liked to do what you call dog fashion. He'd swim around.

Q: Breast stroke?

Admiral MacDonald: Breast stroke arrangement. He used to swim all the time in the Potomac, down at Blackstone Island. Every time I was down there, I'd take samples of water, because pollution was drifting down farther and farther in that area. We were always sampling the water to see whether it was still all right to swim in.

Towards the end of the period, the water was getting pretty damned polluted down that far, and that's about 80 miles down the river. It's 95 miles from Washington to the bay, and Blackstone Island was about 85 miles down there, so we were almost to the bay and here the water down the river was getting polluted.

Anyway, we were always taking samples and nothing ever happened, but the President used to go in for a swim during the summertime when the water temperature was all right.

Vaughan had an aide, a colonel, who always loved to go down there, too. His main job at the time was to take care of these two or three Army communicators who came down from the White House.

I've got to say that Bill Rigdon, who was Admiral Dennison's right-hand man in the naval aide's office, was the man who really got all of these parties organized, as far as Key West was concerned.* He's the one who kept me informed, and he's the one I always dealt with in finding out who was coming, how many were going to be there, and all that business, so that we always were prepared. Bill Rigdon was always with us at Key West, and he really took care of the supervising as far as assignment of guests in the different houses and so forth were concerned. He was Dennison's assistant. I think he retired as a lieutenant commander. In a way, he sort of got the Key West parties organized so that we would know what was going on and let me know. Then afterwards, Bill Rigdon would write the sort of history of each event, with pictures and so forth. We had a Navy photographer and he took a lot of pictures, compiled a lot of the things into a sort of chronological book, publication, and gave it around to the different people.

Q: I think you had one incident involving photography that was

---

*Lieutenant Commander William M. Rigdon, USN.

acceptable to the President, didn't you?

Admiral MacDonald: Which one was that?

Q: Didn't he get angry about someone taking pictures of him in a very informal way or something?

Admiral MacDonald: Actually, the press used to come down there. They were billeted down in the officers' mess, and the Secret Service was down there, too. No, wait a minute, the Secret Service was billeted in the officers' mess at the naval air station there. The press was in there, too, and some of the press had to live out in town. But, you know, the press cooperated with the President's staff. There's one person I have to mention, his public relations officer--first it was Steve Early and then he was relieved by Charlie Ross, who was absolutely great.* He could handle all of those press people beautifully. Of course, at that time, the press contingent that followed the President didn't amount to over a dozen, maybe 15 at the most, sometimes.

Q: Was there an official photographer?

---

*Stephen T. Early; Charles G. Ross.

Admiral MacDonald: Navy, yes. The Navy assigned us an official photographer, but that was taken care of by Rigdon through the naval aide's office, and they took a lot of pictures.

When we were down there, the commanding officer of the station had a fishing boat fixed up, which was a converted PT boat, for the President. We used to use the presidential fishing boat quite frequently. We'd go out fishing down there. We'd have fishing parties, and we'd go over to the Tortugas, which were about 60 miles away. The fishing around the Dry Tortugas is absolutely excellent, but sometimes it was too rough to do any of that.

The President really loved that area down there and, of course, the city just boomed with the fact that the President was there. They now have Truman Boulevard, Truman this, and Truman that. He even made some visits after he became an ex-President. They loved it. The city people had a lot of parties given that included a lot of these local bigwigs. They got very friendly, the head of the radio station there, the mayor of the city. It was great for Key West that Truman loved to go down there, but he really did love it because he could just put on a Hawaiian shirt or something and a pair of slacks and walk right down the beach, and here he was behind the fence of the naval air station. He had all the security in the world. He was not molested by anyone. He liked it very much and, of course, he had these wonderful holidays of walking, playing poker, and he seemed to have a hell of a happy life. But he did have to make the decisions and he had to make some tough political decisions. The guy was a politician and he could make them.

I will say that Mr. Truman was the most loyal person to the individuals that he wanted to be close to. He was loyal. He stuck by General Vaughan through thick and thin. He was a very blunt, frank, outspoken person on many occasions. He wasn't the tactful guy that you would think, but he was sound, and most of his remarks, as he used to express it, came from just good old common sense, good old stubborn Missouri mule sense, and he invariably was right that he did express himself and he was quick to explode in connection with certain things.

I remember a couple of times when we were out at sea and there were some calls coming through in connection with some political appointments and the names that were submitted to him. When he heard a couple of them, he just hit the ceiling and he swore, "the bastard," and so forth, and how the hell was he going to let him get anywhere. I mean he picked enemies and he wasn't going to help them along.

I just happened to think of one thing now. Admiral Dennison and the President, we were out on a trip in the Williamsburg when we got the news about the Missouri running aground. We were out in the Chesapeake Bay. Well, the minute we got the news about the situation, the President wanted to know exactly what it was all about. So Dennison came up and we broke out the charts and we started trying to figure out what the hell had happened, how the Sam Hill could Bill Brown have run the Missouri aground down there in Norfolk.* We talked on the telephone a little bit, and I remember Dennison talking with me because we were trying to figure out what the Sam Hill happened down there.

The thing is that Captain Brown really didn't feel his responsibility; this was the unfortunate part in this whole case. One of the things that was very bad about the Missouri running aground was that the Secretary of Defense wanted to put all the battleships into mothballs. They wanted to do away with them, and it was only because of Truman, who wanted to keep the Missouri going in the Navy, and it was the only battleship we had still on active duty, and it was due to Truman's decisions to keep the Missouri still operating. And here the Missouri runs aground, so it was quite a blow to everyone, particularly in the ship that day!

Q: Bob Dennison had been the skipper.

Admiral MacDonald: Bob Dennison had been the skipper of the Missouri, and it was just one of those terrible incidents.**

---

*USS Missouri (BB-63) ran aground on 17 January 1950 off Thimble Shoals while under the command of Captain William D. Brown, USN.

**As a captain, Dennison commanded the Missouri from April 1947 until January 1948.

The net result was that Truman asked Dennison to fly down there and talk with all the people. Dennison went down there--I don't know whether he told you this or not in connection with the *Missouri* incident. But he went down and talked with the people and they soon found out that the captain, Bill Brown, whom I knew because he had the *Nicholas* with me in the Pacific and was a great skipper, just felt that it wasn't his fault that the ship ran aground.

Of course, the other thing that Dennison had to find out was were they going to be able to get her off--she really ran aground--and whether they were going to get the darned ship off the beach. That happened when Truman was on board the ship, that particular incident, and it wasn't a pleasant period at all.

Q: Did he explode?

Admiral MacDonald: I don't remember exactly what all he said. I think he was just so dumbfounded that the thing had happened that he wasn't prepared for anything. Ordinarily, he didn't lack for expletives.

The only other thing I can recall is that he used to invite me to come down, particularly after we anchored in the evening, if we were going down early, to come down and either join him playing poker or having a drink with him before dinner. I used to go down there occasionally and sit around watching them play, but as far as drinking, I didn't drink there, although the bar was wide open in his section; there's no doubt about it. People used to question me about that, and I said, "What he does is what he wants to do." I didn't participate in the drinking aspect in that ship. But we did, as I mentioned, have cocktails in the other ships, which were noncommissioned.

I would just like to summarize my own thinking in connection with President Truman, particularly now, after the fact of having been associated to a certain extent with Eisenhower and having met Kennedy and even knowing Johnson and having been an aide at the White House under Roosevelt. Mr. Truman, without a doubt, was a great person and probably will go down in history as being one of the great Presidents of the United States, and I base this on the many, many terrific decisions he had to make. They were impossible for so many people. Johnson never could make decisions, and this is why he got out of the presidency. Truman never hesitated to make a decision. He may have been wrong in some cases, but he made them and he stood by them. He used common sense and he was a real, loyal person, even to the extent of consideration of the country. This man wasn't out to make a lot of money; he was a President who saw to the fact that the widows of ex-Presidents were allowed to get a pension. Never before had they been able to get a pension. He also was the one who took care of the pension plan in a very mediocre way of $25,000 for a President, to make sure that the family wouldn't suffer. The fellow was a great person, and I think that we benefited. I really had the most terrific respect for him. He was a fine person. I won't say that he was a great scholar or anything like that; he was just a fine person.

Q: That's perhaps the best compliment one could pay, and having been associated so intimately with him over a period of three years, you really could make an estimate.

Admiral MacDonald: Of course, I wasn't as close as General Vaughan or anything, but I did spend an awful lot of time with him alone and just in those periods I found out that he was just a great, great person. And he wasn't grasping for money or fame or anything like that. He just wanted to do a good job in a sound way. That's about what I have to say about Mr. Truman.

Q: Thank you very much, sir.

Interview Number 7 with Rear Admiral Donald J. MacDonald,
U.S. Navy (Retired)

Place: Admiral MacDonald's residence in Washington, D.C.

Date: Tuesday morning, 27 December 1979

Subject: Biography

Interviewer: John T. Mason, Jr.

Q: Donald, I'm delighted at the prospect of completing this series of interviews with you and completing it by covering the balance of your career in the Navy.

Last time, you talked rather extensively about being skipper of the Williamsburg, and you talked about your boss in that capacity, who happened to be the President of the United States. Now we're ready to leave Washington in 1951, in September, when you took command of an AKA, the Marquette.

Admiral MacDonald: The Marquette was an amphibious landing ship, cargo, AKA class, and her mission was to load up Marines, a lot of their equipment, and so forth, transport them around, and then see that they were landed properly on the beach that they had been set for.

Q: This was to be your major ship command, wasn't it?

Admiral MacDonald: No, it wasn't, no. The Marquette was just an interval. At that time, most of my class were getting command of amphibious ships, having the top commands later on.

We had a very interesting cruise in the Marquette by spending two tours of duty within a year in the Mediterranean.

Q: How many months each time?

Admiral MacDonald: Three months at a time, and then when we'd come back, why, we'd go on landing operations down at Vieques Island.

Q: Who had the Sixth Fleet at that time?

Admiral MacDonald: That's what I was trying to recall. The chief of staff was Captain Parker, Butch Parker, who's a great friend of mine, and I was trying to recall who had the Sixth Fleet.* Butch Parker was the chief of staff, a great friend, and Red Yeager was chief of staff on the cruiser division staff, and while we were over there, of course, the flagship always anchored up at Villefranche.** We were anchored down near Juan-les-Pins, in the Gulf of Juan-les-Pins.

Being friends, I used to see--I call him Butch, but he later

---

*Captain Edward N. Parker, USN. When MacDonald first took command of the Marquette, Commander Sixth Fleet was Vice Admiral Matthias B. Gardner, USN.

**Captain Howard A. Yeager, USN.

became Vice Admiral Parker. I don't know whether you've interviewed him or not.

Q: No.*

Admiral MacDonald: I had known him from the days in California, being in the battleship California. Later, he commanded one of the destroyers in the Battle of Guadalcanal, which was right ahead of the O'Bannon, but that was sunk and he was rescued. But we got together a number of times and it was a very enjoyable cruise. Mediterranean cruises invariably went east and west, depending on the season, but we were so short of ships at the time that when I came back, after a short period we were ordered back again. So out of the year we spent almost six months over there.

Q: Was that because of the fracas out in Korea?

Admiral MacDonald: No.

Q: The shortage of ships?

---

*Vice Admiral Parker was interviewed in 1985 for the oral history collection.

Admiral MacDonald: It could have been on the East Coast. I don't recall exactly now. I'd have to refresh my memory.

It was an interesting cruise, and while I was on my second tour over there, I got orders to come back and take over as head of the Department of Foreign Languages at the Naval Academy. So I was relieved over there, in Marseilles.

Nothing unusual happened in the Marquette. We participated in landing exercises and cruised with the Sixth Fleet.

Q: The Royal Navy was pretty much in evidence still in the Mediterranean, wasn't it?

Admiral MacDonald: It certainly was. When I went back later with a destroyer squadron, we used to get together. As a matter of fact, we operated with the Royal Navy at that time.

Q: In 1951-52, you mean?

Admiral MacDonald: Yes. I used to play tennis a lot with the captain of a British destroyer squadron who was over there, and we used to continue that relationship even in Malta. I happened to be in Malta at the time when Lord Louis Mountbatten was commander in chief in the Mediterranean.* Of course, I

*Admiral of the Fleet Lord Louis Mountbatten, Commander in Chief Mediterranean from 1952 to 1954.

associated with the British all the time on Malta. We had a lot of delightful gatherings together, but Lord Louis Mountbatten brought out his debutante daughter when I was there and I was included in the invitations to be present. I had met him in London.

It was a very pleasant cruise. I enjoyed the cruise in the Mediterranean, and after my Department of Foreign Languages tour of duty, I was assigned commander of a destroyer squadron, and we also had a cruise in the Mediterranean. But we'll cover right now when I went as head of the Department of Foreign Languages.

Q: Was your assignment to the Naval Academy a surprise to you or had you sought it?

Admiral MacDonald: It was sort of a surprise. I was told when I arrived--Turner Joy was the Superintendent at the time and Taylor Keith was his aide--Taylor Keith told me that he was the one who had asked to get me there.* My tour of duty there was for about three years and was just sort of routine in a way but very pleasant duty. One thing that was different from the usual tour of running or heading a department was the fact that I was sent off on the midshipman cruise as chief of staff for midshipmen and

*Vice Admiral Charles Turner Joy, USN, Superintendent of the Naval Academy from 1952 until 1954; Captain Robert Taylor Scott Keith, USN, Commandant of Midshipmen, 1954 to 1956.

Admiral Libby was the task force commander.

Q: Ruthven Libby?*

Admiral MacDonald: Ruthven Libby was task force commander and Charlie Melson was the chief of staff.** He was a captain then. Arleigh Burke headed up the midshipmen cruiser division, and we had two battleships and two cruisers, the New Jersey and the Missouri.*** Of course, I was on the staff of Libby, messed with the admiral, and stood staff watches.

Q: What was your particular duty then?

Admiral MacDonald: I was chief of staff to the admiral for the midshipmen.

Q: What does that mean?

Admiral MacDonald: Well, it means that I was chief of staff for the purposes of operating the squadron. Charlie Melson was the

---

*Rear Admiral Ruthven E. Libby, USN, Commander Battleship-Cruiser Force, U.S. Atlantic Fleet, 1954-1956. His memoirs are contained in the Naval Institute collection.

**Captain Charles L. Melson, USN, whose oral history is in the Naval Institute collection.

***Rear Admiral Arleigh A. Burke, USN, whose extensive memoirs are included in the Naval Institute oral history collection. The cruise described here took place in 1954.

senior chief of staff, there was myself, and then a classmate of mine, Brute Roeder, who later became a vice admiral, was the operations officer.* And Melson, I will say, I never thought much of him at the Naval Academy and I never thought much of him on the cruise. I stood all of the midwatches, staff watches, for the task force, and Charlie would take the evening watch and Roeder had to take the morning watch, so there were just the three of us standing watches for the whole task force, and I had all the midwatches, so I didn't get much sleep on that cruise. But did we put in to some nice ports.

Q: Was this a European cruise?

Admiral MacDonald: Yes, it was a European cruise, southern European. We went to Spain and France and so forth. When we were in Lisbon, anchored there, why, of course, the ambassador was Colonel Bob Guggenheim, whom I knew quite well from Washington, and his wife Polly. They gave some very nice, interesting parties for Libby and his staff, for which Charlie Melson kept all the invitations in his drawer.

Q: Being secretive?

---

*Captain Bernard F. Roeder, USN.

Admiral MacDonald: Yes. Well, he knew that I knew the Guggenheims very well, so I don't know. You've probably talked with Charlie Melson. I don't have much in the way of feelings, but, anyway, it was pleasant. It was during my tour of duty at the Navy Department and was the one sort of unusual event that happened in that type of a life.

Q: Was it only one summer cruise that you went on or did you go on others?

Admiral MacDonald: No, just one.

Q: Tell me about the Department of Foreign Languages. How big was it? What were your obligations there?

Admiral MacDonald: Actually, your obligation--you're also on the academic board, you work with the admiral in connection with the operation of the academic curriculum, the mission, and all that business, but then you run a department which, at that time, had 18 or 20 professors.

Q: Were they all civilians?

Admiral MacDonald: No, there were several. There was one lieutenant who spoke Spanish, who was regular Navy, and we had one Air Force officer at the time. Otherwise, they were all civilians, professors, or assistant professors. At that time, the Naval Academy had a requirement that all students had to take a foreign language, and we had about six different foreign languages.

Q: Oh, you did have, it was more than just French and Spanish?

Admiral MacDonald: Oh, yes, it was Russian, Italian, Portuguese, Spanish, German, and French. Of course, for Russian, Lemieux is still down there.* Professor Lemieux was the authority on Russian. The department ran so that these boys would learn something. We had a very good top professor in each of the different branches.

There was a very interesting thing. Later, when Joy left, Boone took over as Superintendent.

Q: Freddie Boone?

Admiral MacDonald: Freddie Boone, and Charlie Buchanan was the chief of staff.** Boone, being an aviator, wanted to cut back on

*Professor Claude P. Lemieux, who taught Russian and French at the Naval Academy from 1940 through 1979, and again from 1984 to 1985.

**Vice Admiral Walter F. Boone, USN, Superintendent of the Naval Academy from 1954 to 1956; Rear Admiral Charles A. Buchanan, Commandant of Midshipmen from 1952 to 1954.

the humanities, our subjects, and inject more subjects that might qualify people to be naval aviators. Well, we battled this my last year or two down there so we wouldn't lose more and more of our curriculum time.

Q: He was veering toward the trade-school idea, was he?

Admiral MacDonald: He almost felt that every graduate should be a qualified aviator. That was the way he was pointing. We had to battle this thing, but, thank goodness, some of the people over in the English Department were very helpful, because they said the qualifications of the average midshipmen going to the Naval Academy don't know anything about English, don't know how to speak it or anything else. And the best way to learn English is to study a foreign language, because there you learn how sentence structure is put together and that you have to have certain subjects, verbs, and objects, and how to qualify and all this business. So we were able to maintain our full time, under great difficulty.

Q: Did you have some assistance from the Secretary of the Navy?

Admiral MacDonald: Not particularly, at the time. They were trying to cut back in all aspects so that they could get more time for aviation because this was the coming thing. As a matter of fact, the one great thing that happened while I was there that disillusioned me was that I began to feel, toward my third year as head of department, that unless--I even advised some of the sons of friends of mine who were there when they'd ask me the questions--that unless they were really physically qualified to become aviators or submarine officers, because this was the way the Navy was going, that being a general line officer was not a great sort of allure for the future. And when they finally dipped down in the selection list and picked Ramage, way below me, then I decided that maybe I wanted to get out of the service, because I could see the handwriting on the wall.* I was talked out of that, but, later on, when I got back into the Pentagon, I saw how things were going and that was one of the reasons why I asked for early retirement, because unless you were an aviator or a submariner, they were well organized in politics, and the poor old general line officer was almost on his own.

Q: Primarily the aviator, wasn't it?

Admiral MacDonald: Aviators, they were very strong, very cliquish. They looked after their own people, they made sure that they were appointed to the right jobs so they could be

*Rear Admiral Lawson P. Ramage, USN, a Medal of Honor-winning submariner, was selected for flag rank in July 1955. He retired as a vice admiral in April 1970. His oral history is in the Naval Institute collection.

promoted.

Q: Tell me a little more about it. What proportion of the boys would choose some language like Russian or Portuguese? How did it work out?

Admiral MacDonald: Russian and German were probably the two hardest languages, the toughest. In the beginning, probably more people wanted to take Spanish or French if they had a touch of it, maybe, in school.

Q: So it was an easy course?

Admiral MacDonald: It was supposed to have been a little bit easier for them. If they had any background in other languages like Italian or Portuguese, why, they'd try to take that. The exceptional person usually put in to study Russian. Yet, at the time, we knew that this was going to be one of the great languages for the future, Russian. They filled up their quota of people who wanted to study Russian, and they had some very smart fellows. As a matter of fact, one of the smartest was Nicholas Brown's son, who's still in the Navy, as I recall, who was very fluent in French when he went to the Naval Academy, and he took

Russian and stood at the top of the Russian class.* A very attractive fellow and he was excellent.

I think Portuguese probably was the least desirable and Italian probably next. Quite a few people studied German. I had to work with them in order to divide them up as far as professors were concerned.

Q: Your language abilities were German and French?

Admiral MacDonald: No, Spanish basically, and then I had studied German and I had been in France and studied. Basically, my wife's family were German and that's her second language really, but we never really talked at home. I used to take German, even when I was head of the department, study with the head professor. Unless you use a language, it gets away from you very quickly.

Q: It certainly does. Except, perhaps, for reading ability.

Admiral MacDonald: Yes, reading ability, but in German, where everything has to match, like your different declensions and different genders, all different. In English, you have "the," in German you have "die" and "das" and "der." I'm sort of rusty, because we never use these languages any more, but at that time I

---

*Midshipman Nicholas Brown, USN, Naval Academy class of 1956.

was interested in Spanish, which I had done the most study in myself, but I never was really fluent in it. But when you get to a country where they speak the language, it comes back to you a little bit, not completely, but after a while . . .

Q: Did you, as head of the language department, have anything to do with the head of the language department at West Point?

Admiral MacDonald: No, except we had exchange instructors.

Q: You exchanged instructors?

Admiral MacDonald: Yes, that occurred in my period. We'd send only the military; we'd send an instructor up there and they'd send some down here.

Q: So I take it the method of teaching was the same in both places?

Admiral MacDonald: No, they were completely different at West Point. At West Point everything was more on a permanent basis in the department of languages up there. All the people were permanent people.

Q: They were all military but they were all permanent?

Admiral MacDonald: Yes, they were permanent. In other words, the retired military stayed in the job; they were head of department and so forth. They stayed in it, whereas in the Navy, like my executive officer, a submarine officer, just never spoke any language, really, except maybe English, but he was awfully nice. Up at West Point, they were permanent people assigned, just like the professional people . . .

Q: In a university?

Admiral MacDonald: In a university, the same idea, or even like in our English Department down there we had people who were permanent. The head of the English Department was a naval officer, but he had permanent people who were running the classes and so forth.

Q: What was the method of teaching languages at the Naval Academy in that time? Was it somewhat by rote or was the new system, the Berlitz system, coming in?

Admiral MacDonald: It was by rote. I mean they had the textbooks and they had to prepare their lessons and they had certain oral conversation. They had the different dinners where we got an attache and so forth to come down and talk to, say, the Italian group, and the German attache to talk to the German group.

Q: To speak to them in their language?

Admiral MacDonald: To speak to them in that language. A lot of these boys were pretty good and they worked hard at it. The exams, of course, were based on the textbooks. They did change the style of textbooks to a reading type of thing, rather than just grammar and so forth. They had to learn the grammar, of course, but, on the other hand, they did an awful lot of reading.

Q: It wasn't all drill!

Admiral MacDonald: It wasn't all drill, no, and people got a little interested, and if they wanted to work a little bit harder, we had extra study for them and they worked on it harder, if they wanted to.

One of the things we found was that a lot of the athletes had a pretty rough time with these foreign languages, and they didn't have the time to work on it. Trying to keep someone like Fred Franco in the Naval Academy because he couldn't get through the head of the language department--this was a decision I had to make at the academic board!*

---

*Midshipman Frederick J. Franco, USN, football standout in the Naval Academy class of 1954.

Q: Were they somewhat partial to the star athletes?

Admiral MacDonald: Well, Admiral Boone was Superintendent at the time, and he didn't have the same feeling like he has today about having good athletes at the Naval Academy. I don't think he was an athlete at all when he was there, so his interest wasn't exactly along that line, but mine was. Elliott Loughlin, who is down there now heading up the Foundation, was director of athletics.* We worked together, and we finally got some of these athletes in a position where they could stay in the Naval Academy and not be thrown out!

It was an interesting tour. Socially, it was a very delightful one.

Q: I would imagine so. Where did you live?

Admiral MacDonald: We lived on Porter Road.

Actually, several events occurred while we were there. One was when Eisenhower, on his only trip in the Williamsburg, came around to Annapolis and they anchored out there. Turner Joy gave a reception for the President in his quarters, and my wife and I were invited. I had a good chance to talk with Eisenhower in

*Captain C. Elliott Loughlin, USN, was director of athletics from 1954 to 1957. His oral history is in the Naval Institute collection.

connection with the *Williamsburg*, because by that time he had committed himself to put it out of commission, so I talked to him and said, "Mr. President, I think you've made a mistake in saying that you would put the *Williamsburg* out of commission, because maybe you don't realize the advantage of the *Williamsburg* in the way that you can get away from everything quickly, really getting away from all the sort of official duties at the White House."

But he said the unfortunate part was that his brother Milton, when they were campaigning, had hit on the theme of economy and one of the things that he was stressing was to do away with all the luxury items like the *Williamsburg*, and that he had committed himself to follow through on that particular item. Therefore, he was going to put her out of commission. I told him at the time that the *Williamsburg* not only was a presidential yacht, which the people wanted him to have, but we ran the White House mess, set it up with my stewards from the *Williamsburg*, operated Shangri-La--at that time he was just getting ready to change it to Camp David--the Navy, the *Williamsburg*, paid for it, paid for a lot of things, even the painting of the White House because there was no budget money available to do a lot of things. When they went in the private car, we sent our boys in the private car, took care of it, and so forth.

Well, he said he was beginning to realize some of these things, but he'd gone too far in committing himself, so he put the *Williamsburg* out of commission.

Q: We've heard something more recently of a similar nature, haven't we? Carter and the _Sequoia_.

Admiral MacDonald: Well, the _Sequoia_ was never really a presidential yacht. In the good old days, you would have called it the admiral's barge or something. Roosevelt used it temporarily while he was getting the _Potomac_ ready as the presidential yacht. It was not a commissioned vessel. There was an officer in charge in the _Sequoia_, and it was really the Secretary of the Navy's boat.

Q: Yes.

Admiral MacDonald: When Eisenhower put the _Williamsburg_ out of commission, he then took the two boats that I had to go along with the _Williamsburg_ and changed their names, the _Barbara Anne_ and something else. Later, when Kennedy came in, he changed it to the _Honey Fitz_ and a few others. They were not commissioned vessels and they really only had an officer in charge, even a chief petty officer to run them.

Q: But the _Williamsburg_ was actually a yacht and was the successor to the _Mayflower_, was she not?

Admiral MacDonald: Well, there was one in between, the _Potomac_, which Roosevelt had and which later they either gave or sold to the State of Maryland. It was a converted minesweeper which they fixed up as the presidential yacht for Roosevelt. But Eisenhower also changed the name of Shangri-La to Camp David, and the Army, at that time, moved in to take over all of the communications, security, and everything else. They completely changed Camp David from the Navy rustic area that it used to be. When President Truman used to go up there, we used to send a detachment of Marines, just when he was up there. Otherwise, the Williamsburg personnel took care of the whole camp. We did all the work, and the financing was done through the Williamsburg's budget.

That was one incident that happened when we were at the Naval Academy, this visit by the President on the Williamsburg, and that was the last trip she made.* She went out of commission right after that. That was rather early.

Q: You told me, off tape, that after Eisenhower had decommissioned the Williamsburg, she then had a future career when Kennedy became President. What was that?

Admiral MacDonald: Yes. Kennedy gave the ship to Woods Hole for oceanographic and research work, but in order to equip her

*President Eisenhower's cruise in the Williamsburg was 14-18 May 1953. She was decommissioned 30 June 1953.

properly, they had to redesign her.* They turned over the design to a group of marine architects who consulted me at the time in connection with knowing what maybe they could do. And they finally did turn her out as the Anton Bruun, and she was sent out to the Indian Ocean to perform oceanographic duties.** She was out there for some time. I don't recall when they brought her back, but obviously she couldn't have been very satisfactory as a ship because she had characteristics of instability and so forth. I never did see her after they had redesigned her. They probably had to take off all of the heavy air-conditioning equipment and possibly a lot of what we called the pig-iron ballast down in the bilges, where we tried to make her more stable. What they really did, I don't know, but, as you say, she then was sold and became a sort of restaurant motel in Delaware.

Q: Anchored in the backwaters of the Delaware.

Admiral MacDonald: There is a group here that operates these little tour boats, and they were very interested. They also came to me to get a lot of information about it, because they were

---

*After being struck from the Navy list on 1 April 1962, she was transferred to the National Science Foundation on 9 August 1962 for use by the Woods Hole Oceanographic Institute.

**The vessel was renamed in honor of a noted Danish marine biologist. See Stewart B. Nelson, Oceanographic Ships Fore and Aft (Washington, D.C.: U.S. Government Printing Office, 1971), page 188.

interested in buying her and bringing her down here, but with her high structure the way she is, or was, they couldn't get her under the bridges. So they were working on that concept of how to cut her down so that they could get her up and tie her up in Georgetown, where they have a dock for the touring boats, and probably use her just for sightseeing and maybe even as a restaurant-motel type of a ship. The last I knew, because I talked with a friend who's involved in this sort of syndicate, it's not finished business yet. They're still trying to work on this thing, to get her down here.

Q: It seems like an awfully sad fate, however, for a noble ship.

Admiral MacDonald: Surely. The sad fate was when she was decommissioned in the first place. However, I don't think that any President today, with our rapid communications and the way they travel around by air all the time, that it would be very suitable for the purposes we used to use her for, like tying her up at the navy yard here and plying up and down the Potomac River and Chesapeake Bay.

Q: As you pointed out, in Truman's day it was a place to get away from the demands of the presidency. Our present President finds Camp David--he's up there all the time.

Admiral MacDonald: Mentioning Camp David, when the present one was elected, I wrote a letter to him and said, "Here you have a wonderful opportunity to change that name back to Shangri-La. Every President since Eisenhower has changed the name of everything, and the Democrats could have changed it back to Shangri-La."

I got a letter back saying that no, it was too well known as Camp David, but they changed the names of all the other detachments, other ships. Nixon sold the Barbara Anne and some of those. He sold those off, too.

But the funny part, Jack, getting back to when Eisenhower was in Annapolis on the last and only cruise he made in her. I talked to him about this economy that his brother had sold him on, and one of the things I realized was that the Air Force was so anxious to get him--where we were spending only about $100,000 on the Williamsburg, the Air Force was willing to spend millions of dollars to build Lowry Air Force Base out in Colorado for him and headquarters out there, just so that they could get him in their hands more frequently. So there was no economy involved in all of this, because this was the one opportunity, and, boy, they were so anxious. All of the time under Truman, the Air Force felt they were neglected and they never had a chance to do anything like get the President under their control.

Q: Since they've become an independent branch of the services, they've been more aggressive than the Navy.

Admiral MacDonald: Yes, they certainly have. I would swear that enlarging Lowry Air Force Base and building it up as a base, new planes, and all this business--because they spent millions and millions of dollars, where we wouldn't have even spent that in many years the way it was going. There was no economy there. It was just on paper that they were going to do it and this is what they were going to do, but they never followed through in telling how they spent more.

Q: Revert back to the Naval Academy and tell me a little more about the social life you enjoyed there during your three years.

Admiral MacDonald: The social life at the Naval Academy, particularly as head of department, was very pleasant. In the first place, you're assigned very nice quarters and there's a lot of activity going on all of the time. A lot of the social life stemmed around the different heads of departments. We also knew a lot of townspeople in Annapolis and our social life there was very good.

Q: What sort of contact did you have with the midshipmen? Did you have them in the house very often?

Admiral MacDonald: Yes, particularly sons of friends and so forth. We used to invite them in, and when their fathers and mothers would come down they'd stay with us in order to see their sons. The midshipmen used to come over, some of them, people we knew, would come over a lot just to have a place to go. Of course, the commandant did a lot of entertaining, and they had nice parties because they had a couple of young girls who were just about the age to be interested in midshipmen. They had a lot of gatherings and we were usually always included at all of those.

Q: Did you have anything to do with the Board of Visitors?

Admiral MacDonald: The Board of Visitors checked out our whole operation in the different departments and you had to prepare a situation report. They'd call them all in and review what the recommendations might be.

Q: Were there educators on the Board of Visitors in that time?

Admiral MacDonald: The Board of Visitors is appointed by the President and there were, yes, Father Hesburgh and a lot of top people, heads of universities and so forth, including well-known politicians, congressmen.* Dick Lankford used to be on the board, Father Hesburgh, and payoff people, politicians.** The President would give someone sort of a job where he'd get a little recognition. They had people who were pretty well qualified in certain things. We had to meet all of these requirements and standards of being a qualified school.

Q: An accredited school?

Admiral MacDonald: An accredited school. I really haven't given much thought about a lot of things, but you had to always be prepared to defend what you were doing in your department. Of course, foreign languages at the time was not exactly one of those considered most professional. As a matter of fact, as I was mentioning earlier in connection with Boone, who wanted to cut back more and more on this foreign language study, I went over to the archives and museum there and broke out the original papers of the charter and the mission of the Naval Academy, and, right there, from the very beginning, you see that it was a requirement that officers who were going to be gentlemen had to learn foreign languages in their travels, way back in the beginning, and produced this at one of our Academic Board

---

*Reverend Theodore M. Hesburgh, president of the University of Notre Dame.

**Representative Richard E. Lankford (Democrat-Maryland).

meetings, and they weren't too happy. But we did hold the line at that time under great pressure to have the whole damned thing changed. They wanted to take time from the English Department, from the humanities completely, to inject into a built-up aviation program.

Q: And to lose sight of the fact that naval officers, by virtue of their vocation and the fact that they travel around the world, are almost diplomats?

Admiral MacDonald: This was pointed out in the very beginning, that they had to represent the United States, particularly the officers. Of course, even the enlisted men are representatives of the United States, and they also should conduct themselves in a manner that would bring credit on the country and also be capable of being as well educated as possible. But foreign languages in America just were not pushed at all. I think that now there's more circulation of students from other countries, and there's a little more emphasis being put on it today, but there was a period there when just no one learned a foreign language. They were taken out of the courses of a lot of the universities so far as requirements were concerned. It no longer became a required subject to be studied, foreign languages. Just like they dropped Latin practically, and Greek. They just almost disappeared, and yet Greek is a sort of brain--studies that make you think and also awfully good for stimulating your brain by having to think in a foreign language. So many of the scholars really are quite fluent.

Take, for example, the Pope when he was over here talking in different languages. It's such an impressive thing and a thing that people admire in a person, to be able to shift from one language to another, to have that capability.

Q: It's a mark of the educated man.

Admiral MacDonald: Yes.

Q: It has this one aspect, too, it seems to me. We've had in our history a tendency to be isolationist in this country, being self-satisfied with our own land. Languages have the tendency to have you reach out and think of other people.

Admiral MacDonald: The funny part about it is that it's changing again, but 20-some years ago, during the period we're discussing right now, the emphasis had almost gone on making everything who went to school and took a classical course have to have so many points or credits in a foreign language. That disappeared and they could shift into other things like sociology and psychology or something. There's nothing wrong with psychology, but the sociology aspect is terrible!

Q: Kind of an amorphous subject!

Admiral MacDonald: Yes, well, it's the result of this sort of welfare state we have today, but they recognized it way back, and it was all written down in the minutes of the meeting of the Academy Board way back in the Naval Academy's history about great emphasis placed on the students--midshipmen--learning Spanish and French and so forth. That, of course, used to be the whole setup. We only taught French and Spanish at one time, when I was at the Naval Academy. Of course, it broadened out and, all of a sudden, they wanted to take that away from us.

Fortunately, they still have a department down there. I don't know how it's operating today, but they still have one. It's probably one of the least-considered departments at the Naval Academy.

Q: Tell me about your staff arrangements in the Department of Foreign Languages.

Admiral MacDonald: Basically, they had duty professors. Particularly during the summer vacations, if they didn't have duty, they could travel on their own and basically the ones who taught the specific languages, go to those countries and enhance their ability and so forth, and they did an awful lot of writing of textbooks for us. They wrote them the way that the midshipmen wanted them written so that the midshipmen could handle it, and, basically, those were the textbooks we were using. Most of them were produced by our own people.

Q: Who, incidentally, got royalties on them, I suppose?

Admiral MacDonald: Oh, yes, royalties definitely.

The other thing was that we also paid tuition for people to go up to Middlebury during the summer to get their master's and also work on their Ph.D., where they could get accredited along that line. Some of them would spend their summers there when they were not having the duty requirement of staying at the Naval Academy, because we did have short classes there during the summer for the plebes. Not much, but some, particularly extra instruction for athletes.

Q: You did have a number of civilian professors who were also of foreign extraction, didn't you? A man teaching French would very often be a Frenchman?

Admiral MacDonald: Oh, yes. As a matter of fact, we had quite a few. For instance, the people who taught Spanish were basically Spaniards, yes, but a lot of them had been there a long time. When I was back there as head of the department, some of them who were teaching Spanish taught me Spanish. They'd been there a long time, but they had never gotten accredited like getting a Ph.D. or anything, but they were considered professors. This is where the thing was a little difficult.

Yes, absolutely, there were those fellows, but then there were also some Americans, fellows like the head of the German Department, he was an American, but he spoke beautiful German. I think that basically the head of the language branch was a full professor and he had six or more, depending on the size of the classes he had to handle, because every midshipman had to take a language for two years. I think that may be cut back today. We tried to hold onto two years, anyway, and that had been cut from three years. It used to be that we had three years in a language. That was cut back to two. So that your classes were composed of the entire class, whether it was the plebe class or the youngster class, they all had to take a language, so they had to have professors to handle that quota of people.

Well, that was the same in all of the subjects until they started being able to have some elective subjects. Now, I don't know how that works. That's something that came on within the last six or seven years. We also, of course, used to conduct special classes for some of the athletes who were having trouble so that they could stay up academically.

You had your duty watches and so forth assigned to you, just like you would aboard any other ship. You had to be available and handle whatever was going on.

It was a pleasant tour of duty, but I don't know whether it enhances you particularly for the future as far as a naval career is concerned.

Q: Marking time?

Admiral MacDonald: It used to be that they assigned a Superintendent who was sort of a person everyone could look up to, who had established himself in the Navy as a person of great record and so forth, and it used to be older people, so they had great stature, Admiral Wilson, Admiral Hart, Turner Joy.* Those people had made great names in their naval careers. Those are the people who used to go to the Naval Academy as Superintendent. Now it's a different type of assignment at the top, where they assign people who have never really been known in the Navy until all of a sudden they end up as Superintendent. People like Stockdale, who was head of the War College and also the present Superintendent.** They were prisoners of war and this is something that we want to recognize because of what they had to go through, but basically no one had ever heard of them as

*Rear Admiral Henry B. Wilson, USN, Superintendent 1921-1925; Rear Admiral Thomas C. Hart, USN, 1931-1934; Vice Admiral C. Turner Joy, USN, 1952-1954.

**Vice Admiral James B. Stockdale, USN, President of the Naval War College from October 1977 to August 1979; Vice Admiral William P. Lawrence, USN, Superintendent of the Naval Academy from August 1978 to August 1981. Both men were naval aviators shot down and captured during the Vietnam War.

officers of the Navy from what they had done, except for being prisoners of war. It's the same thing as a sort of minority group compensation or something like that.

It's changed a lot. I don't know, maybe it's for the best, but the people do not have the stature that they used to have, and whether that detracts from the image of the Naval Academy, I don't know, because so many things have changed.

Q: Your tour of duty at the Naval Academy was coming to an end and your next tour was . . .

Admiral MacDonald: Commander Destroyer Squadron 34.

Q: Yes, and this was in the year 1955, wasn't it?

Admiral MacDonald: Yes, '55.

Q: Now this was something you really wanted to do, wasn't it?

Admiral MacDonald: Well, basically, at the time I wanted to command one of the big ships. I went up to the department to see whether I could get a cruiser or a battleship command. Arleigh Burke had just gone as Commander Destroyers Atlantic, and he insisted he wanted some people with a little background knowledge about destroyers to be assigned to his command. The next thing I knew, I got command of Destroyer Squadron 34, and I think Burke was behind the assignment. He wrote me a nice letter telling me that he was glad to have me. Well, he wasn't there very long after I reported in and took over command, when he left.

Q: He left to become CNO, didn't he?

Admiral MacDonald: Yes, he left to become CNO, and Joe Daniel became Commander Destroyers Atlantic.* Of course, I'd known Admiral Daniel when he was in the Bureau of Naval Personnel and liked him very, very much.

We were based in Newport, and at that time we had a tour of duty in the Mediterranean. We had to alternate tours of duty over there.

Q: Was this a six-month tour?

Admiral MacDonald: As I recall, it was about four months, the last cruise that I had over there. We operated all around there. We even escorted a lot of--there were a lot of problems even in the Atlantic and down around the Caribbean.

Q: What kind of problems?

---

*Rear Admiral John C. Daniel, USN.

Admiral MacDonald: Convoys, amphibious operations, exercises in the Atlantic in connection with antisubmarine warfare.

Q: We were turning our attention to that subject at that point, were we?

Admiral MacDonald: Yes. It was always a big point with destroyers and particularly convoys--antisubmarine warfare. I don't recall exactly when we went over to the Mediterranean. When we got over there, the Commander Sixth Fleet was Admiral Felt, and Larry Freeman was chief of staff, and Larry was the person whom I relieved as the commanding officer of the Williamsburg.* I operated with the Sixth Fleet and they took the other squadron of destroyers and sent them out to start a watch out in the Middle East area. Don Eller had the other squadron, and he was sent out there on a special task group to establish a patrol setup along the Red Sea and off Jerusalem and Alexandria.**

Q: 1956 was the year of the Suez crisis?

---

*Vice Admiral Harry D. Felt, USN, Commander Sixth Fleet from April 1956 to September 1956. His reminiscences are included in the Naval Institute oral history collection. Captain Charles Lawrence Freeman, USN.

**Captain Donald T. Eller, USN.

Admiral MacDonald: Yes. We were over there in '55 and part of our mission was to observe and find out what the traffic was like. After I got over there, my first stay in the Mediterranean was with the Sixth Fleet in and around the western part of the Mediterranean. Eller's group set up a patrol arrangement where part of his ships were on this side of the Mediterranean, and the rest were in the Red Sea and up the Persian Gulf area, watching the traffic and so forth. The situation was becoming a little volatile over there, and they wanted to see what the situation was because Egypt would not allow Israeli ships to go through the canal, and the British were in the canal when I got over there. The British had their troops still stationed in Port Said. I put in to Port Said a number of times when my squadron was over there, and the British were just getting ready to leave.

The early part, as I recall, was just normal operations with the Sixth Fleet, where we visited different ports and we had amphibious landings around Corsica.

Q: Did you use North African ports, too?

Admiral MacDonald: No, we never went over there. We didn't go over there at all, at least I didn't. I think maybe some of the ships that were sent out on sort of visiting arrangements went over to North Africa, but I didn't. With the destroyers we had to stay more or less around with the carrier and the flagship.

Q: What was the complexion of our Sixth Fleet at that point? How large was it?

Admiral MacDonald: At that time, it was just one carrier. I think there was only one carrier, two cruisers, a tanker or so, and some amphibious ships, and two destroyer squadrons. They conducted amphibious operations at various times, visiting around, and so forth. We'd split up, then we'd rendezvous and have an operation. Basically, the carrier usually anchored off Cannes, and Villefranche was usually the home port for the cruisers.

Not much happened in a way, except that as far as the duty was concerned I enjoyed Mediterranean duty very much. Midway in that particular cruise there, Eller, who had the other squadron, and I shifted positions. I went out to the Middle East and put one division down in the Red Sea and the Persian Gulf, where they would patrol and visit places. We had to submit reports, shipping and intelligence reports of activity in the area. We actually based sometimes in Lebanon but then cruised down, and we always had a ship off Alexandria, one off Israel, and then we'd alternate and visit ports.

I put in to Haifa a number of times and called on the chief of naval operations there, and they'd all come down and tell us what the situation was. Finally I went down to Alexandria and relieved one of our ships and put in there. Every time we went to Egypt, even Port Said, I had to get permission to go up to Cairo from Alexandria. They would check you in and check you out. They knew where you were all the time. In Alexandria, the captain of my flagship and I, we were tied up there and we went ashore and, all of a sudden, at night, when we were sitting in one of these places where we had dined, along came the chief of the Egyptian Navy. This was at a very bad period in relations in connection with Egypt. Dulles had gone out there and they'd decided not to finance the Aswan Dam and we weren't giving them any help whatsoever.*

Q: The Russians hadn't yet come into the picture, however?

Admiral MacDonald: They were just coming in. This was the point. So the chief of naval operations came in; they knew where we were because we were watched by spies all the time. He sat down and said he'd just come from the President.

Q: This was Nasser?**

Admiral MacDonald: Nasser. He'd just come from Nasser, and Nasser wanted a message to get to the United States that he

---

*John Foster Dulles, Secretary of State from 1953 to 1959.

**Colonel Gamal A. Nasser, Prime Minister and Military Governor of Egypt from 1954 to 1956; President of Egypt from 1956 to 1958.

needed help, he needed submarines, he needed patrol boats, and this was all in connection with the buildup in Israel. And if we would not help him, and the British had stopped training--all these guys were British-trained originally, the top of the Navy and the Army, they'd all been trained by the British--if we wouldn't help him, then he had no alternative but to go to the Russians, and they were negotiating with Yugoslavia to have patrol boats built, and they wanted to get submarines and help from Russia. If we weren't going to help them, then they had no alternative but to do this.

I sent the message to Felt and told him what Nasser would have wanted conveyed there, but nothing ever came of it. So after talking with the Egyptians, the top people--the one person I couldn't talk with was our own ambassador whom Eisenhower had assigned over there, an ex-Army guy who used to be his aide.

Q: Who was that?

Admiral MacDonald: Henry Byroade.* He was the ambassador and he had told his staff that no one was to have any contact with anyone in the Egyptian Navy unless he okayed it. Well, knowing this, the Egyptians got to the naval attache, bypassing the ambassador, whom I had called and said I wanted to call on the

---

*Henry A. Byroade.

ambassador, but he didn't want to see me; he didn't want to have anything to do with us. He got kicked upstairs later on. There was no communication between the ambassador and Nasser; the staffs just weren't functioning. That's why they were going out of their way to try to get messages through in a different direction. They weren't apparently very successful. They told me that there would never be--I got this from conversations in Israel--and I wrote a communication that I sent to Felt, a summary of the situation, that both sides felt there was so much hatred involved between the two of them that there would never be any peace in that area unless one side or the other was eliminated. This is the way they both felt at that time.

Q: It looks like the same thing today!

Admiral MacDonald: I could show you a copy of that letter that I sent to Felt as a summary of the situation, that there'll never be any peace until one side or the other is destroyed.

We were out there for a couple of months. My squadron was there for longer, because this was just about the time when, all of a sudden, I got the message to proceed to Monaco. I was ticked off to be the Navy's representative for the Grace Kelly-Prince Rainier wedding, and so I had to turn the squadron over to my division commodore, and went off to Grace Kelly's wedding.*

Q: Had you known her?

Admiral MacDonald: No, never knew her at all and I never really knew who said that I was the one to represent the Navy, because there was Felt still there and Larry Freeman. But on my way there, knowing how some of these things operated, I sent a message to Admiral Felt requesting that I be assigned a car and chauffeur so that I could carry out my obligations of representing the Navy there.

Q: And had some status.

Admiral MacDonald: They okayed it, which made it very pleasant, so when I arrived, we tied up alongside the Italian frigates and representatives of other countries. I made my official call which was required. I did this using the car that was assigned me and that amounted to a flood of invitations.

Q: Was Mrs. MacDonald with you?

Admiral MacDonald: No. I had asked her to come over, and her

---

*Prince Rainier III of Monaco was married on 18 April 1956 to American movie actress Grace Kelly.

father, who was over in Geneva at the time, heard about this and he said he'd pay her transportation if she would come, but she didn't feel like coming. So I went through that ordeal of a week of really nothing but one fantastic gathering after another.

My first meeting was set up by the consul general at Nice with the press. As soon as I arrived, we had a press conference there, and Art Buchwald, who at the time was in Paris, came down with some other newspapermen and they wanted to know what we were supposed to do at Grace Kelly's wedding.

Q: Stand around!

Admiral MacDonald: By that time I had been in communications with the Sixth Fleet's flagship, and they told me that they would assign a detachment of Marines from the flagship to be assigned to my ship and I could use the Marines as a ceremonial setup, which we did at Grace Kelly's wedding. It was a very nice present. The invitations were a very funny thing. You knew that there was going to be an event, but you had to have a special pass for the car. You had to have a special pass, and that was delivered by hand, by a motorcycle rider, just about an hour before the event so that there could be no counterfeiting of any of these invitations. This is the way they really worked it, and it worked out beautifully. You checked in, left your address, and they gave you a list of things but no invitation until just about an hour before the event.

Q: A little nerve-racking, though, wasn't it?

Admiral MacDonald: Well, after the first one or two times, it began to all fit into place. You knew that you would get it; you knew they had to be there. They had a lot of parties for them and, of course, Grace Kelly's father and family were over there in great style. At that time, she was a famous motion-picture actress, so the movie industry, Neiman-Marcus, and all these people of that sort just poured into there. Eisenhower sent over Conrad Hilton as his special representative to the wedding.

Q: The hotel man?

Admiral MacDonald: Yes, the hotel man, who arrived and who was staying in the hotel, so he sent word down that he'd like to see me. I went up and he said, "What am I supposed to do?"

I said, "I don't know exactly. You represent the President and I'm supposed to represent the Navy."

But he fitted into the picture just the way I did. He would get his invitations. Of course, everyone knew who he was and I was very flattered that I should have been asked to represent the Navy at that particular function, when there were people like Felt and a few others over there. I don't know what was in the back of their minds, and I never knew exactly where the original request came from that I be the one. Even to this day, I have never been able to find out who specifically ticked me off to represent the Navy there, but I certainly appreciated it because it was fabulous. The mayor of Monte Carlo entertained at all the different places, and we got all kinds of little mementoes from it, including a medal from Grace Kelly and Prince Rainier.

After the ceremony at the cathedral, oh, goodness, it was a white-tie affair and they had a lot of aristocracy there, monarchs and so forth who still recognized Prince Rainier as something. The church was filled. The cathedral was absolutely filled, packed, and everyone was dressed in top hat and white tie. Of course, we were in full dress with all our medals. The reception was held in the palace afterwards, and this was at the end of the week, after a week of parties, fantastic parties, that went on with circuses and the firing of firecrackers night after night. Oh, gee, what a to-do.

Q: Wasn't Mrs. MacDonald sorry that she missed this, after all?

Admiral MacDonald: I don't know. I've got a lot of material up in my case in connection with this event, pictures, because there were photographers all over the place.

Q: It would have been much easier for you if she'd been with you, though?

Admiral MacDonald: Oh, sure. We'd have had to move into the Conrad Hilton in that case because there was no place for her to stay on board.

I had a lot of the people down on the ship later, Gloria Swanson, the Gimbels, and a lot of people like that. I even had a lot of pictures taken for them and sent them all over the Sixth Fleet and asked for copies. I never got any copies back except very few.

Q: They're in the Navy archives now, I guess?

Admiral MacDonald: I don't know where they are, but they only sent back a couple of pictures, because I had a several photographers with me. The reception was in the big courtyard in the palace and there were a lot of people there, lots of food and drinks, and there was Mr. Kelly who had practically bought up the stamp collection at the post office in Monte Carlo and was giving out these stamps to some of the guests.

Q: There must have been a philatelist there?

Admiral MacDonald: I don't know, but this became quite an important thing. People were trying to get stamps for this one occasion, and the stamp was only printed for that day, special stamps, and they must have sold millions and millions of them.

Q: A good way of raising revenue for the princedom!

Admiral MacDonald: Yes. I have a whole batch of them that were two and a half francs, sheets and sheets of them. I just don't know how to get rid of them, but I've got them. These were all given to me by Mr. Kelly, who was very flashy in a white tie, tail coat arrangement, but it was light blue! But the family looked most attractive. Mrs. Kelly was a very attractive woman, and Grace Kelly's sister was a very attractive person. Of course, John Kelly is one of our trustees now at the Naval Academy Foundation. He was down there last week. He was a famous sculler, single.

So that was the highlight of my trip over there with Destroyer Squadron 34.

Q: Quite a different assignment!

What were your relations with Don Felt?

Admiral MacDonald: I didn't know him at all at the time, until I then came back and Joe Daniel said he had to have a destroyerman down in the CNO. He said, "I want you to go down there and be the destroyerman in the Chief of Naval Operations's office." And the job that I was assigned was deputy ASW, antisubmarine warfare. Burke was CNO and Harry Felt then was Vice Chief of Naval Operations. That's when I really got to know Felt, when he was vice chief. He was a full admiral and an aviator. Actually, that's the beginning of my really getting to know him because I had to work in that operation there. I was deputy ASW, and Warder was the director of antisubmarine warfare at that time.* This is when I came down there supposedly to be a destroyer representative, and it was quite an enlightening tour, because ASW at that time contained the submarine branch, the research and development branch, the mine warfare branch, and a very small aspect of surface warfare. Surface warfare was a different division. We had the seaplane patrols--the aircraft side was under us, too.

There, again, I found out that if you were not in submarines or aviation, you had one terrible time, even with Burke, who bent over backwards not to show any favoritism to the surface force. This was a strange thing. Joe Daniel, when he asked me to come down there to represent destroyers, I don't think he had any idea that Burke was a different person than he thought he was, because Burke really didn't help us on the destroyer side at all. Of course, at that time the submarine people had just made a notch into the surface warfare setup by getting submarine officers

*Rear Admiral Frederick B. Warder, USN.

assigned as commanding officers of destroyers, and they were well-organized. Gee, I ran into that, Grenfell and Warder and Daspit, they were all top submarine people of the day and they had organized a group.* Under me was Pete Galantin, who headed up the submarine branch, and under him were people like Bob Long, who just recently went as Commander in Chief Pacific, and I was in the position of writing up their fitness reports.** Well, I got them all promoted without any trouble because they were submarine people.

I worked with Felt, and, you know, you'd go in and talk with him and tell him what you were trying to do, because I had to work as hard for the other different categories in the Navy as for just surface ships because we were getting the Polaris submarine under way, too. That was the beginning of the Polaris submarine and the beginning of the battles with Rickover, who wanted to control the whole nuclear-atomic energy setup.*** You'd talk with Felt and you'd find out that he was quite agreeable with the way things were outlined, recommended, and so forth, and the next thing you'd know, he'd go up and talk with Burke and he'd give a different story, and back would come the word and it wouldn't be what you thought it was going to be at

*Rear Admiral Elton W. Grenfell, USN; Rear Admiral Lawrence R. Daspit, USN.

**Rear Admiral Ignatius G. Galantin, USN; Lieutenant Commander Robert L. Long, USN, who was Commander in Chief Pacific from 1979 to 1983.

***Rear Admiral Hyman G. Rickover, USN.

all. Felt was Burke's roommate, so this is why Felt had so much power. He could talk to his roommate probably very easily.

Q: Burke told me once that Felt was of particular value to him in those two years Felt served because Felt was not a yes-man; he was a no-man. If he disagreed, he said so, and Burke said he valued this.

Admiral MacDonald: This is true. What I'm trying to say is that he would say yes to you but no to Burke.

Q: I see.

Admiral MacDonald: Maybe Burke never realized this because they were classmates, roommates, and very friendly. I guess you have completed Burke's . . .

Q: I'm still working with Burke. I've done a series with Don Felt, though.

Admiral MacDonald: Yes. Well, I don't know. Of course, I shouldn't be saying anything for the record about those two, but the thing was that in destroyers at that time we just got no help, really, because we were being diluted by commanding officers from the submarine branch getting command of destroyers, so we lost our entity. People who weren't going anyplace in submarines were going into the destroyer program, and Warder, who really was the senior submarine officer in the department, was my boss. It was amazing how they used to have meetings and find out how we want So-and-so to go there and we want So-and-so to take this job so he can qualify for that and so forth. They had it all worked out just per se.

Jack McCain, who's a classmate of mine, was called in and told, "You've got to do this and you've got to do that," but Jack McCain, fortunately, had Burke as a great helper because Burke had worked with Jack McCain's father and Jack then had free access to Burke's office.* He stood way down at the bottom of this class and was quite a surprise.

Q: He was the last man in the class!

Admiral MacDonald: Almost. He was quite a surprise to everyone, but he had the backing and Burke was very helpful. He also had the submarine people's backing because they were trying to get into a position where they could at least get their people placed well, because what had happened--it was obvious even when I was at the Naval Academy, but I didn't mention it at the time in this interview--all of the top jobs were going to aviators or

---

*Captain John S. McCain, Jr., USN.

submarine officers. They were all going to top jobs. The way they did this was that all of the boards, the Advisory Board, of which I was secretary at one time, later on in my second job there, consisted, out of nine people, four or five aviators and two or three submariners. So you can imagine how anyone else could make any headway.

Burke was CNO and he stayed in there for three different tours, the first one to ever do that. He was in a good position. He didn't have to show favoritism; he was at the top.

While I was there I sat on the Ship Characteristics Board for all ship construction, and on the Ship Characteristics Board you had the same thing. You had aviators representing the different divisions, aeronautics and so forth, and everything was always put up to a vote, just like taking the guns off surface ships to put missiles on. The missile division was under the Deputy Chief of Naval Operations for Air.

Q: Who was that? Bob Pirie?

Admiral MacDonald: It was Bob Pirie at one time but later it was--let's see, Bob Pirie was there part of the time.* Jim Russell relieved Felt.**

---

*Vice Admiral Robert B. Pirie, USN, was relieved by Vice Admiral William A. Schoech, USN, in November 1962.

**Admiral James S. Russell relieved Admiral Felt as Vice Chief of Naval Operations in July 1958.

The Ship Characteristics Board used to have to make sure that the design and weapons that went into these new ships were what we wanted and of the latest material. That was one of the things that bothered me a great deal, the fact that missiles were coming along and there was so much pressure to take all the guns and all the offensive power off of even a destroyer in the way of removing the guns and putting on these missiles which, in a way, were basically antiair missiles. So we would have had no defense against a little surface ship, a patrol boat, or anything else. Fortunately, that was stalled for a while. Then the guns got all off, and now they're putting them back on again.

Q: This was an excess of enthusiasm, was it, for missiles?

Admiral MacDonald: Oh, yes, and building up the power in this area. In order to get money, this was the whole thing, it's a fight to get your share or a bigger share of the buck, and the more programs you have that are dynamic, it's just like, as Burke will probably tell you in connection with his fighting to get Polaris money, he's up against the Air Force, who wanted big bombers and all this. It's a matter of planning to get the budget and to produce the glamour type of thing. Just like, when the Polaris submarine program got under way, all of a sudden the Air Force wanted the Minuteman program, put in all these silos. They're always fighting and yet, when you think back, the Polaris program was a successful program as a deterrent, but it took a lot of money and it took a lot of money away from a lot of things.

We were involved in this because we represented ASW, although antisubmarine warfare was also the submarine group that advised Burke, through the submarine branch and up through me and Warder to Burke. We used to have meetings on a lot of this. At one time, particularly when Warder was out on a campaign of selling ASW to all the different Army and Air Force commands, I used to have to go up and defend the programs in Burke's presence, but he always said, "Well, you're doing all this for submarines? What are you doing about the destroyers in the way of protecting them?"

Well, we were tied. He did a good job. Burke had a lot of difficulty in trying to keep control. Rickover was no help because he wanted to maintain absolute control of the nuclear power program in the Navy, and by that the assignment of officers, ticking them off, and so forth.

But getting back to the Characteristics Board, those were the things that were so disturbing, the fact that they wanted to take all of the offensive capability off some of our surface ships before we had adequate replacements. The missiles were not adequate replacements because they were antiair. They were making advanced air weapons and they were starting to work on a dual missile which could serve both purposes but you'd have to shift them. The missile program was an up-and-coming thing in the late Fifties, there's no doubt about that. But as time goes on, they find out that, out in Vietnam and so forth, they have to have surface capabilities.

Q: They found that wasn't the only answer?

Admiral MacDonald: That's right. The missile wasn't the only answer because there were no airplanes to shoot at. They had to shoot probably patrol boats and things like that.

I think I covered working with the big Ship Characteristics Board a long time ago, in my earlier conversations about the destroyers, when I came back from the Pacific.

I stayed in that job of ASW, and the selection board came out, and I was not included on it that year. People like McCain were not either. Then, all of a sudden, between the meetings of the groups, now we've got to get Jack in the right position to go along and so forth, and I had no one to fall back on, except Butch Parker, who was down in the Atomic Energy Division, in the tank down in the Joint Chiefs, who wanted me to do something with it. Basically, they told me that I should move over to general planning, and I became assistant director of general planning.

Q: Was that under the Joint Chiefs?

Admiral MacDonald: No, it was right under Burke, and we did all of the work in the way of drafting, message on the budget for Burke. Rollo Wilson had been the head of general planning.* He had just left and they asked me to come over there after a year in ASW, maybe longer than a year.

Q: Was Felt still there?

Admiral MacDonald: Felt had just left, I think.

Q: He'd gone out to CinCPac?

Admiral MacDonald: He just went out to CinCPac and Jim Russell took over as vice chief, and I will say that Jim Russell was a gentleman. He was a delightful person.**

Q: Gentleman Jim he's known as.

Admiral MacDonald: In my capacity of being his number two man in general planning, Frank Miller, who had been the assistant to Wilson, fleeted up and I took Frank Miller's position.*** Being in that position, I was also secretary to the CNO's advisory

---

*Rear Admiral Ralph E. Wilson, USN.

**Admiral James S. Russell, USN, whose reminiscences are in the Naval Institute collection.

***Rear Admiral Frank B. Miller, USN.

board.

Q: CAB?

Admiral MacDonald: CAB. I was the secretary and so I sat in on the meetings.

Q: That must have been an interesting job.

Admiral MacDonald: I realized what was going on, yes. As I said, you line up there and you see all these representatives. Basically, the Vice Chief of Naval Operations is the senior one on the CAB, and that was Jim Russell. Of course, Bob Pirie was Deputy Chief of Naval Operations for Air at that time.* The DCNO for Operations was an aviator. That went on for one year and Burke worked Frank Miller. Burke, in my personal view, had no hobby except work.

Q: That's right.

Admiral MacDonald: He would be down there in the morning early. He wanted the papers all ready for him by the time he got there at 8:00 o'clock or 7:30, and some nights he wouldn't leave until

*Vice Admiral Robert B. Pirie, USN, whose memoirs are in the Naval Institute collection.

11:00, and we'd have to work all night to get the papers ready for his answers the next morning.

Well, poor old Frank Miller was my boss. He didn't last much longer after he left that job. As a matter of fact, he died shortly thereafter. He just worked him to death, and I wasn't up to this type of operation because I like fresh-air activities, you know, a little bit of exercise occasionally. But I did my job. We used to have to go up and defend our budget. I used to have to work basically on the budget arrangement with the comptroller Wilfred McNeil, who just recently died.

Wilfred McNeil was comptroller and he was wonderful. The Navy budget people were wonderful. I had to coordinate all the deputy chiefs on the budget. This is where I ran into a little difficulty, trying to get the aviators to cut back so we could live within our budget. I know that the deputy up there didn't particularly like the way we suggested that he cut down his recommended task forces and so forth to fit within the budget capability. I don't think they liked it worth one damn, but anyway, Frank Miller would prepare drafts of all kinds of things for Burke, because for some reason or other Burke turned to Miller to do all of this and not to anyone else. Frank was devoted to him, and he could keep the hours that Burke did. The only thing about it is that Burke would come back from the Joint Chiefs of Staff at night, maybe about 7:30 or 8:00 o'clock, turn over all this stuff, and he wanted the answers the next morning.

An awful lot of the work in the Joint Chiefs in connection with policy boiled down to money, appropriations, and budget, and programs, and you have to defend them, and Burke was very meticulous about making sure that he could defend the programs that we were sending up there, because he just wanted it that way.

Well, at long last, after that, I decided to retire, and that's when I retired as a rear admiral.

Q: This was in 1959?

Admiral MacDonald: Yes, October 1.

Q: Felt also was a workaholic, wasn't he?

Admiral MacDonald: Not that much. I don't think Felt would have maintained the hours like that, no. Felt was brought up in that aviation atmosphere and they like to relax a little bit, too. No, I don't remember Felt driving anyone, but Burke drove people himself. He was a hard worker. He wanted things right away. I certainly do think he was very instrumental in getting the Polaris program sold all the way up, which took money away from the Air Force. It also took money away from our ship construction.

Q: From the bureaus?

Admiral MacDonald: From the other bureaus.

He wasn't so powerful up there in the Joint Chiefs, though, because they still had some people represented, as I think I mentioned in one of our earlier interviews, when I sat down and we used to have to review papers sent to us in France. You'd sit down and you'd find that the Air Force had ganged up with the Army to take away from the Navy and the vote was always two to one. The Army wanted the Marines, the Air Force wanted everything that flew in the air, including the planes on the carriers. It was a tough battle. These people were in there to maintain their dynasty, there's no doubt about it! I don't know when they started thinking about the security of the country.

Q: I was going to ask, isn't that the overriding issue?

Admiral MacDonald: The overriding issue is the security of your country, that's right, but putting all your eggs in one basket is not going to be security, I'll tell you that.

The other thing was that in both of these different divisions there, I had to work with Chick Hayward, who was director of research and development.* Although we had our own submarine

---

*Vice Admiral John T. Hayward, USN.

research and development, that later got incorporated into the main department when they split it up as the division of research and development. There was a fellow called Bennett at one time who was the head of research and development.* He was a scientific type. Then, all of a sudden, along came Chick Hayward, who was very dynamic, very likeable, and a great friend of mine. He moved in and I used to sit in on the meetings there to try to protect our own research and development program in his realm of power. Chick has always been a very capable person. It always amazed me that he worked so hard. He had a doctorate in some sort of science, and he was very able, a sort of happy-go-lucky aviator. He also sat in on the CAB. The CAB was overwhelmingly aviation, too, and it wasn't easy for some of those just straight line to make a go of it. I gave up.

Q: Where did George Miller fit into this picture?

Admiral MacDonald: George Miller later came in and headed up special studies, what they call long-range objectives.** Rivero was head of long-range objectives when I was there.*** Here's how it works. As the general planning group, we took programs up to five years, then you run into long-range objectives which take

*Rear Admiral Rawson Bennett, USN, Chief of Naval Research from 1956 to 1961.

**Rear Admiral George H. Miller, USN, Director, Long Range Objectives Group from 1964 to 1967.

***Rear Admiral Horacio Rivero, USN.

them from five years up to 20. They're sort of a think tank up there, but we did have this analytical group that came directly under us, an operational analysis setup, composed of scientists, doctors from different schools like MIT, who used to work out a lot of the problems we'd give them, like how many submarines you need on a patrol line between Greenland and Ireland to keep the Russians bottled up.* They would come up with it, based on speeds of current and so forth. The answer would be, well, you need so many out there and you need such a force to replace them. They handled a lot of the think-tank type of analysis. But they served a useful purpose. As a matter of fact, their head man sat in on all of our meetings with the CNO. He was always there with the CNO, CAB meetings, and so forth, an operational analysis group.

It was a very busy time. But there was no doubt in my mind that I wasn't going anyplace, because there was no place to go.

Q: You could have gone to Pensacola and learned to be a flier!

Admiral MacDonald: Well, I gave up before they gave me up. I just thought I'd retire, retire as a rear admiral, because I thought that would be worthwhile. I talked with Boone later.** He was head of the last selection board that looked over the

---

*MIT--Massachusetts Institute of Technology.
**Admiral Walter F. Boone, USN.

records that I was involved in, and he indicated what the situation was. His whole point of view was conducive to having me decide not to make my career in the Navy any longer.

After that I got out and immediately went to work as a consultant and that was a very nice arrangement, very lucrative in a lot of ways.

Q: This was a free-lance sort of consultant? In the financial world?

Admiral MacDonald: No, I became a consultant originally with Fairchild Camera and Instrument. It was free, and then Thiokol Chemical asked me to work with them, too. At one time I was consulting with three different industries: Englehart Industries, Thiokol, and Fairchild Camera and Instrument. They were wonderful jobs.

Q: Arleigh was with Thiokol, too, wasn't he?

Admiral MacDonald: He was on the board of directors, yes. He went with them because they made the solid propellant missiles, and at the time I was with them they were working on a solid propellant ASW torpedo, a torpedo propelled by a solid propellant. I consulted with them until I got involved with having to learn something about the investment business. I was made trustee of some trusts in New York and I thought I'd better learn the job. I thought I could hang onto a couple of my consulting jobs, particularly Englehart Industries, where I was really most anxious to stay. Charlie Englehart was a friend. And when I put it up to the New York Stock Exchange, they said it would be a conflict of interests; I could be a director or a trustee but I couldn't maintain a consulting job.

Q: That's a fine line of distinction, isn't it?

Admiral MacDonald: I could be a director, but, you see, consulting . . .

Q: You have to give advice?

Admiral MacDonald: You have to give advice. You have to work for them.

Q: Don't you have to also as a director?

Admiral MacDonald: Yes, but not the same way. Consulting, I could be called upon by the company to do certain jobs. Goodness knows, I made many trips out to Thiokol's plant in Utah while they were building the missiles for the Polaris submarines, but this trustee arrangement for a trust in New York, I knew, was going to probably go on indefinitely, so I decided to cast my fortune with going into the investment banking business, and I'm still at it.

I'm able to keep up and I can advise properly, or better than otherwise, how to keep your investments up.

Q: Keeping abreast of inflation!

Admiral MacDonald: Well, it's very difficult, but, of course, the market was up yesterday. It's a very difficult time to know what to do, but if you have good investments, you don't have to worry too much; they'll come back. If you want to make money right now with interest rates the way they are, the money market area is a very good idea to be in because most of them are paying well over 12% interest and that's very, very helpful. I've got a lot of money in it for people. I don't make a lot of money out of it, but I'm not so interested in making money as in staying up with what's going on, and it's a place to go and get out of the house. I'm sure my wife is very happy about that!

Q: I do thank you.

ACTION REPORT

O'BANNON
USS BANNON DD-450

SERIAL 0134 17 NOVEMBER 19

REPORT OF PARTICIPATION IN BATTLE OF GUADALCANAL.

CDR. E. R. WILKINSON'S NARRATIVE REPORT OF ENGAGEMENT WITH UNITS OF THE JAPANESE FLEET IN THE WATERS SURROUNDED BY GUADALCANAL, SAVO, FLORIDA, AND TULAGI ISLANDS IN THE EARLY MORNING OF 13 NOVEMBER 1942.

At 0137 Commander Task Group 67.4 ordered the course changed to north by another column movement. While steaming on this course Commander Destroyer Division 10 in the CUSHING reported over TBS, ships on his starboard bow and also ships on his port hand. Commander Task Group 67.4 then ordered course changed by column movement to 310°. There was considerable congestion at this turn, the leading ships were falling back, we became bunched. The O'BANNON turned inside to avoid a collision with the STERRET, later easing out into column. The ATLANTA closed in close on our port quarter.

THIRD PHASE

(A) The leading ships had just gotten settled on course 310° when word was received over TBS to attack with torpedoes. At practically the same instant searchlight from enemy units were seen on the port bow and on the starboard bow, illuminating our leading ships. Initially our guns were trained to starboard and were prepared to fire on this side when an order was received over TBS for even ships to fire to port and odd ships to starboard. There was a delay of possibly 30 seconds in getting our guns trained out on the target to port. Firing was commenced by both our own forces and the enemy at practically the same instant. Our forward guns were trained on the searchlight on our port hand. Shortly after we had commenced fire something in behind a Kongo class battleship was hit causing the battleship to be beautifully silhouetted at a range of not more than four thousand yards, this ship appeared to be on course approximately north. At the same time I observed on our starboard bow an enemy three-stack cruiser (Tenyru Class) on course about 270°, distance approximately 3000 yards. This cruiser appeared to be firing at the CUSHING AND LAFFEY. Aircraft overhead dropped flares when the firing first started which lit up the whole area so that our leading ships must have been clearly visible to the enemy.

(B) During this period, I was conning the ship, from an amidships position at the forward bridge port; gun fire was evident coming from ships on our starboard bow, distant 10 to 12 thousand yards, as the flashes appeared as coming from low down in the water. While we were firing at the Kongo class battleship, I could distinctly see our bullets hitting her superstructure, flashes, and sparks were coming out of her Pagoda tower. Enormous flames began to appear in and around this ship, her fire ceased and the ship appeared to be dead in the water. About this time I noticed two flashes on the STERRET's stern as if her after guns were hit. It was shortly after this, that the STERRET stopped in front of us and turned left. We closed up very rapidly, orders were given as follows: hard right and emergency full astern. We just cleared the STERRET's stern by about 30 feet. After passing the STERRET we again came back to course 310° and went ahead full. At this time I could only see the Kongo class battleship on our port bow. There was firing on our starboard bow but I could not make out what it was; the Japanese cruiser was not visible nor was the LAFFEY or the CUSHING.

My first thought then was to remain at full speed and cross ahead of the battleship which seemed to be drawing ever closer. At this time the word was received over the TBS to cease fire. It was carried out in this ship. The Commanding Officer ordered torpedoe fired at the battleship on our port bow. At about 0157 our course was changed to the right, while making this turn I was concerned at the proximity of the battleship and thought that we would not be able to turn clear of her, so gave the following orders: hard right and emergency full astern; when it was evident that we would clear safely, all engines were ordered ahead full, and course chan to 090°. The battleship at this time was not firing and was envel in tremendous flames. While on course 090° we were illuminated by searchlights and heavy fire was going overhead, coming from the no Directly ahead I saw the bow of a ship, I can distinctly remember seeing white numbers on the bow, left rudder was ordered to avoid this wreck and we unintentionally passed through a number of survi who were swimming on the surface. They were screaming something. I now think it was "LAFFEY"; a number of our personnel threw life jackets, to them. The firing still seemed to be heavy from the no so that course was changed to southeast, the general direction of channel. At about 0205 the ship was shaken violently by an underw explosion which virtually lifted the stern out of the water. I wa looking out the front port at the time and the airport came down h ting me on the head. I thought the ship had been hit somewhere ab midships. Word was sent down to the repair parties and engineroom to inspect immediately and report what damage had been done. Repo were promptly received that there was no apparent damage but the after engine room reported a rumbling in the port reduction gear a requested that we slow down. The engines were slowed to two thir speed. Considerable firing was still going on and it appeared as Japanese after we had ceased fire were firing at themselves. Two black objects were observed on the port bow at approximately 3000 yards, from one, great clouds of black smoke were pouring. These black objects later turned out to be the HELENA, and SAN FRANCISCO Course was then changed toward the beach and we made a sweep in th bight just west of Kukum. Upon completion of this circle an appro was made to clear through Lengo channel.

FOURTH PHASE

(A) With the use of the fathometer and by staying close to t shore line our position was finally established. We then proceede through Lengo Channel at approximately 18 knots.

(B) During the passage through Lengo Channel information was received from the radar personnel that there was a vessel hugging the shore line, her approximate bearing was on our starboard beam three or four vessels could be seen in Sea Lark Channel. During passage through Lengo Channel, the Commanding Officer definitely established the identity of HELENA, SAN FRANCISCO and FLETCHER ov the TBS as being the ships observed in Sea Lark Channel. The shi on our starboard beam apparently came visible well up on our starboard bow after she had passed Taivui point, this vessel after daylight was identified as the Juneau. At 0358 after clearing Lengo channel we proceeded northeast to join task group 67.4.

2. COMMENTS:

(A) It was quite evident that the enemy were not surprised at our appearance. No doubt one task group of theirs was preparing to bombard Cactus; they had air craft overhead to provide the necessary illumination. The fragment which hit our ship was from an 8" bombardment projectile. The Kongo class battleship with which we engaged appeared to be screening a contemplated landing operation in or near Tasmfaronga. I believe that the ligh cruiser which was observed on our starboard bow was the outer screen of the bombardment force coming down the northeast, the main force of which was 12000 to 14000 yards away when the firing commenced. It is further believe that the Japanese operations for this night had been well and strategically planned in their entirety, and that we completely upset their plans. A submarine had been sighted off Koli Point according to a report which we had received aboard (prior) to midnight of the 12th. It is quite possible that this submarine was covering the channel and inflicted some damage to the ships at the rear of our column.

(B) During our approach to the battle area and while still in Lengo Channel a report waw received on the bridge from the gunnery officer that we had just passed over the track of a torpedo wake. This was not observed by me although I was watching the water very carefully.

3. DAMAGE:

Friendly: I saw two large flashes appear around the after guns in the STERETT. The CUSHING and LAFFEY were observed to be under a cross fire from the battleship on the port bow and the cruiser on the starboard bow. Both of whom were hitting our ships and tearing them down gradually. Heavy explosions were felt and heard throughout the engagement.

Enemy : I did not see any enemy ships blow up and sink but I did observe great fires coming from something in behind the battleship on our port bow and then later huge flames envelope the battleship. Several ships on our starboard hand were on fire but it was impossible to observe who they were.

4. The following recommendations are submitted:

(A) That less use of the TBS be made during the approach to an engagement. Furthermore it is not completely reliable with all the noise that is created during an action.

(B) That the PPI on the SG radar have a duplicate repeater on the bridge.

5. COMMENDATIONS. I recommend that the following officers and men be commended for their performance of duty far and beyond that expected of them in the normal line of duty:

Lieutenant George Philip, Jr., USN, for his maintaining strict and controlled discipline over his battery and personnel during the entire engagement; for being able to take the enemy under rapid and continuous fire; and for his assistance in the destruction of one enemy battleship and possibly one enemy cruiser.

Lieutenant Carl Ferdinand Pfeifer, USN, for the efficient operation of the entire engineering plant during the emergencies which required at two different times, emergenc full speed astern, immediately followed by full speed ahead and after receiving an underwater explosion which caused the vessel to lose light and power was able to make 24 knots.

Richard Nelson LANHAM, QM3c, USN, who was the helmsman during entire action and who obeyed accurately every order which was given to the wheel, through all the noise which was caused by gun fire and explosions, telephone talkers and wind blowing through the ports. His work was so well done that in my mind if he had not acted correctly and quickly we would have had two collisions, one with the STERRET and one with the wreck of the LAFFEY.

James Homer JOINER, EM2c, USN, who had the intelligence and presence of mind when this vessel was shaken violently by a heavy underwater explosion causing the ship to lose light and power, to quickly go behind the distribution board and throw in the switches which had tripped, when everyone else in the engineroom thought that the engineroom had been hit.

That all hands are to be commended for their excellent performance of duty while under the severe strain of continuous enemy fire and the close fire of our own vessels for a period of about 40 minutes.

D.J. MacDonald.

U.S.S. O'BANNON

CONFIDENTIAL DECLASSIFIED

November 16, 1942

From: Executive Officer.
To : The Commanding Officer.

Subject: Report of personal impressions and recollections of the night action with Japanese units in Guadacanal - Florida Island Area, November 13, 1942.

Reference: (a) Article 712, U.S. Navy Regulations, 1920.

1. In accordance with reference (a) the following report and resume of my own personal impressions, recollections and recommendations of the subject battle are submitted.

FIRST PHASE

(A) All hands were called to general quarters at 2003, November 12, 1942. At general quarters, I relieved the officer-of-the-deck and remained on the bridge assisting at Conn in order to free the Captain of the responsibility of keeping station. The ship took station fourth in column order as follows: CUSHING, LAFFEY, STERRET, O'BANNON, ATLANTA, SAN FRANCISCO, PORTLAND, HELENA, JUNEAU, AARON WARD, BARTON, MONSSEN AND FLETCHER. This group of 13 vessels formed what was called Battle Disposition I, simply a column with 4 destroyers, 5 cruisers and 4 destroyers.

(B) This task group was covering the retirement of another task group composed of 4 transports, 2 auxiliary vessels, and their destroyer escort which were clearing Guadacanal Area via Lengo Channel. Our task group cleared Sea Lark Channel, stood east into Indispensible Strait, then southeast and reversed course to due west proceeding to entrance of Lengo Channel. The sea was calm, there was no moon, the ceiling being completely overcast.

SECOND PHASE

(A) At 2400 November 12, 1942, our task group was off Taivui Point proceeding through Lengo Channel, at a speed of 15 knots. My task at this time was to keep the ship in position in column. At 0103, November 13, 1942, we cleared Lengo Channel and changed course to 280°, going ahead at 18 knots. While steaming on this course a bright light was observed sharp on the port bow; this light appeared to be located on the beach; at approximately this same time word was received over the loud speaker that there was a red air raid warning on at Cactus; also word was received from our lookouts that unidentified planes showing running lights were overhead. At 0130 Commander Task Group 67.4 ordered course changed to 310° true by a column movement. It was while on this course that information began to be received regarding radar contacts on our starboard hand. The Juneau reported radar contacts on the TBS.

COMSOPAC FILE

A16-3/(90)
Serial 0270a
~~CONFIDENTIAL~~

# SOUTH PACIFIC FORCE
OF THE UNITED STATES PACIFIC FLEET
HEADQUARTERS OF THE COMMANDER

DECLASSIFIED

~~SPECIAL ENDORSEMENT~~ to
CO USS O'BANNON Conf.Ltr.
DD450/A16 Serial 0134 of
November 17, 1942.

NOV 29 1942

From: The Commander South Pacific Area and South Pacific Force.
To: The Commander-in-Chief, U.S. Pacific Fleet.

Subject: Report of engagement with Japanese units on morning of November 13, 1942.

1. Forwarded.

2. The O'BANNON gave an excellent account of herself. The ship was exceptionally well handled under the most trying conditions. The employment of both the five-inch and torpedo batteries left little to be desired.

3. Concur in Executive Officer's recommendation that [illegible] repeaters be installed on navigating bridge of destroyers.

W. F. HALSEY

Copy to:
Comdesfor SP (CTF-67)
Comdespacflt
CO USS O'BANNON

# Index

to

Reminiscences of

Rear Admiral Donald J. MacDonald

U.S. Navy (Retired)

U.S. Naval Institute

Annapolis, Maryland

1986

www.ingramcontent.com/pod-product-compliance
Lightning Source LLC
Chambersburg PA
CBHW082221090526
44585CB00020BA/2129
* 9 7 8 1 6 8 2 6 9 9 9 0 4 *